LIBERATING LUTHER

LIBERATING LUTHER

A LUTHERAN THEOLOGY FROM LATIN AMERICA

VÍTOR WESTHELLE

Translated by
ROBERT A. BUTTERFIELD

FORTRESS PRESS
MINNEAPOLIS

LIBERATING LUTHER
A Lutheran Theology from Latin America

Cover image: ©iStock 2020; Main Christ of the Basilica of Our Lady Aparecida stock photo by Maggin Torres
Cover design: Kristin Miller

Print ISBN: 978-1-5064-6962-1
eBook ISBN: 978-1-5064-6963-8

CONTENTS

FOREWORD

Writing the foreword to a book by Vítor Westhelle, who was my colleague, friend, and fellow pilgrim, is a task that, at this moment, exceeds my ability. It was only a short time ago that he departed, giving himself to the earth and to eternity. And the emotion of his absence still hovers in the air. What can I say about his theology? What can I add to his texts, which are always pulsating, current, theologically consistent, critical, and challenging? Even so, I accepted this request with a certain trembling that I hope words will help me overcome if they are said with the care that this moment demands. Vítor Westhelle left his mark on our generation of theologians and ministers of the gospel. Perhaps in life he did not get the recognition that he deserved in the church he served with dedication and great affection in Brazil and abroad. But his legacy will continue to disturb us, disquiet us, and make us think. And this certainly makes him a *present* companion for reflection in spirit and truth, as Jesus taught us (John 4:23).

Vítor had a special predilection for eschatological thinking, for reflecting on "ultimate realities," and he wrote some extraordinary lines about eschatology. It's part of his eternal legacy. If I learned anything from reading his texts, it's this: the faith that moves us and by which we give life is and always will be *eschatological faith*, because in it and with it we face the ultimate and final questions about life and death, about the meaning or meaninglessness of our existence in this world.

He once used a metaphor that has reappeared in other texts and that even today I find one of the best for understanding theology and the life of faith in the living God. It goes something like this: *Faith makes us transcend the limits of science, life, and rationality.* Faith helps us to overflow the imposed framework, to go beyond the parameters that enclose us and reduce us to that frame, to the model, to what's already been determined, to what enslaves us in our pettiness and insignificance. Faith surprises us and takes us to unknown pastures, to disconcerting encounters, to experiences that transform or *transfigure* us. This is *liberating faith.* This faith is also a bet, an adventure, an involving-oneself-without-reserve in a depth that is unknown to us, but we believe in it, and it makes us persons, *eccentric* beings. This is an expression I found in Gustavo Gutiérrez, and I use it here because I think it fits with Vítor's thought. We are centered people who know what we want and go after it, and at the same time, we are decentered because we belong to Christ. Christ is in us; he lives in us. We are his, and for him we exist, as when with him we discover ourselves in the least of these, the exiled, the unfortunate, the dehumanized, the *condemned* of the earth, the worthless. In them we find ourselves again sanctified by Christ, who shares his life with them in plenitude. Ah (!), this passion for the *ultimate*.

What is it that might be worth doing in this crazy world, in this ambiguous reality that's always controversial and contradictory and in which we also are ambiguous persons, firm or infirm, animated or hesitant, happy or sad, as if we didn't even have faith and were like people with no pastor? That's the time when doubt assails us and makes us insecure, changeable, without fiber. But precisely there, in deep pain, in our most fragile humanity, in the misery of incomprehension or of negligence, it's at that moment that we discover the possibility of encountering meaning, something alive, the *other*, who decenters us again and causes solidarity, compassion, and love to be born within us. Love gives meaning to living and suffering, to the struggle for life, and to death. And this happens *transfiguratively* when we learn to give our bodies to the Beloved. But at the same time, we let the Beloved keep his distance so that his existence, his journey, can be full.

In the Lutheran evangelical tradition, this means that the life of faith is a hard way of learning what it means to say that we are simultaneously justified and sinners: totally sinners in our human reality, which is precarious and limited, but at the same time, justified in hope, as Paul wrote in his Letter to the Romans (8:24). As can be confirmed by reflection on the texts published in this book, Vítor used exactly this revolutionary hope to characterize the depth of Christian existence.

Let me mention one more source of amazement: Vítor's comments about the women who, in the passage from the Saturday after the terrible Friday of the cross, with its agony and defeat, go out very early on Sunday to the place where he has been put. In this way, the women make an *ultimate* gesture of love and care. This gesture, which is *gratuitous and without meaning*, becomes a *gesture of witness* to something that changed their history and our history and became a *gesture of resurrection*, of a transformative announcement, whose memory we have to honor if we are the *people of Jesus*. He rose again or was raised, if we understand it better. And then, out of all this resurrection amazement, like out of a hat, Vítor pulls a sentence that continues to cause us discomfort. With five words he makes sense of what seems impossible to understand: "It's time to practice resurrection."

When Vítor reached age fifty, I dedicated a long poem to him as a tribute. Since then, fragments of it have been published. Perhaps without knowing it, I made the attempt—even as an extemporaneous bit—to understand something of his theology, which is always profoundly connected with his way of living, teaching, loving, and being loved. I want to proclaim this poem as an homage of sharply felt nostalgia, gratitude, and thanksgiving, as a gesture of love shared by the entire believing and praying community of faith to which Vítor felt united wherever he went in Brazil or outside it. I retrieve this poem to keep Vítor's memory alive among us, in our hearts and in our lives.

When you're a child
you don't think about age.
You want to see time pass,
you want to grow, to get bigger.
At twenty you have enough energy
to transform the world.

But time passes, and you mature.
You learn (or unlearn) many things,
Other stuff you forget,
and, fortunately, the essential remains,
the pit of the fruit—nothing against the pulp,
of course.

At fifty you've enjoyed time and nostalgia.
But from the mountaintop you insist on looking far,
sounding eras, places, peoples,
seeing beyond the horizon.

My friend, on your day I want to greet you
openly, with all my heart,
the way you know me.
How good to have known you one day,
with your sparkling, restless eyes:
a far-traveling friendship
that I plucked on the green fields of struggle.

You are one of the culprits who made me
walk toward the indigenous peoples
—Lori was my other accomplice—
and you can weigh the good
that this choice did us
and the fruits it gave us.

Magisterially you practiced
an inter-trans-disciplinary theology
that travels casually among many (other) fields
without sophism, but with great honesty,
in the church and in the university,
in the small encounter, in the study commission,
in the classroom, in advising.
Always the same Vítor, amiable and inflexible

when the subject is truth,
love, and hope.

One day we'll have your systematics in hand.
What new thing will it give us?
I can't imagine yet,
but I think I can risk this:
In it we'll have the integrity of someone
who learned to love the small gesture,
the small fish, the forgotten stone,
the nudity of the cross without flowers,
what seems garbage but reveals itself precious.

Amid the vicissitudes of life,
questionings of existence are not lacking,
the life-crisis awaiting around every turn
or—without warning—on the page of a book
read with more attention.

Our life is not flat or
linear with everything in its proper place.
We're never fully
in place. We're pilgrims of utopia.

In the revelation of places
often we discover ourselves
as ideas out of place,
as quite strange pedestrians
amid the general apathy.
And even so, searching,
feeling our way like the blind, at times,
but stubborn like sniffing bloodhounds.

I found a little four-line poem by an anthropologist and educator whom Vítor knew well and who taught us to *pray with the body*. His name is Carlos Rodrigues Brandão, and the poem is included in a book prefaced by Rubem Alves, another of Vítor's companions on the journey and a person of patient reflection. With this poem I want to connect myself to all the people who, with this book, desire to express what we feel in our hearts when we begin to sense that we will no longer write letters to Vítor or receive from him those words that consoled us when frustrated or that filled us with joy when we discovered the *new, something new*, something unusual, which he pointed out with his usual elegance and humility. Since Vítor was a lover of poetry, I think he would be happy to know that now he is rocked by the Wind that sows lives, worlds, worthy people in every place, because there is no place in which the Wind of the Spirit of Life fails to penetrate and comfort our lives, so weighed down with ambiguities and frustrations but also, at the same time, with joys and hopes that no one can take away from us. In conclusion, here is the poem I promised:

Rise Again

May my body
nourish a cedar seedling.
May my soul
rock it in the wind.

Prof. Dr. Roberto Zwetsch
Escola Superior de Teologia (EST)
São Leopoldo, RS, Brazil

TRANSLATOR'S NOTE

Vítor Westhelle once described his own writing style as baroque, and evidence of that style inevitably remains in translation. But wherever necessary and practical, I have broken up long sentences into more manageable blocks and rearranged the syntax so that the reader can more easily follow Westhelle's complex train of thought.

I have translated into English everything that was in Spanish, French, or Portuguese, and those texts, though often difficult, are quite understandable in translation. But several times Westhelle includes quotations from the novel *Grande Sertão: Veredas* by João Guimarães Rosa. These are brief quotations but ironic and paradoxical in the extreme. I have tried to capture at least something of their meaning.

Where Westhelle quotes from Wendell Berry, John Donne, and John Milton, he uses Portuguese-language editions of those authors, and I have translated those quotations back into English. Where he quotes Shakespeare, he again uses a Portuguese translation, but I have chosen to quote directly from the original English.

Westhelle also makes frequent use of the Latin and German vocabulary that is a standard part of the classically trained theologian's lexicon. I have left such words and phrases untranslated. If necessary, the reader can consult a dictionary of theological terms.

Finally, the reader may note that, though Westhelle is a brilliant and careful thinker, he is not always so attentive to supplying the bibliographical data one would expect to find in footnotes. In this regard, I beg the reader's indulgence for the author's sake. He wrote these articles mainly for discussion with his colleagues, who were generally familiar with the articles, books, and other materials he used and did not need to have all the information that other readers, many years later, would want.

Robert A. Butterfield, translator

THE CROSS, THEOLOGY, AND ROSES

THE SOTERIOLOGICAL SIGNIFICANCE OF THE CROSS IN THEOLOGY

I read about the crucified Christ,
the only-begotten Son,
sacrificed to flesh and to time,
and to all our fear. He died
and rose again, but who does not tremble
for his pain and loneliness
and the sixth hour of darkness?
Unless we cry like Mary
at his tomb, thinking him
lost, Easter morning will not come.

—Wendell Berry, "The Way of Pain"[1]

The Cross of Theology

Just imagine. What difference would it make for all of theology and preaching if Jesus had died in bed of old age? This is a hypothetical question, of course. But it helps sharpen the senses for trying to understand the first theological problem that a small band of Jews, both men and women, faced after the leader of their movement, a carpenter from Galilee, was judged to be a blasphemer and handed

Originally published in *Estudos Teológicos* 30, no. 3 (1990): 224–43.

[1] Wendell Berry, "The Way of Pain," in *Collected Poems* (San Francisco: North Point, 1985), 210. Here retranslated into English from the Portuguese version used by Westhelle.

over to the imperial power to be executed as a political criminal. The punishment was death by crucifixion, brutally humiliating but by no means uncommon. Rebellious slaves ended up on the cross, and so did political subversives, which the Roman Empire had in abundance.

From this event, which was undoubtedly scandalous, there arose an inevitable insignia: the cross. The significance of the cross brings with it a profound ambiguity rooted in the very history of its adoption as the Christian symbol par excellence and in its use through the ages. From the mystical interpretation that sweetens the suffering on the cross to the embarrassing partnership of the cross and the sword that characterized the conquest of America, the cross is far from having a single meaning. Consider this song from the Chibchas, natives of the Northeast of South America, to illustrate the "cross" that the cross of theology carries: "I climbed up to high ground / There I sat down / I found a cross / And I started to cry."[2] Such embarrassments continue. The cross was slow to become a Christian symbol. There is no evidence of its use before the end of the second century. Other symbols, such as the anchor, the fish, and the lamb, preceded it. Used marginally during the third century, the cross became the hegemonic symbol of Christianity only with Constantine, who combined it with the monogram XiRo and used it in 312 AD as the emblem of his victorious army (*in hoc signo vinces*). Moreover, the swastika, adopted much later by the Nazis because of its supposedly Nordic origin, was already relatively widespread at the time of Constantine, possibly as a disguised mark of the cross on Christian tombs of the first few centuries. The origin of the swastika, however, antedates Christianity, being common to ancient Europe, Asia, and America.

Salvador Dalí, a harsh critic of domesticated Christianity, brilliantly expressed in two of his paintings the way the cross has become a mystical fetish. The better known of these paintings presents Christ on a cross that is suspended in midair and projected toward the infinite as if in flight. It's a cross that doesn't touch the ground and leads to infinity. It's a cross suspended in a cosmic drama without

[2] Guillermo Alberto Arévalo, ed., *Poesia Indígena de América* (Bogotá: Arango, 1998), 23.

contact with reality. Dalí adorns the scandal of this drama with levity. Old Dalí, with all his sarcasm, would have laughed if he'd seen his cross used as a pious decoration in ecclesial spaces.

There is no doubt about the importance of the cross as a central symbol of the Christian tradition. In the beginning, its connection with the crucifixion was a bit vague and designated more the cosmic dimensions of the work of Christ (Eph 3:18) than the event of the crucifixion itself. The specific use of the cross by Constantine made it a symbol of victory over the powers of death and evil. Only around the eleventh century did crucifixes appear as a realistic representation of the event on the cross. Since then, popular devotion associates the cross with the suffering of Christ and makes the days of the passion (especially Good Friday) into the most important time in the spirituality of the liturgical year. The Reformation somewhat modified the history of the cross's symbolism. While Lutherans maintained the cross and crucifix, Calvinists avoided them as decorative pieces until the beginning of the twentieth century, and the Anglicans did likewise because of Puritan pressure, though they used the cross and the crucifix in ritual actions. But whether present or absent in decoration, the cross has never stopped inhabiting the popular imagination ever since the followers of the Nazarene were overcome with amazement at his fate.

The ambiguity of the symbol is not an immediate judgment on the event to which it points and that it reveals. The event of the crucifixion, however, is in itself received, presented, and interpreted in such a way as not only to make possible different understandings of the significance of the cross but also to explain why the cross of ignominy, to use Luther's expression, is adorned with roses. What happened to turn this "happy exchange" of the righteous man who suffered for the sinner into the unhappy trade-off that sublimates the suffering into devotion to the sufferer? As the popular song says, "They forget his passion so as to live the passion of the Lord."

It was in this situation of many crosses that Luther became the voice denouncing the absence of a theology of the cross. Theology had made of the cross a symbol of glory. In a text that, strangely, is both famous and little known—that is, the "Ninety-Five Theses"—we encounter this warning: "Out with all those prophets who say to the people of Christ: peace, peace, when there is no peace. Blessed are all the prophets who say to the people of Christ: cross, cross, when there is no cross" (theses 92–93). In these two theses, the contrast between peace and cross suggests that the cross indicates conflict and crisis, while the parallelism of "there is no . . ." reflects the inability to recognize reality such as it is. For this reason, Luther will define the "theology of the cross" as that which "tells things as they are."[3] The symbol and the image became a means of concealment. The scandal was undone; there were too many roses.

It's important to try to understand what happened in the interpretation of the event of the cross to make possible such a varied and problematic reception of this event, which became the principal symbol of Christianity. A few questions serve to shape the arguments elaborated here. Namely, what is the relation between cross and salvation when it is affirmed that Christ died for us? What is the relation between the life and the passion of Jesus? Did Christ also live for us? And what is the resurrection, seal or event? How does the passion of Christ relate to suffering in the world? What determines the necessity of the passion? And finally, if Jesus had died of old age in bed, what difference would it make?

There is no doubt that it was a scandal. When Paul assesses the soteriological value of the cross in 1 Corinthians 1, he is not able to do it without superimposing paradoxical images: madness, power, scandal, wisdom, scorn, sanctification, humility, redemption. More than twenty years already separate this classic text from the event of the crucifixion, and the amazement has not gone away. There still resounds the terrible cry of the crucified: "Eloi, eloi, lama sabachthani?" (Mark 15:34; Ps 22:1). In Mark (and Matthew agrees), this cry has its clear, exalted meaning when it is followed by the report of the misunderstanding of those who were at the cross and thought that Jesus was "calling for Elijah." It's as if Mark said, "We who were following him and knew him, *we* know what he was saying." The expression appears as testimony to the scandal. Already Luke, a few decades later, exchanges the reference

[3] Martin Luther, *Obras Selecionadas*, vol. 1, *Os primórdios escritos de 1517 a 1519* (São Léopoldo-Porto Alegre: Sinodal-Concordia, 1987), 50. On the theology of Luther, see Martin N. Dreher, "A *theologia crucis* de Lutero e o tema da teologia da libertação," *Estudos Teológicos* 28, no. 2 (1988): 137–52.

from Psalm 22 for the expression of confidence in Psalm 31:5: "Into your hand I commit my spirit." Clearly, Luke omits the misunderstanding. As Riobaldo (a character from João Guimarães Rosa's novel *Grande Sertão: Veredas*) might say, "Hearing the cry of the person suffering is different from experiencing it yourself." And so it is that people decorate the garden of skulls (Golgotha) with flowers.

Except for a few women observing the crucifixion from afar, the followers of Jesus, including Mark, wanted no part of that cross. For them, death was already outside of life. It is at the very least intriguing that the oldest synoptic source, Q, records nothing about the passion of Jesus. How was it, then, that this event ended up being the catalyst for the entire soteriological significance of the work of Christ, to the point where Paul can say, "I decided to know nothing among you except Jesus Christ, and him crucified" (1 Cor 2:2)? In this way, the crucifixion becomes the Archimedean point for understanding what God did in Christ. The question became "How?" replacing Jesus's question of "Who?" (Mark 8:27–30), which only the centurion at the cross will be able to answer as he recognizes the Son of God in suffering and death (Mark 15:39), something Peter failed to do (Mark 8:31–33). The implicit question (How?) in the announcements and reports of the passion brings with it this search for understanding how death can mean life. How did salvation work? In this way, Christians began to overcome the scandal that shocked those who participated in messianic practice: What happened to Jesus, the Nazarene (cf. Luke 24:19)?

"Religion decays, the icon remains; the narrative is forgotten, but the representation still magnetizes. . . . In fact, history democratizes our sympathies." This sentence from a novel by Julian Barnes could be applied to the life and passion of Jesus. The icon remains; the representation mystifies by itself. But the crucial scandal—the scandal of the cross—is reduced to didactic models, which not only remove stumbling blocks but also point to central elements of the event.[4]

---

[4] This has been one of the central points of Latin American theology's critique of the models of reconciliation. For more on this, see the study by Luis Marcos Sander, *Jesus Cristo, o Libertador: A Cristologia da libertação de Leonardo Boff* (São Leopoldo: Sinodal, 1986), 135–45. See also José Comblin, *Teologia da Reconciliação: Ideologia ou Reforço da Libertação?* (Petrópolis: Vozes, 1987).

That's what models do; they explain. But they don't get us involved or entangled in the plot. Throughout history, models come one after the other, determined by the social and religious contexts that delimit their relevance.

The Cross in Theology

Before speaking about models, it's important to recognize that there are two types of arguments developed in relation to the passion. The first understands the passion of Christ as being determined by the drama of his own life and mission—either as martyrdom or as a necessity of God's economy of salvation—but not possessing in itself any soteriological value. In this case, there exists a direct continuity between the life and death of Jesus. In the second type, which ended up being victorious in the tradition, the cross is in itself salvific and more or less linked to the life of Jesus. Around his life, the history of salvation develops. So that an understanding of the soteriological value of the passion might be possible, it was important to underscore the discontinuity between the life of Jesus and his death, even to the point of affirming that his death was a political or religious misunderstanding (Bultmann). But let's see, in brief, how these arguments are elaborated. In the first argument, it's possible to distinguish two plans (schemas). In the second argument, there will first appear motifs that call for the connection between death and reconciliation and then the models that provide structure for theories of reconciliation.

First Argument: Plans

The Gospels agree that Jesus confronted death of his own volition. He was aware of the traitor (Mark 14:42) and did not allow any resistance to his being arrested (Matt 26:52–56). He introduced himself to the people who were arresting him so that he might drink from the cup that the Father had prepared for him (John 18:4–11). To explain all that, two possibilities appeared.

The first sought to explain the passion based on the image of the martyr/prophet. According to this image, an explicatory schema is constructed that posits Jesus as the victim of martyrdom at the hands of the religious leaders of his own people. Israel kills its prophets (Luke 11:47; 13:33–34; Acts 2:22–23). But Jesus is not simply one more prophet. God legitimates his practice (ministry) through the resurrection (Acts 2:24; 5:30–31; 10:40). From this emerges the schema of contrast.[5] Much of this schema was not preserved in the tradition, but there exist clear indications of the way it oriented ancient interpretation.

In the context of intertestamental apocalypticism, the emergence of the prophet of the last days is associated with the image of the blasphemer who comes to contradict the law, according to Daniel 7. Since this interpretative schema is associated with the mission among the Jews—because only in this religious and cultural context does it make sense—the frequent mentions of the charge against Jesus as a blasphemer (Mark 14:64; Luke 5:21) and as a trickster (Matt 27:64; John 7:12) serve to indicate the background that shapes this schema. Either Jesus is a blasphemer or he's a prophet who reveals true blasphemy. The problem was defining who this Jesus was in the religious context of Judaism. Thus it is also important to know how this Jesus interprets the law (Mark 10:2). He is presented as one who has authority—that is, as one who is authorized (has "the morals") to express the very meaning of the law. It is worth remembering that, in the time of Jesus, interpretation of the law is disputed among the Sadducees, Pharisees, and other groups. There is no unanimity in interpretation. This whole dispute must lead to a climactic resolution. And therein lies the secret that true interpretation reveals: the spirit of the law and the law of the Spirit: "You stiff-necked people, uncircumcised in heart and ears, you are forever opposing the Holy Spirit, just as your ancestors used to do. Which of the prophets did your ancestors not persecute? They killed those who foretold the coming of the Righteous One, and now you have become his betrayers and murderers. You are the ones that received the law . . . and yet you have not kept it" (Acts 7:51–53).

---

[5] For a discussion of this schema, see Edward Schillebeeckx, *Jesus: An Experiment in Christology* (New York: Crossroad, 1981), 274–82; and Wolfhart Pannenberg, *Jesus: God and Man* (Philadelphia: Westminster, 1974), 244–47.

The true prophet is proved in martyrdom (Neh 9:26). This interpretative schema may be at the root of the Pauline understanding that replaces the law with Jesus as the subject of salvific action (Gal 1:16; 3:2–5).[6] Jesus himself replaces the law as the light of the world. This schema, however, still does not attribute any special significance to the event of the cross but interprets Jesus on the basis of his practice, acts, and teachings.

The difficulty with the schema of contrast, apart from the sparse scriptural base that remains of it, is that it remained confined to the Jewish religious context and made sense only in that context. The question changed shape, however, with the failure of the mission to the Jews, which led to the questioning of its relevance. This schema also presents difficulties when it tries to justify the ultimate character of Jesus's prophetism—he is not only Elijah redivivus—by making the resurrection the criterion that differentiates Jesus from any other prophet whose martyrdom legitimates his practice. This difficulty is emphasized in the parable of the rich man and Lazarus, which attests to the uselessness of the resurrection as proof (Luke 16:31). In the Jewish tradition, the guiding principle was to be wary of receiving extraordinary proofs not corroborated by Scripture. Paul was ready to declare anathema an angel who might come to add anything to what he was teaching (Gal 1:8). And that view is supported by the rereading of Deuteronomy, which affirms the proximity of the law and the comprehension of its immediate meaning, for which reason it censures anyone who seeks its significance elsewhere: "It is not in heaven" (Deut 30:12). For divine corroboration of the authority of Jesus to be effective, it needed to authenticate itself, since to this generation no sign will be given (Mark 8:12). False prophets are the ones who offer signs (Mark 13:22).

The other schema that seeks to explain the death of Jesus deepens the questions theologically and changes the subject of history. Now it's no longer the prophet/martyr who suffers the consequences of his

---

[6] Schillebeeckx, *Jesus*, 280–82. Juan Luis Segundo, working independently, offers a similar formulation of the argument in his interpretation of Romans, *El Hombre de Hoy Ante Jesus de Nazaré II/1* (Madrid: Cristandad, 1982), second part, "A Cristologia Humanista de Paulo."

practice; it's God, who, in his salvific project, consigns him to death. The action emanates from God. Contrary to the schema of contrast, in this schema the passion is an end in itself and is imposed by the divine project as a programmatic necessity: "The Son of Man must undergo great suffering" (Mark 8:31; also Mark 9:12; Luke 17:25) or "The Son of Man is to be betrayed into human hands" (Mark 9:31; also Mark 10:33; 14:41; Luke 24:7). A typical way in which this schema develops is found in the report on the road to Emmaus (Luke 24:13–35, esp. vv. 25–27). The context is again Jewish but is no longer a function of mission. Instead, it involves catechesis, which was also developed in the context of Judeo-Christian communities. Joachim Jeremias points out that to interpret these texts, one can practically do without the Greek text of the Bible.[7]

The basis of this schema is a theological reflection that is much more developed than in the previous schema and that possesses an apologetic character. It already goes a step beyond the schema of contrast. It asks whether the schema of contrast had to turn out the way it did. It questions whether death serves only to legitimate what the practice of Jesus already contained in itself. Moreover, the very form of Jesus's execution brought with it new embarrassments. It was not like the death of Stephen, who is taken from the Sanhedrin to be stoned, thus emphasizing the religious character of his trial, along the lines of the schema of contrast. Jesus was put on the cross and was the type of condemned man that a Jew easily identified as one cursed by God (Deut 21:23), a passage that Paul refers to in Galatians 3:13. The problem was demonstrating the *dei* (it is necessary) of the divine plan. Here we still have no expiatory interpretation. Jesus does not die for the sake of sinners; he is delivered into "the hands of men." The Aramaic parallelism between "Son of Man" and "human hands" (Mark 9:31) forms a play on words (*bar nascha / bene nascha*) that is highly allusive, indicating that the formulation of Mark 14:41 and Luke 24:7, which substitutes "sinner" for "human," is a redaction already influenced by a soteriological interpretation. The central motif in this idea of the man being handed

[7] Joachim Jeremias, *Der Opfertod Jesu Christi* (Stuttgart: Calwer, 1963), 24.

over to men is that the essentially human (the Son of Man) becomes an object of manipulation when he is delivered into the "hands" of men. This schema finds an echo in the tradition of the suffering of the righteous man as reflected in the late wisdom literature. For example, in Psalm 34:19, "Many are the afflictions of the righteous." The classic elaboration of this idea is in Wisdom of Solomon 2:12–20. In Stephen's speech, which is based on the schema of contrast, there already arises an element of this schema of design when, in Acts 7:50, Jesus is identified as the righteous man. We see that the various traditions are being mixed, but in none of them do we find expiatory elements. The suffering of the just reveals the impending punishment of the impious, an idea reinforced by the inversion of their fate. The suffering just man will be glorified (Ps 34:19b; 5:1–7). The absence of the fourth canto of the suffering servant of Isaiah 53 as the framework for this schema reveals the nonexpiatory character of the necessity for suffering, which could have been shown by an appeal to the canto of the servant who takes on himself the iniquities of all.

The schema of design reveals an in-depth theological examination that relativizes human action as a function of the divine project. The idea that it's necessary for God's will to be accomplished is emphasized by the apparent absurdity of the suffering of a righteous man. The "myth of punishment" in a direct schema of retribution (guilt-punishment) nourished by Genesis 2–11 is amplified and becomes more dialectic. The resolution is eschatological. In the partial experience of history, what one sees is the inverse of the correct relation of retribution: the just man suffers. But based on the totality of the divine project (*sub specie aeternitatis*), one can affirm that this is the correct resolution of retribution.

The problem with this schema is that the life and death of Jesus end up being only judgment on the world. The chaff and the wheat are found together, as are the sheep and the goats. They await the final showdown only to find out, with great surprise (Matt 25!), that they were either one or the other and that chaff does not become wheat, nor do goats become sheep. There is no answer to the question about the historic difference that Jesus makes. He proleptically manifests judgment. This connection with judgment gave rise to redemptive interpretations of Jesus.

The Motifs

Melanchthon said that knowing Christ is not knowing his nature but knowing his benefits. This "utilitarianism" will mark the reconciliatory visions of the cross. The cross itself is effective for salvation. The fundamental models that explain the salvific efficacy of the cross arise from soteriological motifs in the New Testament. At the origin of these motifs is the *hyper* formula: Jesus died for our sins, for us, for many (all). The formula applied to the cross is typically Pauline, though it was part of a more ancient kerygma (1 Cor 15:3). The formula also appears in the tradition of the eucharistic supper (Mark 14:24).

In the context of this formula, the first motif that develops is that of redemption (ransom) through the life choice of one who offers the blood of life to the very end. This becomes clear in the tradition of the supper, though there the expiatory element is not yet directly linked to the cross. The blood poured out is a metaphor for the diaconic giving of a life. The only other synoptic text that bears the *hyper* formula (Mark 10:45) corroborates this interpretation. The "ransom for many" is inserted in the context of the discussion about power and service (Mark 10:35–45).[8] These texts suggest a certain dependency on Isaiah 53:12, which would confirm the fact that the soteriological idea of redemption/ransom does not reside in a sacrificial act of death in itself but in the life lived for others. The motif of redemption/ransom appears originally as giving, like the good shepherd who goes in search of the lost sheep or like the father who, instead of punishing the son who returns, rewards him. Therefore, redemption/ransom is not understood in a literal sense; the question is not even asked to whom the ransom is paid.

With Paul, the motif of ransom receives more rigid outlines, sketched in terms of the social relations of a slave-owning society.

---

8 Xavier Léon Dufour, *Jesus y Pablo ante la Muerte* (Madrid: Cristandad, 1979), 89–94.

The sinner is not lost; he's the slave of another master and must be ransomed at a certain price (1 Cor 6:20; 7:23; Gal 3:13; 4:5). Here the subject of slavery is the law, thus breaking the schema of design. Jesus is no longer the supreme expression of the law but the end of the law (Rom 10:4). Through the cross, the wall that the law raised preventing reconciliation was torn down (Eph 2:14–16). The law condemns and punishes the effects of sin. The law condemned Jesus for the result of his practice (actions). That's where the victory is. Jesus was made sin—not a sinner—for our sake (2 Cor 5:21). By condemning sin while thinking it was punishing the sinner, the law destroyed its own power to indict. Thus it is that Jesus overcomes the law. The motif of ransom in this formulation will be influential for the formulation of the triumph model in the objectivist version of reconciliation, which will be discussed below.

In Paul, we find still another motif linked to the theme of overcoming the law, a motif that Jeremias classifies as penal.[9] This motif is intimately connected with the preceding one but has some peculiar characteristics. The death of Jesus is seen as the punishment that we should suffer because the law accuses us. Therefore, God hands Jesus over to suffer the necessary punishment (Rom 4:25; 8:3, 32). So that this could occur, Jesus was made into a curse (Gal 3:13). Here Paul refers to the text of Deuteronomy 21:23, which declares accursed him who is hung on the tree. Paul's solution is ingenious, showing that the cursed one on the tree is cursed only for us. As in the motif of ransom, here also the condemnation of Jesus annuls the accusatory power of the law when Jesus replaces us on the cross. This motif is at the root of the model of vicarious satisfaction, though, in the penal motif, substitution does not mean satisfying the legal demands that kept the law in force. Here the substitution makes Jesus the representative of God's love for humanity as well as the representative of humanity in its sinful condition before God.

Another influential model in the formulation of the redemptive character of the cross is found in the tradition of the Lord's Supper,

---

[9] Jeremias, *Opfertod Jesu Christi*, 16–17.

which interprets Jesus as the paschal lamb. There the death of Jesus is connected with the formation of a new alliance/covenant (1 Cor 5:7–8; 11:25), a community of those redeemed through participation in the act of remembrance, thus fulfilling the promise of Jeremiah 31:31. The blood poured out does not have an expiatory character in the sacrificial sense, but it produces a new covenant, with a new people formed not genetically through the corrupt descendancy of Adam but "nutritionally" through participation in the supper that remakes the body. As a matter of fact, there's nothing new in the words of Ludwig Feuerbach: *Der Mensch ist, was er isst* (Man is what he eats). An *ex opere operato* ritualism is, however, expressly rejected by Paul when he warns that participation in the body requires a worthy subjective posture (1 Cor 11:28). This motif emphasizes human involvement in the condition of sin. Jesus, through his obedience to the Father (Rom 5:18–19), forms the New Adam in whose body we participate. The motif of covenant will be important for the construction of the subjectivist versions of reconciliation.

Little by little, the organic relation between the life and death of Jesus has been deteriorating, and a sacrificial vision of the event of the cross in itself is beginning to take shape. The tradition of the paschal lamb is connected with this motif (as well as with the motif of covenant), and Paul had already made this connection (1 Cor 5:7). But its more complete elaboration occurs later than Paul. This motif is the core of the Letter to the Hebrews, which emphasizes the definitive and perfect character of this sacrifice, in which the priest is himself the immolated victim who vicariously expiates our sins. This idea of sacrifice should not be understood as a literal interpretation of what happened on the cross. The image is suggested as a metaphor. The interesting part of this motif is that it picks up the cultic language of expiatory sacrifices, though, in the practice of Jesus and in the ancient traditions, there is no basis for such an interpretation. Jesus corroborates the prophetic opinion that the practice of mercy and justice is superior to all sacrifices. But the return of this motif, which echoes through the centuries of Christianity beyond the Jewish context, harmonizes with a religious search for purity and with the awareness of the human incapacity to achieve it, all of which forms a sort of universal matrix of religious expectation of reconciliation.[10] In relation to contemporary science, research on altruism has shown that it is possible to explain the self-sacrificing individual as a function of the adaptation of a genetic type, in the case of parents in relation to children or of individuals in relation to the nation. This altruism is explained by the so-called egotism of genes, which can sacrifice individuals as a function of its own adaptation of genetic markers. In other words, sacrificing oneself for someone who is "genetically" close can be explained as a biological mechanism. What cannot be explained biologically is sacrificing oneself for a stranger or an enemy. In this sacrifice there exists a redemptive element that genetic egotism is incapable of explaining. In these (theological) circles, there has been a rediscovery of the importance of the sacrificial motif for explaining the death of Jesus, who, as Friedrich Nietzsche preached, loved not only the person close to him but also the person far away.[11]

The Models

Let us move on from these motifs that sought to articulate answers to the why of the cross so that we can now assess interpretative models that, by making use of these motifs, developed theories of reconciliation. The movement is on a continuum that begins with perplexity about the cross, passes through affirmation (the "It could only be so" of the schemas), and arrives at the significance (the "What difference does it make for us?" of the motifs). Up to this point, the enigma is very much alive. The motifs still preserve the amazement. They are metaphors that say that the cross is ransom, punishment, covenant, or sacrifice, and at the same time, they deny the identity of the cross: it is not exactly ransom, punishment, sacrifice, or covenant. Thus the

---

[10] A reevaluation of the sacrificial model drew renewed energy from Frances M. Young, *The Sacrifice and the Death of Christ* (Philadelphia: Westminster, 1975). Gerhard Forde also performed such a reevaluation: "A obra de Cristo," in *Dogmática Cristã*, vol. 2, ed. Carl Braaten and Robert Jenson (São Leopoldo: Sinodal), locus 7.

[11] This argument has been developed especially in the dialogue between religion and science and is recorded in the journal *Zygon*. See, for example, Philip Hefner, "Theology's Truth and Scientific Formulation," *Zygon* 23, no. 3 (1988): 263–79; and Ralph Wendell Burhoe, "War, Peace, and Religion's Biocultural Evolution," *Zygon* 21, no. 4 (1986): 439–72.

metaphors keep the meaning of the cross open. A metaphor suggests but does not define. But with models, the metaphor disappears, and explicatory structures are constructed that satisfy arguments based on reason.

There are two basic ways to understand reconciliation, and in truth, these are extremes that allow for a series of intermediate compositions. One way is objective reconciliation; the other is subjective reconciliation. This terminology is meant to aid understanding. The objectivist theory affirms that reconciliation is an event external to human subjectivity and thus comes before justification and conversion. It's what happens outside of us but for us (*extra nos–pro nobis*). The subjectivist theory affirms that reconciliation happens in and through human disposition and therefore comes after justification and conversion. It's what happens for us and in us (*pro nobis–in nobis*). What identifies these two theories is that the event of the cross has meaning for us and therefore presupposes the *hyper* formula that grounds the soteriological motifs.

In the objectivist theory, we find two principal models: the triumph model and the satisfaction model. The first is also referred to as the classic or ransom[12] model. The term *ransom* indicates that this model is inspired by the ransom motif. But contrary to the ransom motif, which had a metaphorical meaning, now the meaning is literal, and the parties to the ransom negotiation are defined. The term *classic* (Gustaf Aulén) is used because it was the first reconciliation model in the history of the church. It is appropriate to call it the triumph model because it's based on the vision in which the cross of Christ represents victory over the tyrannical powers of evil.

The triumph model began to take shape in the second century and was based on an important question for Christians—namely, if in Christ we have new life, and this life is qualitatively superior to that of the Old Adam, why is there resistance and apostasy? Irenaeus

[12] Translator's note: Westhelle uses the Portuguese noun *resgate*, which means "rescue," "redemption," or "ransom." These three terms can be thought of as interchangeable.

defended the existence of a "dominion of apostasy" governed by the forces of evil. The work of Christ was to give his blood as ransom to deliver us from that dominion, which, though not legitimate, possesses power. Based on this principle, Origen developed a reconciliation model that is almost a Greek comedy. Origen interprets the "ransom" in Matthew 20:28 as the price paid by God to the devil to liberate the world from the influence of the devil's tyrannical power. A negotiation is set up between God and the devil, its object being dominion over the world, and the medium of exchange is Christ. The devil controlled us until that exchange was made; the life and death of Jesus were the payment that freed us from slavery. But how was it that the devil entered into this negotiation? He was fooled and tricked! He was told that he had power over Christ, but he didn't know that he couldn't exercise that power because the key to exercising it is the sin committed by the sinner. Jesus, in his perfectly human form, attracted the devil, who wanted to ensnare him. But Jesus was innocent, and brought to suffering and death as a sinner, he triumphed over the devil. The enticement consisted in the fact that this information—namely, that the devil would not have real power over Christ, given his innocence—was concealed from the devil. This notion of trickery was then attributed to the text of 1 Corinthians 2:7–8: "But we speak God's wisdom, secret and hidden. . . . None of the rulers of this age understood this; for if they had, they would not have crucified the Lord of glory."

The fantastic, mythical construction of this model has the merit of recovering in theology, in an extremely realistic way, the cosmic dimension of the struggle between good and evil, for which the world is a battleground and in which the fight is between tyrants and ordinary people. This theme, like that of tricking the devil, recurs in various cultures and religions. For the Christian, the cross is what defines and symbolizes this battle. But its result is still not complete. Apostasy still has its territory. Origen goes so far as to suggest that the expiatory suffering of Christ continues in heaven, where the battle of a war already won continues. Here we have, in a very realistic formulation, what Pascal said: "Jesus is in agony until the end of the world." Exaggeration aside, in this model, sin appears definitively as an objective, structured reality behind human subjectivity. Thus are avoided both the problem of merit in the reconciliation between God and the world and the exclusion of the divine wrath as a function of love or vice versa. It then becomes possible to explain why the wrath of God against evil and the forces of tyranny is at the same time an expression of his love for anyone under the dominion of evil. In this model we have the first systematic presentation of what in Latin America is called *structural sin.*

Models always caricature what is real. In the case of the triumph model, various limitations immediately get our attention. If its merit is in linking the incarnation to suffering, then it must be noted that the cross in itself has no special role to play except as the devil's treaty of surrender, because there the devil saw that he had been defeated and had taken the bait by thinking Jesus would be his prey. It's interesting to compare this model with Martin Scorsese's film *The Last Temptation of Christ*, in which this question is presented the other way around; it's the devil who tricked Christ by taking him off the cross and thus impeding the consummation of his expiatory work. Surprisingly, this inversion reveals a strong point of this model. In a scene in which Jesus, spared the cross, meets Paul, who is preaching Christ crucified, Jesus introduces himself to Paul and advises him that he is still alive. But Paul rejects him in favor of the kerygma based on Jesus's death. The dialogue suggests that, more than the actual fact of death, what counts is the announcing of that death. The model tries to show that Jesus's death is the culmination of a battle waged, from the moment of incarnation onward, with the tyrannical powers of evil, and his death consummates the victory instead of the defeat. Thus this model restores the original idea of ransom not as the backroom deal made by gentlemen/lords for the purchase of a slave but as a gentleman/lord who becomes a slave to make slaves lords of their own destiny. Why did God become human? In this line of thought, Irenaeus responds: so that human beings could ascend to God. The incarnation is understood as a "recapitulation" of creation. Christ acts correctly where Adam (= humanity) erred. Hence Irenaeus's maxim "Without [God's] assuming [our humanity], there's no redemption."

The most decisive criticism of this model is that it describes a suprahistorical drama in which no human being participates actively and in which the human being is only the spoils of war. This model was accused of not seriously considering the gravity of sin (Anselm). It was also criticized for granting too much power to the devil, to the point that God had to use stratagems ill befitting his sanctity (= transparency); namely, the devil was conned. Finally, beginning with the Enlightenment, this model was attacked for its selection of images, which were judged as excessively mythological, fantastic, and contaminated by a dualism that was foreign to illuminated reason and contrary to the modern cosmovision. Nevertheless, I recognize that Hegel will review this model in his philosophy of religion, in which the dialectic immanent in history is the expression of the internal dialectic of the divinity itself. The great distance between Hegel and the theologians of the first centuries, in regard to the images used, barely conceals the similarity between their versions. One difference, however, seems to be foundational: the cosmic struggle is expressed not as a duality of forces in combat but as the dialectic intrinsic to the divine being as it expresses itself in history.[13]

The central question in the triumph model is power. The model arose in a Christianity that was on the margins in regard to the relations of power. In fact, being more victims than subjects in these relations, Christians understood this model as a cosmic battle of which human beings are the object. After the constantization of Christianity, this model remains as a backdrop but is no longer reworked or deepened, even in the work of a great theologian like Augustine. It remains only a "relic of a common Catholicism" (Adolf von Harnack). But the question begins to change. It's no longer "If Christ triumphed, why doesn't his power make itself felt?" but "If by the cross the church triumphed, what has gone wrong?" The problem is not in the executive [branch] but in the judicial, where the problem is how to correct the problem of guilt and sin. Thus guilt and sin

[13] For an introduction to the concept of reconciliation in Hegel, see Luis Henrique Dreher, "Os Atalhos e os Atalhos da Cristologia: Um Estudo sobre a Relevância da História para a 'Cristologia da Reconciliação' de G. W. F. Hegel, 'Trabalho de conclusão: Escola Superior de Teologia,'" first semester of 1990.

emerge as the main concern, and with this concern there arises in the church a penitential practice through which the person tries to satisfy God, from whose love the person has distanced himself.

In this context, the most influential and elaborate model of reconciliation in the Western church emerges. Its author is Anselm of Canterbury, who, at the end of the eleventh century, developed his argument in one of the most famous books of theological literature, *Cur Deus Homo?* (Why did God make himself human?). For Anselm, the gravity of sin had not been sufficiently considered in the model of triumph. In his view, sin is not rendering to God the honor owed to him; it's an offense against the honor of God. And the problem is how a human being can be pardoned without staining the honor of God. Hence the cosmic struggle with the devil disappears. Now God is only the agent both of wrath, by virtue of his justice, and of love, by virtue of the necessity to repair the damage caused by sin. Appealing to God's love while disdaining his justice would be sentimentality. Justice demands reparations and satisfaction through compensation for the damage caused. Anselm's starting point is the legal maxim of German jurisprudence: punishment or reparations (*poena aut satisfactio*). However, this repair of the damage done to God's honor can be done only through a meritorious act that offers to God something that placates the sin. But what could that be for a human being, who already owes everything to God? Giving to God what one already owes to God doesn't repair anything. The one who owes is the human being, but the debt is such that only God could pay it. How, then, would the human being be pardoned? Answer: Through the God who becomes human so that, as a human being, he can pay the existing debt in the name of humanity and thus maintain the bond between God's justice and God's love, which offers the world the God-man. Because of Christ's innocence, he didn't need to die (death being the price for sin), but condemned on the cross, he infinitely satisfied divine justice.

The logical clarity of the argument based on juridical principles and anchored in the profound psychological experience of guilt made the model of satisfaction a powerful instrument of medieval theology, and this model was even incorporated into the Protestant orthodoxy of the seventeenth century (actually, after Luther broke with this model—though he occasionally used its language—it was restored by Melanchthon and Calvin). But its effects have especially touched piety, hymnology, and popular liturgy, right up to the present. When the Black church in the United States sings its spiritual "He Paid My Debts," the model of satisfaction is operative. If, on the one hand, it is affirmed that Christ already did everything for us, then, on the other, it is an accepted fact that we deserve infinite punishment. Anselm was correct in affirming that his model elevated to the maximum the gravity of sin. So grave is sin that all we have left to do is to recognize that our guilt is infinite. And all the more serious is our sin (as Peter Abelard demonstrated) that it demands an even greater sin, which is the crucifixion of Christ, for which we are all responsible. The image of the cruel God who can't give any more than he has already given and whom no one can pay is closely associated with the payment of promises that appear as subsidiary negotiations with the sacred through saints, since with God himself, negotiation was delegated to Christ, the negotiator of the unpayable debt.[14]

At the beginning of the twelfth century, Abelard immediately pointed out the major difficulty with this model. He correctly asked, If, for the relatively small sin of Adam, such a massive dose of satisfaction was necessary, who would be able to repair or satisfy the great sin committed in Christ's condemnation? Whom should one pay for this death? Who or what might serve now as reparations for such damage? If the crucifixion occurred as a function of divine justice, what justice is it that demands the death of an innocent man? Moreover, would God really be satisfied to see his Son dead for the sake of repairing the damage to his honor and justice? Luther felt this model suffered from an irreparable legalism and was incitement to a penitential (though not meritorious) practice stemming from an insuperable feeling of

---

[14] For a study of how Anselm elaborates the first ideological support for the totalitarianism of the capitalist market, see Franz Hinkelammert, "Economia y teología: Las leyes del mercado y de la fe," paper presented at the Consulta Nacional Sobre Dívida Externa a Igrejas, March 27–30, 1989. See also Hugo Assmann and Franz Hinkelammert, *A Idolatriada do Mercado: Ensaio sobre Economia e Teologia* (São Paulo: Vozes, 1989).

guilt. In regard to this model, he recalled the Latin maxim *summum ius summa iniuria* (law in the extreme is injustice in the extreme).

We can now introduce the subjectivist version. In the objectivist models, the human being has at most a supplementary and secondary function in the reconciliation process. Reconciliation is an objective fact whose benefits affect and condition human existence. When the subjectivist version arises in the twelfth century with Abelard, it already manifests an awareness of human coparticipation in providence, a characteristic that will go on to be affirmed in both Pietism and Puritanism and in the liberal theology of the nineteenth century. We can, however, recognize elements of this version in the Gospels, where Christ is associated with the image of teacher, just as, in the first centuries AD, Christ appears frequently as legislator, teacher, doctor, or example.

It's difficult to speak about the subjectivist model because, unlike the objectivist models, it doesn't have rigid outlines. But some elements stand out with different emphases.

To understand this version, it's important to know its point of departure: reconciliation is understood as an initiative of God's unconditional love. Abelard, who had already been Anselm's main critic, understood this love to be expressed most radically in the fact that God assumed human nature and remained obedient unto death, thus serving as teacher and example. This expression of love awakens in us a response that springs from faith in this love. Love is the manifestation of justice (Rom 3:25). We are reconciled with God through Christ because with his love, we are redeemed from sin and from fear. Therefore, God delivers Christ not as ransom to the devil or as reparations to satisfy divine justice but as a superabundant gift of grace from God for the benefit of humanity.

In Abelard, this version is only partially developed because he got a scolding from his contemporary Bernard of Clairvaux, who accused him of making Christ only a teacher of virtue: in the same way that it wasn't by Adam's example that we became sinners, it won't be by the example of Christ that we'll be reconciled with God. This criticism still resounds in Luther when he insists that, rather than being an example, Christ is a sacrament. But the Reform movement itself, though it broke down the structures of the medieval cathedral, permitted the resurgence of the subjectivist version in various quadrants, just as, in orthodoxy, it reedited the model of satisfaction.

A more radical formulation of the subjectivist version appears in association with the name Fausto Sozzini, the leader of an Anabaptist group that migrated in successive exiles from Italy to Poland, where it ended up being dismantled by the Jesuits in the middle of the seventeenth century. For Sozzini's followers, inspired by John Duns Scotus, the divine will is totally determinative, being in no way conditioned either for condemnation or for pardon. For this reason, one can't even speak of God's assuming the human condition, since that would already be in itself a determination imposed on his will, which in a certain manner would be conditioned to humanity. Christ is the human miracle that God caused to be born of a virgin (!) so that, through his life and example of perfect love and "active obedience," even unto death, he might manifest to us the divine love to which we have access through faith. God exemplified this love even by taking Jesus up into heaven. One can recognize in these arguments elements of the schema of contrast dealt with above. Death in itself, the cross, has a confirmatory function, authenticating Jesus's life practices. In this way, elements of rationalism are brought together with elements of supranaturalism.

Beginning with Immanuel Kant, who limited religion to practical reason and moral action, Sozzinism turned to theology by other, covert pathways. But before that, Pietism had already raised the flag announcing that Christianity was not about knowing but about doing (Philipp Spener), and this doing is the result of interior regeneration by means of faith. Such regeneration concerns the subject of faith and not its object. Faith is believing itself (*fides qua*) and not the content of belief (*fides quae*). The arena of reconciliation is neither in the cosmos where the struggle of God and the devil takes place nor in the juridical forum in which reparations are awarded for damages. The arena is human consciousness. Here we're back to the active obedience of Sozzini. From there to liberal theology is just a step. In liberal theology, the central problem is linked to the Enlightenment's cry for the autonomy of the individual. The possibility of a true faith must recognize that the idols in which people found comfort (the so-called proofs of Christianity: the miracles, the fulfillment of prophecy, and eventually, the expansion of Christianity) were not the proper support for a radical faith—the only true support being absolute dependence on God, even without proof. Friedrich Schleiermacher will seek to give more definite shape to this subjectivist version of the doctrine of reconciliation while avoiding a model of mere moral influence. Schleiermacher thinks he can achieve his aim by means of a historically based observation. The reconciling activity of Jesus is not in the simple example that Jesus sets but in the reality of a historical community that forms around him. It's by belonging to this community, of which Christ is the head, that the believer participates in the reconciling process itself, which takes place in this body (this community) as the body of Christ. Later, Albrecht Ritschl takes up this motif by emphasizing its eschatological character and defining this historical community as the decisive mark for the establishment of the kingdom. He also incorporates elements of the motif of covenant. The action of Jesus that leads to his death acts on his disciples by communicating the divine consciousness that was in him and was perfect. The work of reconciliation is not that of the human consciousness that recognizes in Jesus a mere example to be followed but the work of Jesus, who attracts disciples to his perfection, throughout history, by the proclamation of Jesus as the archetype of the new life. Whoever resists Jesus's magnetism convicts himself of sin and alienates himself from grace, which is experienced by living in community. What is the reconciling work of Jesus? He lives the perfection of the consciousness of God by demonstrating it in his life unto death, through which he communicates to us the love of God and attracts us to participate in the eschatological community.

The subjectivist version has received attention from various theological currents. But the difficulty that always presents itself is that of reducing Christ to a religious hero. All the reconstructions of this version attempt to make certain concessions to objectivism so as to avoid reducing Christianity to a moral exercise.[15] Their great merit

[15] Compromise formulations can be found in the Christologies of Emil Brunner and Paul Tillich.

lies in linking reconciliation with divine love and definitively valuing human participation in the process of reconciliation.

This version has sensitized middle-class consciousness in the search for a modernity that guarantees the autonomy of the individual and that cherishes the nostalgic dream of communitarian interactions that would compensate for the fragmentation in capitalist modernity. But this is also the model that, with a little retouching, made possible the formulation of political theology, in which Christ's work is not directly salvific but becomes so through its effects. Political theology affirms the memory of the passion of Christ (*memoria passionis Christi*) as the subversive element that reveals in the established order the agent of suffering or the incapacity of the system to face existing suffering. The memory of the passion also reveals the weak point of all systems of domination, which, when trying to give meaning to the existing order, utterly fail when they confront the lack of ultimate significance that death brings. For this reason, they need to conceal death. But the passion of Christ reveals, in a radical way, this lack of significance that all systems hide, because the death of Jesus was the death of a righteous man. Christ effects reconciliation not by some objective victory over evil but as the subject behind human subjects who moves them in their search for meaning for a life lived in the midst of the system's necrophilia. Christ, by his inexplicable death, creates the fundamental dissonance in the minds of his followers, who recognize, in all the systems that conceal death, the barrier that separates people from life.[16]

These subjectivist versions receive various criticisms. The basic question is in regard to their suppression of the mystical and to the practice of faith that tends to be replaced by pedagogy. If Jesus's life were meant to be summarized as an example, as motivation or a mobilizing force for awakening the consciousness of divine love in the search for reconciliation, then Christianity should consist of a nation of advisors rather than a nation of priests.

---

[16] See Helmut Peukert, *Wissenschaftstheorie-Handlungstheorie-Fundamentale Theologie* (Düsseldorf: Patmos-Verlag, 1976); and Johann Baptist Metz, *Glaube in Geschichte und Gesellschaft* (Mainz: Matthias-Grünewald, 1977).

Theology on the Cross

The attempts to rework the significance of the cross for theology need to be understood as the result of what appears to be the original of the Gospels themselves. The followers of the Nazarene were perplexed by the way their leader ended up. The search for meaning calms the perturbed conscience and arises like a kind of celestial compensation that soothes the restless heart. We might call it the asylum for victims of terror. If that were enough, though, we'd be happy to experience the contentment of the satisfied, of those who no longer question or feel scandalized by the terrible curse. Not only the type of argumentation that a model contains but the simple fact of becoming a model is already a way of adorning the cross with roses. A model closes the discussion. It has one meaning—only one. For the sake of resolving the infinite drama, we suspend in the air all the finite crosses of death with which we cohabit. In a world of crucified people, an outrage greater than that of the very cross of Christ is robbing it of its scandal, thus untying the knot of our perplexity face-to-face with daily crosses. The Christian tradition itself never made a dogma of the meaning of the cross, contrary to what it did with other themes of theology. It retained only the *hyper* formula. It was theologians who made models from the interjection "cross-in-credo." And these models emptied the cross into the credo, like Scorsese's devil, who takes Christ off the cross to put him into the kerygma. This poem by the Spaniard Antonio Machado registers a critique of devotion to the Christ of agony:

> Who will lend me a ladder
> to climb up the tree
> to remove the nails
> from Jesus the Nazarene?
> (*popular Flamenco song*)
> Oh, the song, the singing
> to Christ by the gypsies,
> always with blood on their hands
> always to remove the nails!
> The song of the Andalusian people,
> who every spring

> go begging ladders
> to climb up the cross!
> The song of my land,
> which throws flowers
> at the Jesus of agony,
> and it's the faith of my elders!
> Oh, you are not my song!
> I can't and won't sing
> to that Jesus of the tree,
> but rather to the one who walked on the sea![17]

Machado presents popular piety as that which goes in search of ladders to take Jesus down from the cross. But before ordinary people thought of doing that, it was theologians who, like the friends of Job, set out looking for ladders to remove the *signifier* from the cross and lift him up as the *signified* of proclamation.

The search for the relevance that the cross has for us leads us to affirm its suprahistorical meaning, since only in that way is the event liberated from its historical particularity so that its importance for all of history stands out.[18] And there's the paradox: the more we resolve the question of its significance, the more we distance ourselves from the signifying event that generated our search. Tillich (rightly) corrects the tendency to separate the life of Jesus from his death as a way of separating the particular from the universal: "The story of the cross of Jesus does not relate an isolated event in his life but the event toward which the story of his life is directed." However, Tillich simplifies and sublimates the scandal too much when he immediately ends the sentence, saying, "and in which other events acquire their meaning."[19] The problem is that before assuming any significance, the cross that is the culmination of the life and practice of Jesus is a scandal. This is the scandal of particularity, the scandal of that cross inserted into a historical context.

---

17 Antonio Machado, *Poesias* (Buenos Aires: Losada, 1877), 149–50.
18 Emil Brunner, *The Mediator* (Philadelphia: Westminster, 1947), 504–5.
19 Paul Tillich, *Systematic Theology* (Chicago: University of Chicago Press, 1957), 2:158.

But what, then, should we say? Would the only appropriate response be silence in the face of the unfathomable mystery of this tragic enigma? Should we be informed by the neopositivism of Wittgenstein, for whom death is beyond the world of facts and thus is a matter for which there is no appropriate question or response and that belongs to that about which it is impossible to speak?

Religion is always the celebration of a question and the search for an answer that invariably is "beyond." Therein lies the truth of this sarcastic comment by Mário Quintana, who says that he doesn't understand why people change religions. Why would anyone need to change doubts? Not that all doubts are equally harrowing, but they are celebrated differently! Silence on religious issues only establishes the dimensions of the exclamation points and question marks that conclude questions and answers.

If Christ is the answer, it's not enough only to know exactly what the question is; it's necessary to recognize that this answer is pregnant with an even greater question that transcends it. It's not enough to remove the roses that cover the cross; it's necessary to recover the fear, the indignation, and all the passion. This is Luther's definition of a theologian of the cross: (S)he's the one who tells it like it is. But that is only an exclamation or an interrogation; it doesn't offer a ready-made solution. Even if the comparison may seem spurious, I don't think that we're reading anything different in Marx when he says that "given that the truth of another world has disappeared, the task of history consists in establishing the truth of the world that is here." And in the same context, he speaks about religion as the "sigh of the oppressed creature" and the "opium of the people." He also says that "criticism does not rip the imaginary flowers from the chains so that the human being must bear these chains without consolation or fantasy, but so that he may throw off those chains and be able to gather living flowers."[20] The question ends with an exclamation: *Cur Deus Homo!* And it's fitting to have an examination of the answer.

---

[20] Karl Marx and Friedrich Engels, *Sobre la Religión*, ed. Hugo Assmann and Reyes Mate (Salamanca: Sigueme, 1974), 94.

The mystery that leads us in search of an infinite resolution brings us back to the small lights. The search for meaning is inherent in fear and amazement. Therein lies the reason for schemas, motifs, and models that attempted throughout history to resolve the enigma of the crucifixion. But dialectically, they led to its dissolution. The important thing is to overcome the indifference of those who no longer ask questions, either because they already know the solution or because they refuse to recognize the enigma and the scandal. The attempts to give meaning to the cross are these small lights that illumine parts of a path. Some lights help us better than others to find our way. Some flash for an instant, blinding us and making us believe that we've seen everything already. But they are not the sun that unmasks the darkness. As metaphors, the attempts to interpret the cross preserve the tension between the meaning and the mystery; they maintain the resolutely irresolute passion.

In the discussion of the interpretations of the cross, I have sought to indicate relevant images for the construction of metaphors that help situate us facing the perplexity of the cross of Jesus so that we can keep open the question about the crosses that support death in the modern world. But the radicality of the cross cannot be concealed. Only in this way will we be able to seek the path that separates Calvaries from already empty tombs. This is the manner in which we can practice the resurrection today: celebrating questions and examining responses.

THE VOICE THAT COMES FROM NATURE

Whenever the elements of the world
are corrupted by mistreatment,
God will cleanse them through the suffering
and rigors of humanity.
God offered all creation to human beings
for their use.
But if this privilege is abused,
God permits creation to punish humanity.

—Hildegard of Bingen, 1098–1179

To Begin the Conversation

In the land of Brazilwood [Brazil is named after a particular type of red-colored wood once plentiful and highly prized by Europeans for dyeing cloth], the ecological crisis has already been announced for what it is. From the tree that's the color of a red-hot brazier, we got our name. The tree has gone away, carried off by caravels, themselves made of wood. The construction of those ships practically deforested Europe.[1]

The term *ecology* arose in the mid-nineteenth century to designate the interrelation between plants and animals in their ambient zones. Only in the middle of the twentieth century did this term begin to be applied also to human communities and to receive

Originally published in *Estudos Teológicos* 30, no. 1 (1990): 16–26.

1 Christian Schuetze, "Waldgeschichte und Weltgeschichte," *Der Ueberblick* 3, no. 89: 5–8.

general acceptance as the science that studies the structure and development of human communities in their process of adaptation to the environment, including the effects produced by that process.

In short, it's a new term designating a new problem typically linked with our Western society. It's one of those problems that humankind has set itself to resolve. Expectations regarding this problem are optimistic. After all, as Marx would say, if we know how to define the problem, we'll know how to resolve it. But we are also stalked by the apocalyptic specter of the inevitable immensity of the questions involved. Attacking the problem leaves us with the impression of having a short bedsheet that covers our legs but uncovers our arms. At least it seems as if those are the options. In order not to inundate the Amazon region, we have to construct nuclear power plants, but to avoid constructing nuclear power plants or inundating Amazonia, we need thermoelectric plants. That is, we have the choice among (1) destroying the tropical forests, (2) not knowing how to dispose of nuclear waste, and (3) using fossil fuels that will aggravate the greenhouse effect.

The presupposition, of course, is that we will continue to need electrical energy at increasing levels. But questioning that presupposition or adjusting growth to alternative forms of energy, like solar, is a prescription that has its undesirable side effects too, especially for the two-thirds of humankind who suffer from underdevelopment. That's why environmental proposals originating in the Northern Hemisphere sound as if they come from a gambler who wants to leave the table while he's winning.

I cite an example tied to the question of the hole in the ozone layer caused by chlorofluorocarbon (CFC) gas in aerosols, refrigerators, and air conditioning units. Almost all refrigerators function with this gas. Refrigeration of food is one of the most effective means of reducing diarrhea, which is the major cause of infant mortality in underdeveloped countries. A 35 percent reduction in the production of this gas by 1999 was approved by twenty-four industrialized countries in 1987 in the Montreal Protocol. It is reasonable to think that expansion of the use of CFCs south of the equator at the same levels at which it has been used in the Northern Hemisphere would be catastrophic. But who decides that the four billion poor people in this world can't use refrigerators the way rich people do and that the poor can buy only non-CFC devices, which are much more expensive and not even available in poor countries? Confronting the ecological crisis involves us in one of those problems in which the following advice may be valuable: if you want to kill the king, get him with your first shot.

In fact, we're facing one of those problems that require a radical approach, a reorientation of the very presuppositions with which Western society has coexisted for the last five hundred years—namely, we need to Orientalize Western ways. A radical option is one that goes to the root of the problem. The ecological problem implies the totality of existence. Thus it is a fundamentally religious problem.

The Face of Sin

Ecological problems are enmeshed in a network of broad questions. All interconnected and overlapping, they reveal the groan of creation, its Good Friday. It's nature itself that's speaking to us and, like God to Noah, announcing the independence of the end. Eschatology has already ceased being the exclusive discipline of theology. We live with the terrible realization that, unlike anything in previous eras of history, we arrived in the middle of the twentieth century at the point that we control the means to destroy the basis of life as we know it. Along with the triumph of progress, we inherited the dirty burden of knowing that not only did we eat the fruit from the tree of life; we put the ax to its trunk. Robert Oppenheimer, who developed the atom bomb used by the United States against Japan, expressed very well the awareness of lost innocence when he declared in 1948, "Scientists have met sin."

Today, we recognize three orders of crucial problems linked to the environment: (1) the atomic problem, (2) chemical problems, and (3) the demographic problem.

The atomic problem has two aspects. One is war, and the other is energy. Of all the problems we face, none has done more to alert the world to the possible destruction of life on this planet than has the threat of nuclear war. The current weakening of the spirit of the Cold War and the first gestures toward the dismantling of nuclear arsenals removed from our minds the image of the horseman of the apocalypse astride an atomic bomb. But the use of nuclear energy is far from convincing anyone of the safety of its methods. Atomic fission involves risks that Three Mile Island and Chernobyl had the effect of removing from the realm of the hypothetical. Moreover, the development of technology and its application are far ahead of the capacity to figure out what to do with atomic waste, which remains active for centuries. Finally, the application of nuclear energy for medical purposes is already responsible for the largest radioactive accident since Chernobyl. The case of the capsule of Cesium 137, inadvertently opened in Goiânia (1987), reveals the tragic irony that our best intentions can be converted into bizarre tragedies.

Chemical problems have increased vastly, from the question of ozone to household pollutants. The wearing away of the ozone layer caused by releasing CFC into the atmosphere has, in the regions of Antarctica, already reached the 50 percent mark and permits the penetration of UVB rays. Besides skin cancer, UVB can cause changes in the genetic code (DNA), and the consequences of such changes are unpredictable.

Carbon dioxide, launched into the atmosphere by the use of fossil fuels, results in a thermal barrier that impedes the liberation of heat. This phenomenon is known as the greenhouse effect and is already responsible for an average increase in temperature of 0.5°C, with a projection of 3°C by the year 2030. If that doesn't seem like much, it's helpful to remember that such an average increase can represent the melting of the polar ice caps and the consequent rise of sea levels by seventy-five centimeters. Considering that one-third of the earth's population lives within sixty kilometers of ocean coasts, migration alone would have unthinkable consequences. Beyond that, the greenhouse effect, while it increases the humidity of the atmosphere and the level of rainfall, extracts moisture from the soil even more rapidly. This would cause an increase in the rate of germination, especially of weeds, and would thus require increased application of herbicides in agriculture.[2] In the case of Brazil, even without the consequences of

[2] Gerald Barney, *The Physical Environment*, mimeo, February 15, 1989.

the greenhouse effect, the use of agrotoxins quadrupled in tonnage from 1965 to 1980.

To these problems, one must add the question of garbage produced by large cities, plus the water pollution caused by the use of nonbiodegradable products and mercury pollution, which in some areas endangers flora and fauna and puts human survival itself at risk—not to mention the frequent ecological accidents caused by spills of chemical products or combustibles in our waterways, lakes, and seas.

Finally, we have the problems related to demographic expansion, which coincides with various aspects of the ecological crisis. To get an idea of what this expansion means, the human population of the planet took five hundred thousand years to reach a population of 250 million at the beginning of our era. It then doubled around the year 1650. It reached one billion in 1830, two billion in 1930, and four billion in 1975. These are the intervals in years for doubling: 1,650, 180, 100, 45. In fact, what took place was a demographic explosion, from the seventeenth century onward. But that does not mean overpopulation.[3] The problems related to the demographic explosion are caused by unequal occupation of spaces and resources.

The Malthusian thesis of the geometric expansion of the population and of the arithmetic increase in the production of foodstuffs was proved false. What is true is that the distribution of resources and spaces takes place in an unequal, centralizing way. This centralizing model has forced populations into an irrational occupation of space, which, in the case of Brazil, is expressed in the policy of colonizing the Amazon region and consequently destroying the forest and its inhabitants. On a worldwide level, the process of colonizing Asia, Africa, and Latin America already brought with it the destruction of 42 percent of the tropical forests.[4] The destruction of the forests is an aggravating factor in the greenhouse effect. Demographic expansion

---

3 On this question, see my article "Planejamento Familiar: Genocídio Planejado?," in *Proclamar Libertação*, ed. Harald Malschitzky and Uwe Wegner, vol. 12 (São Leopoldo: Sinodal, 1986), 77–86 (esp. 78–80).

4 Ulrich Duchrow and Gerhard Liedke, *Schalom: Der Schöpfung, Befreiung, den Menschen Gerechtigkeit, den Völkern Frieden* (Stuttgart: Kreuz, 1988), 18.

becomes a problem because it reduces the flexibility or the margin for human error in the occupation of space. This is not intended to raise an apocalyptic shout to denounce the dangers of overpopulation, precisely because estimates are that the world's population will stabilize when it reaches fifteen billion, which is a number within the planet's capacity for absorption. The critical point ecologically is inequality in the occupation of spaces and resources.

In point of fact, we are objectively getting closer to one another. The consequence of the effects of our actions occurs more rapidly. An indigenous tribe living in its habitat can throw its waste products into the river for centuries without any negative implications for the ecosystem. But if this is the practice of a large city, the negative results are already well known. The ecological movement and the organizations in defense of the environment have encouraged the expression of concrete struggles ranging from the problem of garbage to nuclear energy. But everyone realizes that the crux of the issue is the posture we assume in relation to nature. Whatever change we make in confronting the ecological problem necessarily, though not exclusively, passes through the reformulation of this posture.

Dominate and Subdue

Discussing the problem of ecology in theological terms demands a series of mediations. In the first place, we're not talking about a major biblical theme, and very little about ecology is directly dealt with in the history of the church.[5] Moreover, Jesus's anger at the fig tree (Mark 11:12–14:20) or the folkloric narrative of St. Boniface's decision to cut down a sacred oak tree to show the power of the Christian faith against paganism will certainly not be the most sympathetic images we can lend to the ecological movement. But the arguments against the Judeo-Christian tradition are quite a bit more serious.

---

[5] Matthew Fox, "Creation-Centered Spirituality from Hildegard of Bingen to Julian of Norwich," in *Cry of the Environment: Rebuilding the Christian Creation Tradition*, ed. Philip N. Joranson and Ken Butigan (Santa Fe: Bear, 1984), 85–106; Richard Woods, "Environment as Spiritual Horizon: The Legacy of Celtic Monasticism," in *Cry of the Environment: Rebuilding the Christian Creation Tradition*, ed. Philip N. Joranson and Ken Butigan (Santa Fe: Bear, 1984), 62–84.

In a famous 1967 article, "The Historical Roots of Our Ecologic Crisis," Lynn White Jr. caused a furor but received equal support by affirming that "our science and technology arose from the Christian attitude toward the relation between man and nature."[6] This attitude might be the result of the dominant axiom in the Judeo-Christian tradition, according to which nature has no other reason for existing except to serve the human being. The P narrative of creation in the Hebrew Bible has this peculiarity: the last act of creation is the human being, from whom all the rest of creation acquires its meaning and at whose disposition all the rest is placed. In White's view, Christianity, which inherited and deepened this notion, ended up being the most anthropocentric of all the religions that the world has ever seen. Hence the contradiction that we live with. Man is the crown of creation (Ps 8), but he turns against his biological support and destroys it. White's argument is that "Judeo-Christian teleology" (that everything involves the redemption of man) is the framework within which the development of science was possible in the West. But it's in the mysticism of Eastern Christianity and in the piety of St. Francis of Assisi that White himself seeks the religious antidote for the troubles of the West. He goes so far as to propose St. Francis of Assisi as the "patron saint of ecologists." Let's remember that thirteen years later, John Paul II took the hint and declared St. Francis the "patron saint of ecology."

White's argument rests on two pillars: first, that the understanding of the *homo-natura* relation constitutes the fundamental opposition in the Judeo-Christian tradition, and second, that this opposition, which privileges man at the expense of nature, constitutes the foundation for the development of technology and science in the West.

As for the first point, White's interpretation depends on the reading of Genesis 1:1–2:4a. The question of dominion and subjection (vv. 26 and 28), as well as the affirmation of the earth creature (Adam) as the image of God, can lead to the interpretation White suggests if that question and affirmation are taken out of context. In truth, the priestly narrative of creation culminates not with the human

---

[6] Lynn White Jr., "The Historical Roots of Our Ecologic Crisis," *Science* 155 (1967): 1203–7.

being but with the day of adoration and rest, which includes all of nature and justifies the Jubilee year.[7] Therein lies an important break from the narrative pattern of the Babylonian myth of creation, from whose influence the P narrative suffers (having been written in the Babylonian exile!). After the creation of man, the Babylonian myth focuses on the institution of the monarchy and the temple cult.[8] The question of the image of God also emerges against this background. In the myths of Egypt and Mesopotamia, this image is attributed only to the king.[9]

In this context, the question of dominion appears as a democratizing task. Its reference is only to the animals, which at the same time are not included in what is intended for human consumption (Gen 1:29). To have dominion over the animals is to establish a peaceful coexistence with them. At least until the Neolithic Period (3000 BCE), animals represented an existential threat to the human race, which was estimated to number one hundred thousand. Today it is thought probable that the world's great steppes were the result of humans' hunting with fire during the Pleistocene (six hundred thousand years ago). Viewed in their proper context, the question of man's image and dominion is an affirmation of the need to get along peaceably with animals and is an indirect negation of the domination and subjection of human beings by other human beings. In that way, the question touches on the ecological problem in reverse. That is, human communities are the weak link in the equilibrium. It's not the *homo-natura* opposition that characterizes Genesis 1:1–2:4a, which is the biblical text considered most problematic in relation to ecology.

What's correct in White's argument is that the ecological crisis is intimately connected to the development of science and technology in the Western world. But the roots of this crisis, though they arise in a Christian context, result not from Christian theology but rather from the vision of nature that dates back to the sixteenth century. Copernicus took the first step in this direction. The great impact of

7 Milton Schwantes, *Projetos de Esperança* (Petrópolis: Vozes, 1989), 32–35.

8 Claus Westermann, *Creation* (Philadelphia: Fortress, 1974), 51.

9 Nelson Kilpp, *Teologia do Antigo Testamento*, mimeo (Preleção CAT-EST), 1988.

his astronomical discovery was not to put the sun at the center of our system but to deny that the world has a center.[10] Matter, in its extensiveness, no longer possesses a stable and objective reference point. It's always relative to the possibility of its observation by the human mind. From this idea results the dualism of Descartes between the thinking thing (the mind) and the extended thing (matter), which is only an enormous mechanism to be exploited and manipulated through knowledge ("thinking points").[11]

This dualism lies behind science and technology, which view nature as a simple object of knowledge for the purpose of human use or interest: to know in order to predict, to predict in order to have power (or knowledge is power). Only the mind has power in itself. Nature is only a manipulable object. This dualism, which today characterizes the Western world and determines the type of relation that we have with nature, has its origin at the beginning of modernity, in the early days of capitalism, which can be understood only from the standpoint of nature as an object to be appropriated—that is, to become the property or material extension of the thinking being. We do not find such dualism in Judeo-Christian thought. It's a typical fruit of modernity.

Sacred Confusion

Between apocalyptic pessimism and the optimism of those who expect technology to provide the solution to the intricate problems of ecology, there is a path of hope. But contrary to the other historic problems we face (land, housing, health, education, wages, foreign debt, etc.), the problem of ecology brings different challenges: first, because it permeates all the other problems and, second, because its solution requires a change in the paradigms that inform the values of our society. The ecological problem is different from all the others in that it is not primarily a technical problem; it doesn't involve making certain adjustments. Rather, it involves a reorientation in our understanding of our relation with nature, including the nature in

[10] R. G. Collingwood, *The Idea of Nature* (Oxford: Oxford University Press, 1978).
[11] Max Scheler, *Man's Place in Nature* (New York: Beacon, 1961), 71–77.

us, our bodies. It's a cultural problem that goes to the root of culture itself—that is, to its religious substance. Hence it involves fundamental questions that are starting to be discussed and that negate the Western system of thought and of capitalism, which sustains this system socially, politically, and economically. Among the ideas to be negated, we have the belief in progress as accumulation, the absolute and irreducible valuing of the individual, and the confining of religion to subjectivity. To confront these ideas, I suggest we examine three basic questions.

First, from Hobbes to Leibniz to recent positivists, the individual is the irreducible and determining component of the social fabric. "The individual," said Nietzsche, "is the latest creation." The collective, civil society, is composed of contractual arrangements among these individuals so as to affirm their interests: man is the wolf of man (Hobbes). What disappeared with modernity is the community as the center of decision-making and of defining individuality, where reason and passion were still not separated, where solidarity is organic, and where spatial and ambient limits—that is, the place of your community—are constitutive of your organicity. To think of politics and ecology together as one thing, on the basis of community, is the challenge facing us. An analysis of class is fundamental to evaluating the question of justice in society, which is implied in the question of ecology. But to abstract the communitarian question from the ecological question and to remain in the binomial class-state would impede an appreciation of the cultural diversification in the life of a group, of its soul. It's in the recovery of the concept and reality of community as an instrument of social organization and of the structuring of the exercise of a group's power that politics and ecology can begin to be thought of holistically. Ecology speaks to us about the internal "logic" of a habitat, its spirit.

Second, another question is that of work. Fundamental for the Western world, where capitalism arises and finds affirmation, is the understanding of work as the appropriation of nature as a function of human interests. Nature in itself loses value, and the product extracted or made from it and defined by its use is what also determines its value. The accumulation of this value is what determines the scale of progress. Abuse is built into the value of its use. The dualism that separates matter from spirit or mind and turns matter into a means to be added to the subject who exploits it in order to accumulate capital is characteristic of Western thought. This attitude is not restricted only to nature outside the human being. The very nature of the worker himself, his body, is treated in the same way—that is, on the basis of the result that one expects to accumulate from the worker, not on the organic relation of the human being with external nature. Marx referred to this treatment of the worker as metabolism (Stoffwechsel).[12] To focus on work based on its organic process and not on its dead result accumulated in capital requires a fundamental reorientation of our social values. It requires an understanding that work, before it is an intervention, is an organic process that grounds human existence itself. This idea brings us close to the Yahwistic concept of creation, where the order to guard and cultivate the garden (Gen 2:15) is directed to the very living being (*adam*) who was formed out of the earth (*adamah*, Gen 2:7).

A metabolic understanding of work offers the possibility of approaching the problem of justice so that human interests are not the only thing at stake and so that nature is regarded as a font of resources to be equitably distributed. This approach also promotes respect for the voice that comes from nature as the very extension of human corporeality, with which it is organically linked. This organic link is what reveals, in Luther's words, the "majesty of matter." This means that the concepts of distributive and retributive justice must be subordinated to the attributive concept of justice, according to which everything that is, simply by being, possesses claims implicit in its being. The basis for such a concept comes not from laws as positive and circumstantial expressions of these claims but from the very foundation of everything that is, whose dignity is based on the affirmation that it is divine creation. Certainly, human justice possesses a value that distinguishes it qualitatively from the claims of the rest of nature, simply

---

[12] On the relevance of this concept for rethinking the ethical question, see my article "Labor: A Suggestion for Rethinking the Way of the Christian," *Word and World* 6, no. 2 (1986): 194–206.

because it is the human being who recognizes and establishes these claims. But there also resides in the human being an incapacity to love with the love that unites what is separated. And whenever the human being is silent and does not recognize what is just, nature will raise her voice until even "the stones would shout out" (Luke 19:40).

A third question is that of spirituality. The great movements of spiritual renewal that take place starting in the seventeenth century (Pietism, Methodism, Puritanism) share the fundamental characteristics of modernity, with its clear distinction between subject and object, between grace and nature. Cartesian dualism is transfigured but is not overcome. Although the critical basis for recognizing truth and grace is feeling rather than reason, it's still the atomized individual who floats over this world, suspended by faith in the supernatural. Pietism may recognize the recovery of elements of the mysticism that Luther inherited from Germanic theology, but these elements were adjusted to new times. Pietism is also a fruit of this era. The ecological crisis today demands a spiritual renewal that finds more inspiration in medieval mysticism (Hildegard of Bingen, Francis of Assisi, Mechthild of Magdeburg, Meister Eckhart, and Julian of Norwich, among others) than in Pietist renewal. What distinguishes these medieval figures and makes them relevant today for ecology is their appreciation of nature as a place of epiphany—that is, as divine creation. However, this does not mean what it meant in Scholasticism, which sought to find in nature the laws that would reveal the divine mind. Mysticism attempts to bring present mysteries into close proximity to the divine creation that surrounds us.

If we understand nature as an expression of the divine mystery, in the sense that nature simultaneously reveals and conceals that mystery, we have the opportunity to find new ways of representing God. For example, Meister Eckhart did one such new representation in dealing with the classic question of Augustine: What has God been doing since eternity (creation)? To which Eckhart responded, without any of the philosophical torments of the Bishop of Hippo, "Since all eternity, God has been on a birthing bed, giving light."[13]

---

[13] Fox, "Creation-Centered Spirituality," 98.

The attempt to reformulate the question of revelation by means of new images distinguishes mysticism from Scholasticism. In mysticism, nature manifests the divine mystery, to which reason cannot attain. In Scholasticism, nature reveals to reason the creator hidden behind his creation. It is this same distinction that Luther preserves by separating the theology of the cross from the theology of glory. For Luther, God is not to be found behind creation, where he is sought through reasoned arguments, but God is *in* creation. Creation is the wrapping or the mask (*involucrum* or *larva*) of a God whose face we will never see. This notion of mysterious and irremovable packaging in which God is wrapped but that is not itself God grants to nature a sacred dignity without falling into pantheism. It avoids looking at nature as a profane object without turning it into the universal source of revelation. God remains hidden in what is not God, but even so, God is definitively present in it: the finite touches the infinite. This is a God who, paradoxically, offers himself without mediations (sacraments or reason) but always next to them and indirectly with them. This revelation is the *mediated immediate.* It doesn't happen because of mediations, but neither does it happen without them. This conception is linked to the mystical understanding of knowledge through participation in the mystery, and it is distinguished both from subjectivist pietism, in which there is no mediation for grace (except faith itself: *fides qua*), and from ecclesial orthodoxies, in which institutions, sayings, and rites are the mediating precondition of grace.

An Initial Proposal

The question about work, community, and mysticism reveals that the ecological problem requires a total reorientation of the way we consider the relation between the human being and his environment: a metanoia. This is a profoundly spiritual and religious task given that it's based on the presupposition that our best intentions resulted in drastic mistakes (*I cannot not sin*). Facing the ecological question demands overcoming humanism through the recognition that everything that is in humanism has a basis that is not in us—that is, humanism comes not from the side from which we come but from the darkest depths of that other side.

In the Christian tradition, baptism has served as a sacramental expression of the renewal of Christian existence. It's an expression with which we affirm the newness of life and the death of our former existence. But baptism is not only this renewal of the individual by water and the word linked to it; it's the overcoming of the individual as an individual for the affirmation of community existence. This "rebirth" is the founding element of the community. Thus it is not an event restricted to the individual conscience. It's not the death of the individual so that he can be reborn as another individual. It's the death of the individual so that he can be reborn as a new corporeality. That's why the question of the baptism of adults or infants is misconstrued when the criterion is conscience and not the integration of the body into a new sphere. What's involved here are the senses and not reason. For this reason, when we affirm the simultaneous character of the word and the element, we talk not about words directed to the conscience but about the divine "logos," which is "contained" within the water itself and in whose name its celebration is authorized, as Luther affirms in the Large Catechism. Framing baptism this way, I suggest that it is an ecological sacrament in which the water, divinely qualified by the word, is neither what washes away our sin nor an external sign or representation of a "spiritual" transformation, these being the two interpretations that Luther rejects. The water is the element with which divine creation operates through nature, not to make it immaculate but to renew it, by binding the human being to the nature from which he is formed. Symbolically, it's what permits the clay (*adamah*) from which the earth creature (*adam*) is formed not to disintegrate into dust but to be rehydrated and reintegrated into the natural cycle by this universal element that interconnects all ecosystems. The loss of this constitutive dimension of baptism is responsible for the way this sacrament has lost its corporative, communitarian, and creative dimension.

It's fitting to recall, as a final note, that nature as creation is not in itself divine. The respect due to nature derives not from its merits but from the right to life, which in the last analysis guarantees human life, especially for those who are on the margins of existence. It's not necessary to emphasize that natural processes are usually violent, that the struggle of the species is real, and that the survival of the fittest occurs at the expense of those who don't adapt. This, at least, we learn from Darwin. What's in question is the new datum that arises in the present century. It doesn't seem, in the three or four billion years of the evolution of life and of natural tragedies, that there has ever been a species on earth with the power to destroy life as such. We have acquired this power. And this truth is so decisive because the destruction and manipulation of nature begin with the destruction and manipulation of the body of people who are being exploited. *Ecce homo!* Perhaps in this way also we come closer to the mystery of the incarnation. God could not have emptied himself any more completely than by choosing human form from among all the varied work of his creation. Otherwise, "consider the lilies of the field."

MISSION AND POWER

THE HIDDEN GOD AND THE INSURGENT POWERS

Denunciation of the Conquest and Expropriation of Spiritual Territories

Almost seventy years ago, José Carlos Mariátegui defined the conquest of Latin America as an "essentially military and religious" undertaking. "The missionaries," he wrote, "did not impose the gospel; they imposed the cult, the liturgy."[1] What we remember of this conquest is nothing more than the intransigent imposition of a religious crust/shell associated fraternally with a structure of power under which the most diverse forms of religiosity were swarming. What, finally, do we remember of all that? From Porto Cabrália,[2] we remember the first and second mass, the fantastic social and ecclesial order achieved with the "reductions" of the Guarani. We remember the emotional narratives of the missionaries who described the fascination of the natives with the great liturgical presentations, like the first mass, and the attitude of the indigenous people as they kissed the cross in imitation of Cabral's crew. But we also remember the lamentations of Manuel de Nóbrega over the natives' inability to live out and practice the evangelical virtues and learn the contents of Christian catechesis. Another memory worth mentioning is the statement made by Oswald de Andrade, which centuries later had the effect of making us all feel

Originally published in *Estudos Teológicos* 31, no. 2 (1991): 183–92.

1 José Carlos Mariátegui, *7 ensayos de interpretación de la realidad peruana* (Lima: Amauta, 1979), 169, 173.

2 The first Portuguese settlement in Brazil was Porto Cabrália, named for Pedro Cabral, the commander.

like indigenous peoples—that is, still anthropophagically fascinated by the trinkets from overseas but stubbornly resistant to catechesis and to mission: "We were never catechized. We live by virtue of our right to sleepwalk. We made it so that Christ was born in Bahia or in Belém do Pará."[3]

The connection between the cross and the sword, between mission and power, does not appear to have been unreasonable or an abuse that perverted the gospel, as is frequently suggested. This connection did not exactly inhibit the announcement of the gospel. Rather, it would be more correct to say that this very connection concealed and denied the gospel!

The celebration of the five-hundredth anniversary of the conquest reopened the discussion of mission and power in ecclesiastical circles. In Christianity, with the possible exception of the churches of the Orthodox rite, whose break with Western Christianity dates from 1054, no other tradition can plead historical innocence in regard to what the conquest represented for the practical definition of what mission has meant for Christianity over the last five hundred years. The Reformation will come almost three decades after Columbus. It's for this reason that the "Message of the 8th Assembly of the Lutheran World Federation" in Curitiba, Brazil (1990), calls upon the Lutheran communion to use the occasion of the five hundredth anniversary of the conquest "as a time of repentance and not of glorification" and to commit itself to protecting and guaranteeing the rights of indigenous peoples. Even the fact that Bartolomé de las Casas was accused of being Lutheran because of his defense of the indigenous against the *encomienda*[4] should not be taken as anything more than an epithet for "heretic" (an epithet, moreover, that Las Casas surely refused with his usual vehemence).

---

[3] Oswald de Andrade, "Manifesto antropófago," in *An Anthology of Brazilian Prose*, ed. R. L. Scott-Buccleuch and Mário Tèles de Oliveira (São Paulo: Ática, 1971), 388.

[4] See "Introdução" by Hans Magnus Enzensberger to Bartolomé de Las Casas, *The Devastation of the Indies: A Brief Account* (New York: Seabury, 1974), 6.

There is no reason to doubt that 1992[5] will be a year in which Christendom will intone more mea culpas than hymns of triumph. Will we, then, celebrate the emergence of a period of penitence that, with tears of contrition, will erase the stain of five hundred years of conquest? What agenda will govern this act of penitence that already is starting? What sort of tears are now being shed, tears of contrition or crocodile tears?

If the conquest was the imposition of the cult by means of power and the imposition of power by means of the cult, the proof of evangelical sincerity possesses, then, a plausible verification: the dissociation or inversion of the relation between mission and power. If the gospel was hidden in the way that mission and power were related, the gospel will also be discovered only when this relation changes radically. What signs might point to such a change? It's important to pay attention to the ecclesial and political agenda behind this preoccupation with purifying Christianity of the guilt of conquest. What do people say today about mission? Will we find in the missionary banners today being held high any inscriptions that redefine the relation between mission and conquest? Or will the past simply be whitewashed?

In the Europe now unifying, the order of the day is re-Christianization. The challenge lies with those secularized segments of the population, especially in eastern Europe. In Africa and the Middle East, the growth of Islam has encountered a Christianity no less willing to fight hand to hand for spiritual territory. The Persian Gulf War did not fail to get framed as a new Crusade. The accidental (?) bombing of a Christian church in Baghdad receives disproportional attention in the midst of the tragedies of war because it indicates what might be an alleged error by the allied legions.[6] In the Americas, the growth of Pentecostalism, the affirmation of Umbanda and Candomblé, the rise of oriental religions, and increasing

[5] Translator's note: This article was written in 1991.

[6] Translator's note: Westhelle is suggesting that because of the history of conquest in the West, even some current events, like the bombing of a church, tend to be interpreted as part of some conquest involving the imposition of religion. Such is also his point regarding *Lumen* 2000, a year-long evangelization project.

secularization have encountered responses and raised concerns, both from the Protestant side, with its proposal to evangelize a still pagan continent, and from the Roman Catholic side, with its program of new evangelization, together with the imposing project *Lumen* 2000.

The memory of the five hundred years of conquest comes at a time when the world is seeking a redefinition of its ideological and religious domains. Old strongholds fall or suffer profound redefinitions. It's worth reflecting on *The Communist Manifesto*'s characterization of modern times: "All that is solid melts into air." But more than all that, what already seemed to have evaporated has solidified once again. There are people talking about a religious renaissance. That's an exaggeration. What's happening is that religion is returning to the surface of discourse as the ideological fields that divided the world and that frequently adopted religious ideas are being dismantled. With the weakening of ideological confrontation on the geopolitical stage, religious expressions become manifest.

In virtue of this situation, the subject of mission comes to prominence, and it does so because the dismantling of ideological opposition in the geopolitical division of the world not only exposes the religious idealizations of groups, sects, confessions, and churches but also brings to consciousness the demarcation of the limits incorporated in the various proposals. Mission returns as a privileged item on the Christian agenda after more than a half-century in which, if mission was defined as the flame that fed the life of the church, it was mostly not presented as a project aimed at seducing people's conscience or at expanding the institutional domains of a religious system. Mission returns now with a certain expansionist (and nasty) habit of a triumphant Christendom. Since the end of World War II and the subsequent division of the world into ideological blocs that consolidated after the war, the West has impregnated with its style of life even the areas most remote from its sphere of influence. It is in this period that the ecumenical movement emerging from the World Conference of Life and Work has flourished, substituting for or taking the place of projects by the missionary societies. With the modest exception of proselytizing and expansionist efforts always associated with the idea of sects, Christianity has come to understand its action in the world as *diakonia*. In a world already divided, it was necessary to seek a common testimony that would be affirmed in service. The motto of the Life and Action movement, "doctrine separates, service unites," delineated the space in which this common testimony would be expressed. The dominant ecclesial model for conceiving of the presence of the church in the world was that of the servant church.

The shifting ecumenical movement now opens a new chapter. In a world that is magnetized around a hegemonic pole, the big question once again becomes mission. Might not the relative position of the capitalist West on the world stage be the hidden motivation for seeking a common testimony? Might not Hegel be right in saying that when a political party becomes strong, it divides itself? At the risk of sounding a bit cynical, we might say that in the absence of the major enemy who could invade the farm, now would be a good time to move the fences and take over more territory. Or to put it a bit differently, might international capitalism feel so sure of its present and future that ideological and religious disagreements in its midst can now be tolerated?

From Diakonia to Mission: Two Agendas and One Problem

The period now closing offered the church exemplary opportunities to recognize and reevaluate a practice that many times was deceptive and imperialist. In this period, there was born the awareness of five hundred years of a conquest that confused the cross with the sword. The diaconal model of the servant church, the church for others (Bonhoeffer), arose out of the necessity of repairing the effects of the conquistadors' enterprise. However, in this period, one must also look for a fundamental error that I believe is responsible for the weakening of the diaconal dimension. The missionary task had received only vague definitions. In a certain way, everything was mission, and nothing was mission. In a comparison among cultures and nations, or even among distinct religious spheres of influence, the differences among expressions of faith were relegated to a plane/level distinct from what was understood as service. Ethics and dogmatics remained separate from each other. Despite the efforts of theologies of liberation to define themselves as reflections on Christian practice, the great diaconal efforts resulted in attempts to put into practice certain ethical convictions that arose from evangelical imperatives and were fed by guilty consciences in thinking that prioritizing religious issues would be a return to proselytism. Theologies of liberation were themselves always tolerated and even encouraged when they were understood as the articulation of a Christian ethic, an effort to put correct doctrine into diaconal practice. But these theologies were frequently censured when they dared, on the basis of experience, to "correct" or reformulate doctrine. For the Roman Catholic Church, ecclesiology became holy ground. For Protestants, Scripture (and for Lutherans, in particular, the questions of grace and sin) became untouchable. The church that puts itself into service does so on the basis of an impermeable doctrinal sphere, a set of ideas that establishes its structure of power. This same impermeability of the sects and missions, with catechizing and expansionist intentions, took that doctrine and called for conversion. Now the relation is inverted. Mission arises as a specific task, a function to be performed, just like diakonia. This means that the relation between power and mission, as well as between power and diakonia, had not been thought through.

For our discussion, it's important to make clear that power is not only the result of the use of force in a situation of conflict; power is the means of affirming a structure (whether biological, sociological, political, economic, or cultural) when that structure is confronted by its limit or by what represents its negation. In all such encounters, power is exercised as a form of self-affirmation, whether the encounter involves conflict or not. For this reason, diakonia and service are also forms of the exercise of power. An ecclesial structure exercises power when it faces its limit. This is normal and endemic to any structure. The problem lies precisely in the connection between ends and means. If power is defined as a means of self-affirmation, the demonic aspect in the use of power resides in having it as an end and not as a means. The result is not only the compulsion and violence that deny the other's identity, his differentness, but the negation of the very being of the one who exercises the violence. This is the tragic observation in the fado [Portuguese-style song] that tells the other side of the conquest: "Navegar é preciso, viver não é preciso"

(Navigating is necessary; living is not). The means of self-affirmation that ends up destroying the other, the world of the Amerindian, is the force that turns against the very one who uses it, since what was destroyed was not a power that threatened the structure of the Iberian world but rather a face that offered the conquistadors the opportunity to recognize their own identity, their own humanity. This was the great contribution of Las Casas. He succeeded in demonstrating, in his victorious dispute with Juan Ginés de Sepúlveda, that it was the Spanish face itself that was disfigured in the destruction of the Amerindians. In this sense, the death of the other is also self-negation. What remains is power as an end in itself. McLuhan's famous phrase "The medium is the message" is the diagnosis of a situation in which the other is at most or only a sort of alienation. The conquistador has no face; he's the sword. The missionary has no message; he's the liturgy/cult that's being imposed. On the question of both diakonia and mission, serving and announcing, when power is not exercised as self-affirmation in the face of other power structures, implicitly recognized as such, it becomes demonic. Thus Loisy's observation assumes a critical character: "Jesus announced the Kingdom; what came was the Church." To paraphrase, the missionaries came because of the gospel but brought only the liturgy.

Strategies and Values of the Kingdom: Two Examples

Since Nietzsche, the Christian faith has been interpreted as promoting a religion of the weak, the resentful, and the cowardly whose will to power is perfumed by the incense of impotence, weakness, and incompetence. The slogan "not by power but by the word" (*non vi sed verbo*) might conceal the imperialism of a language that imposes power. Curiously, when Latin American theology proclaims God as a God of the poor, weak, and persecuted and attributes dignity to the shameful, voices are raised on various fronts to denounce this "new" theology. They accuse it of being responsible for violence, revolution, destruction of the existing order, and a seeking after power. The recent case of the discussion around the chair of feminist theology at EST [Escola Superior de Teologia in São Leopoldo, RS, Brazil] brought back the same ghosts.

Nietzsche's accusation is that the exercise of power is concealed within an ideology of weakness in the same way that sexism is concealed within a discourse that condescends to women by negating their right to self-affirmation from the structures of power. The refusal to recognize the power implicit in any structure is at the service of that power. And since its exercise is dissimulated, it becomes all the more vile. In the case of the conquest, the official discourse was that the conquest extended the benefits of Christianity to peoples who had no law, no king, no religion. The conquest was not presented as an exercise of power. Explicit violence arose when there was also an explicit self-affirmation of the power structure of a people.[7] Thus it is that the dissimulation of power that in fact gets exercised is the most vituperative form of its exercise, since from the outset it negates the power of others to affirm themselves. With the help of an example, I intend to show that the Christian faith is—that is, should be understood as—neither abandoning power nor affirming it as an end in itself but rather affirming it as an intransigent defense of the insurgent powers.

In chapter 6 of the Gospel of Mark, we find two quite familiar pericopes. What is not so well known is the way they were placed together for the sake of contrast. Without going into exegetical details, I will emphasize the presentation of these two strategies as used by two agents of transformation in the face of the dominant power and as the self-affirmation of a subservient power. The pericopes are those of the death of John the Baptist and the feeding of the multitude.

The text begins by presenting the problem (vv. 14ff.): Jesus and John are leaders and agents with popular legitimation. Might Jesus be comparable to John? Is Jesus John resurrected, the one who continues John's mission? The response is contained in the comparison of the two pericopes. Both men are feared by Herod (here representing the dominant power). Both are respected by the people. But they have different strategies of power. John is preoccupied by the sin that fell upon the nation because of its corrupt leaders. He calls for repentance

[7] See the case documented by Miguel Léon-Portilla, *A conquista da América Latina vista pelos índios* (Petrópolis: Vozes, 1987).

and knows that those who should be directing the nation along paths of justice and righteousness are not fulfilling their obligations. The shepherds are feeding off the flock. John does not question the formal organization of power but denounces the reason for which power is not fulfilling its function. He accuses Herod of being personally responsible for these failures. The Gospel narrative recalls that this was the reason for John's incarceration. Even in prison, John still believes that something can change so as to correct the errors of the system. He believes in the conversion of the people who occupy positions of power, but he does not realize that power can be corrected only through an awareness of its limit—that is, through a recognition of what is beyond its structure. The text says that John spoke with Herod about the law and its demands and that Herod listened to him with a good mind.[8] The scene of the party that follows shows, however, that power has an intrinsic logic greater than the conscience of the individual who represents power. A power structure does not change through the conversion of minds. John is decapitated in a symbolic allusion to the separation between head and body, king and people, conscience and structure. After his death, his body was buried. A body without a head prefigures the fate of his disciples, who disappear from the scene and are not mentioned again in the rest of the Gospel. There's not a shadow of a doubt about the integrity of John and the importance of his activity. The pericope is inserted where it is to contrast with Jesus's strategy, which is presented immediately afterward.

The scene changes. The characters are Jesus, the disciples, and the people. The place is no longer the court, with the macabre banquet of absolute power, but the countryside, with its festival of sharing, communion, and life. The text is well known. I point out only what is important for the comparison of the strategies and visions of power. Instead of attacking those who hold power, Jesus focuses his attention on the people, who are thought of as a flock without a shepherd. The problem is not in the head; it's in the body. And the problem is hunger. Jesus's rejection of the charity-based proposal (go buy bread)

[8] Translator's note: Mark 6:20.

and the liberal proposal (every man for himself) prepares the way for the emergence of the self-affirmation of a power opposed to that of Herod. The question is organizing the people on the basis of sharing the little there is. The reason this text moves slowly in discussing the process by which the feeding of the multitude occurs is to make it very clear that any magical interpretation is to be rejected. The process matters. Even Herod could give bread, but Jesus offered the people a structure of self-affirmation. Jesus was not "greater" than John, as John might have said; Jesus was different. He brought a power with him—not the absolute power that would change everything but the power to relativize the powers by confronting them with their own limits. He achieved in his own person and through his actions a mystery that the people could never expect from a Herod messiah. With Jesus, the people would have to hope for themselves. Therein lies the central issue of the famous messianic secret. In the pedagogy of Jesus, revealing himself as the Messiah could take place only when the people themselves could understand that they, the people, were part of the very subject of the messianic action. The insurgency of subservient powers is what makes it possible to affirm that the kingdom is already here by virtue of the self-affirmation of the excluded but not yet here because the structures of power are relativized but not yet overcome. Power is perfected in weakness because absolute power is the negation of the one who holds it. Weakness perfects power because it relativizes power. The death of Jesus, which was different from John's, should be seen in this light. Certainly, Jesus's death resulted from the effectiveness of his mission, just as was the case with John, but Jesus's death was also a sacrifice for the continuation of the messianic consciousness. The difficult passage from John 14:12 thus assumes relevance: "Very truly, I tell you, the one who believes in me will also do the works that I do and, in fact, will do greater works than these." Heinrich Heine, the poet and Marx's companion in exile, said that the initiator must die in order not to become an apostate. It would be even more correct to say that the messiah dies so that the messianic movement may continue. His resurrection confirms his practice but does not turn him into a perennial angel on earth.

A Song of Liberation: The Living Foundation

Rather than thinking that this pedagogy leads to an enlightenment interpretation of the gospel, according to which the ultimate objective would be to affirm the autonomy of the human being, his total freedom, and free will, it is important to remember that the reference to God as the ultimate foundation of all reality is constant in this exercise. The relativization of the powers is the condition for the recognition of divine power. This is the heart of the narrative. Jesus lifts his gaze to heaven and blesses the lack of abundance. Different from John the Baptist, the reference is not to the law and the structures that sustain it but to the divine basis itself that sustains everything by faith alone. Faith is the name that is given to this ultimate confidence that sustains life in spite of all appearances, chances, and probabilities. That is why, from this confidence, radical faith draws the ultimate consequences, affirming that all the limits imposed even by the biological cycle of an individual have been overcome. This faith relativizes the very power structure of the biological organism—not by raising death as the absolute, uncrossable barrier but by relativizing life by the resurrection of the body.

Faith is what makes it possible to sustain with hope the incongruency between the foundation of life and the daily experience that denies us the space where life can flourish. The Lutheran tradition refers to this understanding of faith when it distinguishes *fiducia* from a faith propped up by external, contingent data (*notitia*). The evidence offered to our senses, the calculus of probabilities of what might happen given a certain course of events, and the control that we are capable of exercising over variables that condition our reality all cover up a more profound reality, a mystery that we cannot comprehend but that reaches out to us through faith. Betting on being surprised is what a person of faith does. To operate on these terms is to break with the causal thought of "Jews" and "Greeks" seeking signs and wisdom (1 Cor 1:22). It is this faith, as participation in the mysterious foundation of life, that gives power to those who apparently have no power and that guarantees them an "extra life." The insurrection of the power of the mutilated is always a story about resurrection.

Obviously, these observations cannot be verified by reason, even if reason affirmed them. But for theology, whose job it is to discourse about the mysterious "logic" of God, these affirmations are necessary and indispensable resources for interpreting certain characteristics of the religious experience. Religion is not the inversion or imitation of reality. Religion affirms a deeper reality that appearances only distort. Religion is the leap beyond the dark reality that obscures the mystery, toward what Luther called the *deus absconditus sub contraria especie*, a God whom we do not encounter directly in the pages of the official history and who presents himself not as a *deus nudus* but rather as wrapped and disguised in his own creation.

The Church and the Insurgency of the Powers: A Revelation in Disguise

I was saying that the theme of mission again becomes prioritized as an ecclesial task at this, the end of the second millennium. I suggested that the central problem is in the discussion between power and mission. One can at least suspect that when this discussion does not take place, mission is being confused with imposition. In relations of subordination, there can be neither mission nor communication. The awareness of this difficulty has led many theologies to detour around the classic approach that has oriented missionary thinking—that is, mission as sending to announce the reality of the resurrected one as the Lord of life. The problem that affects Christianity is that the means by which this announcement is made ends up frequently imposing a structure of power; instead of the gospel, it imposes the cult/liturgy. To avoid these problems, Christians have come to think of mission as deriving not from revelation but from the incarnation. The incarnation becomes the interpretative paradigm for justifying a missionary inculturation. The question concerning the differential and the specifically Christian remains open. Finally, incarnation is not dissolution; it brings division and conflict and has a resolution. Paul himself, when he tries this strategy in Acts 17, in his Areopagite discourse, goes along very well until he talks about the pending judgment and the resurrection. Then he loses his audience. But he couldn't fail to do that and justify himself as a Christian. Suggestions to postpone the resolution, following the example of Jesus, who lived thirty years and then preached for only three, or the example of the people of Israel, who prepared themselves for more than a millennium for the announcement of the gospel, are exactly that: postponements.

What remained outside of these reflections is the basic question of the subject of mission. The embarrassments caused by arbitrary missionary actions that motivated a project of inculturation are reactions to badly framed questions. Let's just see: it seems that the only reason for abandoning the revelatory motive to justify mission is that this motive would bring with it impositions of ecclesial power. Such an interpretation supposes that the church is the storehouse of revelation, hence the fear of confusing mission with conquest. But that can be justified only on the ecclesiological premise that the church is, in some way, the perfect society. The necessity for fleeing from revelation as a motivation for mission comes undone when the supposition that revelation is given to the church disappears.

The subject of mission is not the church. Mission is *missio dei*. And what is announced—that is, the content of mission—is the revelation of God. The comprehension of this revelation comes not through signs and wisdom but in the cross of a God who reveals himself in weakness and infamy. The comprehension of this revelation is on the reverse side of the evidence, on glory's opposite side. God is incarnate in the world—not in the church. The church is neither the subject nor the object of mission but rather its means, the liberated space in which the presence of God on the inverse side of the world is celebrated. The church is not the place where mission is born but only the place where the announcement resounds. That's all it means when we affirm the church as a creature of the Word, of a Word that is other and whose otherness consists in presenting itself in what does not resemble God. Therefore, revelation is celebrated, welcomed, and discerned in the church but is not created, maintained, or guaranteed in the church. Revelation is not the message of the church for the world but the message of God, who, through his disguised presence in the world, creates and re-creates the church. This is what the Nicene Creed confesses in affirming that we believe the church—not *in* the church.

The church, in its institutional reality, is not exempt from the endemic search for power. But the church's nature is ambiguous or even contradictory. It is also *ekklesia*, the assembly of those who are called to opt out of the system. In a paradoxical formulation, one might say that the church is a "dysfunctional organization." This is the meaning of Romans 12 and 13, which, on the one hand, call for nonconformity and, on the other, call for effective participation in society.[9] The constant tension between adaptation and rupture is here the same tension that separates utopia from effectiveness. An emphasis on one pole leads to sectarianism and irrelevance. Emphasis on the other pole leads to acculturation. A church that is always reformed is one that is constantly seeking this equation. But this is not a simple rational calculation. The church's effectiveness in history has been achieved not always through adaptation but through actions and dispositions that contradict the rules of institutional survival, such as asceticism and martyrdom.

It was in vulnerability that the effectiveness of the church as a witness to the mission of God was affirmed. The church lives as a bordering space between rupture and continuity, between utopia and a (real) place, between the cosmos and revelation, and it has a sacramental character that celebrates the presence of what is hidden and disguised on its reverse side. It's in this frontier area that the church also carries out its kerygmatic function by offering itself as the environment in which resound the shouts and silences that keep forming words in which the Word dwells. For this reason, let us speak of the church not as the repository of faith and its contents but only as the congregation of saints-sinners who form the space in which faith organizes hope, where the insurgency of the powers in weakness is celebrated. Then people will no longer say that the church has a mission, in the same way that it has a school or a bank account, but that mission has the church, the way a city has its plazas.

---

[9] On the interpretation of these chapters, see Vítor Westhelle and Sérgio Sauer, "Romanos 9–14: Desafio de Paulo a uma Atuação Libertadora na Sociedade," *Palvra Partilhada* 7, no. 3 (1988): 4–20.

CROSS, CREATION, AND ECOLOGY

THE POINT OF ENCOUNTER BETWEEN THE THEOLOGY OF THE CROSS AND THE THEOLOGY OF CREATION IN LUTHER

I. The Impasse

In 1967, Lynn White Jr. published his article "The Historical Roots of our Ecological Crisis," and by making the Judeo-Christian tradition responsible for the Western attitude toward nature, he lit a fire in theological circles that were too preoccupied with maintaining their christological juggling act on the main stage. Although White didn't have Christology as such in mind when he developed his critique (something his followers would add later), the message was heard loud and clear: a theology too focused on *homo perditus et deus salvator* ends up emphasizing the relation with God at the expense of a more incisive vision of nature, including human nature. The human being himself is disembodied.

A theological response was not long in coming. It came in the form of a theocentric perspective in theology equipped with a tenacious critique of what was called "second-article unitarianism" (H. R. Niebuhr). This theocentric course correction renewed the emphasis on a theology of creation and began to stimulate the muscles of that atrophied classic of dogmatics. The proposals were legion. They went from the renewal of a Thomistic reading, which looked at nature sympathetically as an infrastructure for the manifestation

Originally published in *Estudos Teológicos* 34, no. 3 (1994): 291–300.

of grace, to visions of nature and creation as the "original blessing" (M. Fox) or as mother earth incestuously raped by her own sons.

In Protestant theology, the preeminence of the theology of the word caused the resurgence of a theology of creation with peculiar characteristics. Protestants opposed the Roman Catholic tendency to take nature as an epistemologically positive given for the construction of the knowledge of the relation between creator and created. Instead, Protestants were inclined to favor an epistemological approach of negative value: knowledge of God is not contiguous with knowledge of nature. Although there was resistance to a radical rejection of natural revelation (the case of E. Brunner vs. K. Barth), the significance of creation remained tied to the history of salvation: creation is the first salvific act.

Until very recently, political theologies and theologies of liberation harbored a suspicion with respect to the theology of creation. In various ways, it was suggested that the preoccupation with the theology of creation sucked the energy out of theologians, who then no longer took seriously the political and social challenges that originated from the history of suffering. A red theology, the argument went, would not mix with a green one. But this certainly changed, mainly after the peoples of the Amazon and other indigenous peoples of the world vindicated the urgency of mixing green and red in an earth-colored theology, a brown theology.

Despite the acknowledged emphasis that Luther put on the theology of creation, the Lutheran tradition has, in recent times, clearly shown its embarrassment in dealing with the subject. With the exception of a few important works on the subject in recent decades (particularly H. Bornkamm, R. Prenter, J. Sittler, P. Watson, and D. Loefgreen), Luther's emphasis on the theology of creation got filtered through the infamous orders of creation, and the legacy of this filtering was an ecstatic vision of nature and an ideological posture that was no less disturbing. In response to the inheritance of *Ordnungstheologie*, Lutheran theology tried to restore its credibility and its lack of ideology in the postwar period through an emphasis on the theology of the cross. Luther's concern with creation as a theological theme was almost totally abandoned, being viewed as a well-intentioned and even suggestive inventory of theological motifs but as too badly organized to serve as the basis for a theological argument.

The difficulty that we then encounter for the task I'm proposing here is establishing the possible and necessary linkages between the theology of the cross (with its affirmation that "God can be encountered only on the cross and in suffering"[1]) and the theology of creation (with Luther's affirmation that there exists a double knowledge of God).[2] These two apparently contradictory affirmations form the disputed issue. Would Luther have accepted the distinction between special and general revelation, and is that what he meant by the phrase *duplex est cognitio Dei*? If he did, that would be nothing more than an unfortunate atavism to be rejected by anyone who considers the cross as the central and specific point of divine revelation, constituting both the identity of God and its relevance for the definition of the divine immanence and the divine economy—what God is and what God does.

On the other hand, that exclusive emphasis on the cross and the christological concentration that results from that emphasis have been viewed as an obstacle to the growing awareness of our ethnic, cultural, and anthropological relativity or to the growing ecological sensitivity of people who are prepared to read in the book of nature the hieroglyphics of divine revelation. Might these be two distinct and incompatible ways of organizing a Lutheran theology? A creation theology without the cross and a theology of the cross without creation?

II. The Transparent Mirror

I would like to suggest that the basic difficulty we encounter in postulating that question has to do with the conceptual distinction between the visible and the word, between the creature and the creator, between the exterior and the interior, between what the senses are capable of registering—and reason is capable of understanding—and what grace reveals to the heart. I use these categories instead of approaching this problem in its traditional manner—that is, as a problem of the relation between the first and second articles of

---

1 *At Deum non inveniri nisi in passionibus et crucem* (Weimar Edition 1, 362, 28s). Henceforth WA.

2 *Duplex est cognitio Dei* (WA 40/1, 607, 28).

the Creed[3]—because, before being a common dogmatic issue (and normally it's been treated as such), it's an epistemological question that refers us to the mode of cognition of the reality of God and its respective limits. Therefore, the correct *locus* for this discussion is not, as previously thought, either the doctrine of creation or the doctrine of redemption, or both of them. The issue belongs to the doctrine of revelation, and making that assertion already takes the discussion out of the scope of dogmatic theology and locates it in the very fundamentals of doing theology. It belongs to fundamental theology, as I will now start to explain.

In Luther's thought, there is a paradoxical and asymmetrical relation between those two groups of categories mentioned above. It is through that relation that Luther develops the understanding of the double knowledge of God. To simplify the argument, I will take only the opposition between the visible and the Word. By "paradoxical relation," I mean that, in Luther, one of the categories (the visible) indicates and points to the other (the Word), but in so doing, the first category is simultaneously negated. The paradoxical relation implies the rejection of any analogical rationality, even if it's within an apparently analogical relation. In other words, the paradoxical mode of argumentation is always an ironic form of discourse. That is, it appears to accept the obvious but then brings it up as a problem. Luther did this frequently as a tactic for remaining simultaneously within the discursive parameters of institutionalized truths while constantly transgressing those parameters. By "asymmetry," I refer to the fact that what appears to be the case at one pole of the categories presented (here I'm using the category of the visible as an illustration) not only is reflected and mirrored at the other pole but is expressed at the other pole in a way that is always surprising.

Let me exemplify this phenomenon with some well-known images that Luther used to describe creation. Especially in the commentaries on the Psalms, we find statements that speak of nature as full of parables, metaphors, and signs that in a certain way point to the divine reality. But at the same time, Luther will deny emphatically

[3] Translator's note: The Apostles' Creed.

that those parables, metaphors, or signs permit a direct knowledge of God. The visible simultaneously presents God and conceals God within the paradoxical and asymmetrical schema that I'm talking about. As Luther put it, only faith can see creation.[4] This means that the vision of what nature may be is at the same time also our blindness to nature. Between the simultaneous vision and blindness there exists no analogical relation. The "mechanism" by which we can connect creation to the creator is not external. In other words, there does not exist in Luther a decoder by which nature, seen by us, can point to a certain avenue by which we can infer divine reality.

The famous metaphor of nature as the mask (*larva*) or wrapping (*involucrum*) of God points to the same ironic form of thinking. This can be better exemplified if we consider the origin of the metaphor of the mask. Luther adopted this motif from the medieval carnival. There the mask served as a means of caricaturing reality and revealing it but, at the same time, concealing it on its own reverse side. The mask presents the popular projections of social and political life along with the burlesque touches permitted within the space of the festival. But restricted to that space, the mask also disguised the true social relations of daily life (not very different from what happens in the Brazilian carnival). The carnival mask allowed a passing glance that alluded to the invisible and intentionally distorted it. Nature, for Luther, is the carnival of creation, where a disguised God passes for the devil and the devil dances like a god. In Luther's words, "The devil is not the devil unless earlier he was God."[5]

The same type of reasoning applies to the motif of the wrapping or covering. It reveals a presence but denies to our sight any evidence of the essential, of the contents. It even denies the certainty of its existence. A person who receives a wrapped present is convinced of the existence of some invisible contents, if in fact there are any, simply out of confidence in the giver of the gift.

Visible things (*visibilia*), including all of nature, do not permit any direct access to revelation. However, just as a gift does not come

[4] WA 38, 53, 24s.
[5] WA 31/1, 250, 24s.

without wrapping or as reality is not explained except with masks, visible things are what gift us with divine reality. In the visible, the presence of God is a "mediated immediacy" (J. Bailie). Yet this same affirmation attests only to the absence of the divine. God is absent precisely in his present, in his gift. To depend on natural reason for finding evidence and indications of the divine presence will reveal only the idol of a heart (*idolum cordis*) that is thirsty for knowledge and that lives on miracles. The visible becomes an idol when seen as an image that reflects the invisible captured by the observer's gaze. But at the same time, the visible can be a figure of the invisible when one's gaze is not fixed upon it but instead is free to go beyond it, as is the case with icons. The relation between the idol and the icon is of great importance for understanding Luther's ambivalent posture in relation to sacred images. To express the paradoxical relation of the visible that both grants and denies the presence, I have recourse to an oxymoron, a paradoxical expression. It involves a transparent mirroring in which what is reflected is not the visible presence as such but its absence manifested in its own reflection.

That does not mean, however, that the visible is a matter of indifference or is neutral in regard to knowledge of the divine. The *Deus vestitus* (the potential idol) is also simultaneously what protects us from the *Deus nudus* (the irresistible abyss of being). The God dressed in his own creation is the representation of what cannot be represented. By affirming his absence, the hidden and wrapped God offers his presence. The dressed God is the God of religious experience in which and by which human beings open themselves to what transcends real existence but, at the same time, close themselves off from the radical experience of otherness.

For Luther, this is the importance of the "majesty of matter":[6] it impedes our knowledge in order to convince us of the need for the self-revelation of God through the Word. It's exactly in this sense that the thesis of the double knowledge of God is affirmed, even if in paradoxical and asymmetric terms. What Luther said with respect to the efficacy of liturgical elements is exactly what could be said also

6 WA 39/II, 4, 32.

with respect to nature in general or about the visible as such—that is, not because of them but never without them.[7] As Luther would later affirm in the Heidelberg Theses,[8] God cannot be found behind creation, nor can God be inferred from it. God can be recognized only in and through creation. However, even that "in and through" would be badly understood if we didn't grasp that what creation reveals is only the hiddenness, the absence of God. And that hiddenness is to be found exactly in the visible, the only place where God's presence is given and where the gift is detectable only by its wrapping.

Behind the notion of the *Deus absconditus* is the conviction that the visible in general—that is, nature—presents us with a dressed and wrapped God who, as such, remains a mystery. The idea of the *Deus absconditus* should not be interpreted—as has so often been the case—as a moral matter to explain only the presence of evil as an *opus alienum*, as God's strange work. For Luther, the hiddenness of God is also an ontological statement. God is hidden not only in wrath but in all external things, in what is, in general, visible. From popular piety to the most sophisticated theologies, the reason the hiddenness of God has been interpreted only as a manifestation of God's strange work is that it is through evil that human beings become aware of the impossibility of knowing God through the visible. But that is only part of the story and is a great failure of Lutheran theology in the twentieth century. For Luther, God is hidden as much in the beauty and goodness of nature as in its evil and ugliness. The fact is that it is always tempting to find evidence of the divine in the good and the beautiful and to reject evil as a pedagogue. This is what Luther calls idolatry. It's not that the beautiful and the good are false teachers, but like a fetish, they absorb one's gaze and become idolatrous projections of the heart, separated from what's evil and sinister. The good that I observe and see in the nature that surrounds me also hides the evil that I don't see. But how does one explain that?

In Luther's view, evil is part of God. Only the evil work of God has epistemological primacy in knowledge of God. This is the reason that

[7] WA 19, 72–73.

[8] WA 1, 354, 17ss. (theses 19 and 20).

the cross and suffering have primacy in what we know of God. God should not be praised for the greatness of creation, despite the evil that resides in it; God should be praised in the midst of evil, where the continuing divine creation creates reality based on the annihilating power of evil. Because of this force—the annihilating power of evil—the creative power of God is manifest in and through that same power. It is this creativity, and not evil in itself, that makes the knowledge of God possible. This is the fundamental thesis supporting the doctrine of creation out of nothing (*creatio ex nihilo*).[9]

Responsibility in relation to nature flows, then, from the awareness of our participation in the annihilating power of evil—that is, from an awareness of our sinful condition. For Luther, nature did not fall, and neither was *human nature* an accomplice of the sin of Adam; nature suffered the curse of evil because of *human action*. Thus he can say, "Not only in the churches do we hear that we are burdened with sins. In the fields, yes, practically all creation is full of those sermons, reminding us of our sins."[10] Therefore, Luther uses the motif of the mask not so much to show that God is hidden as to emphasize that we hide ourselves by not recognizing the mask for what it is, either because we try to contemplate the bare face behind the mask or because we simply ignore it.

The hidden God places before our eyes masks by which and in which we recognize ourselves as in a false mirror, since God's mask reveals the other side of the good with which creation was originally endowed. Human beings are called to recognize themselves in that transparent mirror, as much in its beauty as in its ugliness. Thus the *Deus absconditus* is also simultaneously the *Deus revelatus* because and only because the hiddenness of God, when recognized as such, incites the emergence of the *homo revelatus*. Therefore, the cry of the Reformation to let God be God corresponds exactly to the motto "Let nature, including human nature, be nature." Auschwitz, Hiroshima, the hole in the ozone layer, the massacre of the Yanomami, and family

[9] Here Luther assumes the negative interpretation of evil as formulated by Augustine as *privatio boni*.

[10] WA 42, 156, 24ss.

violence are masks of God raised up for our self-recognition. In them, we measure ourselves; in them, we see ourselves while recognizing what we did or failed to do with nature. For this reason, what we have in the experience of evil is not only a mask of God but, in fact, a broken mask through whose cracks we fearfully contemplate the abyss of being. This is the reason, and the only reason, that evil as a cracked mask becomes for us a teacher: through its cracks, we recognize the vain attempt to encounter a smiling face behind the mask. The cracks in the mask elicit in us only the *horror vacui*.

III. The Transcendent Depth of the Word

If the visible is the projection of our own beauty and ugliness, the Word is always the word of the other. If I am capable of possessing what I see (since the visible is conceptually reducible to me), the Word always comes from beyond the limits of my dominion. Without the Word, reality loses its focus and its end, since the visible has no window on the transcendent and, by definition, on the immanent. What the visible reveals is not the other but, in fact, only what we are or are becoming. The Word, by contrast, is the creative force of the continuing divine creation. And in that continuing creation, the Word gives itself to the visible in a continuing incarnation. It's the transcendent force capable of bringing into reality what does not exist (*creatio ex nihilo*).[11] If reality loses its meaning without the Word, it's the presence of the Word that attributes finality to reality. This is the conclusion: the presence of the Word constitutes, restores, and creates the real. Without the Word, we slide into the abyss of nothingness.

The epiphanic presence of the Word as transcendence in immanence performs its constant re-creation in nature, its sacramental character. It's in this sense, and only in this sense, that we can affirm the ubiquity of God in creation itself. This affirmation flows not from our capacity to see beyond the visible but from the fact that the visible becomes transparent, and in its transparency, the visible has no

[11] It is necessary to remember that the origin of this concept, in 2 Maccabees 7, is the experience of the annihilating force of evil; for this reason, it's an existential response to the problem of theodicy and not a cosmogonic argument.

"beyond." In this way, the visible, by virtue of its sacramental character, does not become magical. That transparency, as was said above, is a reflected transparency that redirects our gaze to the depths of our own existence. And this is not a simple reflex, since depth, in the eccentric [and excentric] anthropology of Luther, is that which is outside of us and that which redirects us to the Word. Thus nature loses all pretense of otherness, of being other than itself, of being sacred in itself. This is the same as saying that we also lose the illusion of being strangers to nature. This idea is at the heart of the exclusively Lutheran conviction of *finitum capax infiniti*, since the infinite is never reached in the visible but is always present in the visible in its transparent mirroring.

The mysterious or sacramental character of the ubiquity of God through Christ, the coeternal Word, is defined by Luther in the context of his discussion about the three modes of the presence of Christ. It's in the third mode of presence that, according to Luther, Christ is "as deeply and closely inside of all creatures as God is in them."[12] It is precisely this text of Luther's that is cited in the Formula of Concord to prop up the argument that affirms at the same time the real presence in the Lord's Supper and the distinction between sacrament *stricto sensu* and the affirmation that all creation includes the disguised, sacramental, or mysterious presence of God.[13] For the authors of the Formula of Concord, what distinguishes the mysterious or sacramental character of the divine presence in the sacrament in its strict sense is not the combination of element and Word, of the visible with the audible, since this is common to all creation. What distinguishes the sacrament as such is its use (*usus*) in the ritual tradition instituted by Christ. Nature in general includes the continual sacramental relation between the Word and the visible.

But before we fall into the idealism of a theology of the Word, it's important to emphasize that the otherness of the Word confronts me only if I agree to take the visible for what it is. In reference to the

[12] WA 26, 156, 24ss.

[13] Livro de Concórdia, *Confissões da Igeja Evangélica Luterana* (São Leopoldo: Sinodal, 1993), 628, 101ss.

theology of the cross, Luther claims that "a real theologian says things as they are."[14] To ignore the visible, to flee from the "majesty of matter" in search of the pure Word is to remove the cross from the world (something like what Salvador Dalí does sarcastically in his paintings of the crucifixion). Ignoring the visible is nothing less than another version of the theology of glory, with this difference: the theology of glory that Luther criticized took the visible as the mediation of the invisible, whereas, in the theologies of the Word, one observes an immediate leap to the invisible without realizing that the invisible—included in the visible—is only the transparency of the visible itself.

Suffering, the unbearable image of the visible, makes the visible transparent when the suffering seen is the suffering in which humans, as humans, know that they are its active agent. The victim, the pain made visible, is not in himself redemptive, but the way of the cross passes through the pain, since the suffering of the victim is the transparent mirror set up before the victimizer. In Luther, there is no ontological distinction between natural evil and moral or human evil. The cross of Christ serves as the archetypal form that suffering assumes in the Christian narrative (the suffering of God in himself). That suffering manifests the *Deus revelatus* when it is recognized that that suffering is being caused by the powers of evil engendered in the human heart. The Augustinian formula of *non posse non peccare* receives in Luther the following subtle interpretation: the recognition of the universality of original sin is the condition for knowledge of God and is not an invitation to a penitential act. The confession of the centurion in Mark 15 is of such theological importance not because he knew Jesus's actions and teachings but because he knew he was one of those who imposed suffering on Jesus. The centurion saw himself in that mask when it became for him a transparent mirroring of his condition. And that confession was a shout of terror as the centurion exposed himself to the inscrutable absence of God in the wounds of a tortured man.

In the cross of Christ, general and particular revelation meet, since divine creativity is witnessed at its point of origin, in the annihilating

[14] *Theologus crucis dicit id, quod res est* (WA 1, 354, 21s.).

force of evil. Therefore, the cross is the material criterion by which the visible becomes constitutive for knowledge of God in the same way that the theology of creation (*creatio ex nihilo* or, what is the same thing, creation from evil) is the formal criterion for recognizing God in all the suffering of the world. Through the theology of creation, the cross of Christ becomes "essentially identical" (R. Prenter) to the suffering of the world and to suffering in the world. Through the theology of the cross, the suffering of the world and suffering in the world are recognized as the focal point of the creative activity of God.

The suffering of nature, including human nature, assumes a privileged, sacramental character not because of suffering in itself but because in suffering and through it, creation is continuously remade. The primacy of the Word in God's process of creative redemption is, for human beings, only a passive primacy that permits them to face suffering without dissimulation. On the human side, the response is always an action, which, in this case, is giving glory to the one to whom all glory belongs. Work, human effort, is thus not meritorious when and because it assumes that doxological character.[15] This practice—giving glory to God—is done, then, not for the redemptive merit of the work achieved but because it becomes the only way to express our confession of human sin, through which evil has insinuated itself inside of all nature, including human nature.

IV. Possibilities and Critiques

From everything that's been said, we can now conclude that, for Luther, the care of nature is the response of faith that God is the cause and origin of all creation. Human beings are poets from a medieval carnival, creating and decorating masks through which we protect ourselves and are protected from the terrible vision of the abyss, the vision of the *Deus nudus*, of the *horror vacui*. And we human beings are, at the same time, the ones who break those masks and thus expose ourselves to the wrath of the divine absence. For this reason,

[15] See the definition in article 10 of the Augsburg Confession: "It is taught, moreover, that good works should be done and must be done, not so that one may trust in them for meriting grace but out of love for God and to his praise."

ecological responsibility is neither a romantic or mystical response to the good that creation represents nor conformity to a natural law. Our response is a doxological act by which we express our repentance and renewal, which spring from the depths of the void revealed in the cracks of a broken mask. There is no reason to fear that nature has become artificial (K. Marx). In truth, this is the great contribution of Luther to the modern understanding of nature: what is to be feared is a vision of nature that, whether bucolic or scientific, protects us from the experience of the cross and of suffering. Far from a naive and pristine view of nature and also far from the modern divorce between man and nature, Luther's theology offers the criterion by which to confront the evil in society and in nature: the visibility of the silent suffering of the innocent is what opens the space in which the creative Word resounds like a strange, alien sound, calling for our response. Every vocation is a service in and through divine creation, but not for the sake of divine creation. There are no exemptions; we are the nature in which we irrevocably intervene. The focus of ecological responsibility is not the preservation or protection of a nature that we might suppose is external to us. The focus is on the knowledge that we have and the power that we exercise in and through nature. "Only faith can see creation" also means that outside of nature, what we see is our intervention, our own artifice.

But not everything is magnolias. I have tried to show that it's a mistake to think that, in Luther, there's an incompatibility between the theology of the cross and the theology of creation or that there is some kind of incoherence between general revelation and specific revelation. The problem is not found there. I have suggested that Luther advances far beyond the limits of the classical and analogical theology of the Middle Ages toward an already highly modern vision of nature. This he does by dismantling the opposition between the natural and the artificial. The problem that I encounter in Luther is found elsewhere. Although Luther learned how to go beyond medieval constrictions in his conception of nature, he remained bound to medieval thought in his understanding of social institutions (*ecclesia, politia, oeconomia*). The anthropological reductionism in the Lutheran conception of the equation between sin and redemption made it impossible to understand sin and evil in their social and structural dimensions, though Luther did succeed in doing it in relation to nature. *Addito grano salis*, nature was artificial for Luther, but institutions were natural. The nature that we see is not the creation we believe in; rather, it's the product of our knowledge and power. The inability to recognize that that knowledge and power take root in social, economic, political, and ecclesial institutions and are not simply the result of original sin is the weak link in Luther's theology. In this sense, E. Troeltsch was correct in denouncing the medieval character of the Reformer's social thought, even though Luther went far beyond the limits of his time in his comprehension of revelation, where the theology of the cross and the theology of creation meet.

BETWEEN ABEL AND CAIN
THEOLOGICAL COMMUNICATION IN LATIN AMERICA

I. Rivalry

The ontological form of communication is rivalry. Attempting to escape the profound silence of animals thrown into the arena, we seek out the other in a desperate desire for recognition. It's the desire to be desired. However, as soon as we venture into this frenetic search, we encounter the living image of the other, who, in recognizing us, at the same time robs us of the absolute character of the existence that our own solitude grants us. The first manifestation of communication, this bestial quest to be recognized as a person, is murder. The death of the other is the most complete, primary, and fundamental achievement of direct communication between human beings. As the perfect consummation of the communicative act, murder is the satisfaction of desire by its suppression. It eliminates the possibility that the other doesn't love me.

This image comes from Maharal, the rabbi of Prague in the sixteenth century, his legal name being Yehudah Loew Ben Betsal'el.[1] It's not the well-known myth of the Tower of Babel, which always illustrates for us the mythical confusions in the human attempt to communicate. Instead, Maharal uses the leitmotif of Cain and Abel to frame the unhappy, tragic, and original human experience of direct

Originally published in *Estudos Teológicos* 32, no. 3 (1992): 264–77.

[1] I owe to André Neher the interpretation of these intuitions of Maharak. See André Neher, *Le puits de l'exil: La théologie dialectique du Maharal de Prague (1512–1609)* (Paris: Calmann-Lévy, 1966).

communication. Cain and Abel, assassin and victim, symbolize the elemental human search for communication.

The myth of Cain and Abel establishes the experience of horizontal dialogue. For Western civilization, this is the fundamental and tragic myth of the possibility of human communication. But it's an almost-forgotten myth in the theological tradition. All that remains of it is Yahweh's social question, "Where is your brother?" The Cain and Abel myth is far from being able to compete with the myth of Adam, which Paul Ricoeur calls "the anthropological myth *par excellence*."[2]

The Cain and Abel myth tells the story of our origins: how it is that we are here and what went wrong. The myth of these two brothers has been "disowned" for having been found just too strange. The Judeo-Christian tradition does not identify with it, and neither does it identify other peoples as descendants of Cain. In short, it is forgotten as a founding myth. As Hermann Gunkel put it, it's a "troubled narrative."[3] But it's part of the collection of the Judeo-Christian tradition. Why might this narrative have been preserved yet not connected with ethnographic identifications, as usually happens with myths? Might this narrative be too far from our daily experience to acquire significance? Or might it be so close that we lose ourselves in it?

In the narrative canonized in the Bible, until the myth of Cain and Abel appears, there is no word from one human being to another. Humans weren't mute, but their communication was vertical. Adam spoke with God. Eve spoke with God. God spoke with Adam and Eve. Adam and Eve ate the fruit and multiplied. As Maharal tells us, it was as if they knew the risk they were taking as the original couple if they wanted to initiate their style of life through words and dialogue. The absence of direct verbal communication maintains a bearable coexistence and demarcates the absolute limit of each being, the limit of solitude.

With the two brothers, things were different. Here we have two human beings, distinct and separate, each with his word to express the desire to be desired, to be recognized. But each one is a being for

---

2 Paul Ricoeur, *The Symbolism of Evil* (Boston: Beacon, 1967), 232.

3 Hermann Gunkel, *Genesis* (Göttingen: Vandenhoeck and Ruprecht, 1969), 49.

himself; each one is only a part. The desire for completeness is what engenders the tragic outcome. The part must become a whole. But the space that the other occupies delimits my existence and is the reflexive awareness of my finitude. The other, the part that doesn't belong to me, has to be annulled as something other, as different. This is what theology calls *hybris*, which is sin in its ontic form; it's the turning in on oneself as the center of one's self and of the whole world. The word directed to other people is tragic in the classical sense—that is, it betrays one's own intentionality. It represents a break with *hybris* and at the same time is the most radical manifestation of *hybris* in that the other disappears. The first death begins with horizontal communication: "Cain said to his brother Abel, 'Let us go out to the field.'[4] And when they were in the field, Cain rose up against his brother Abel, and killed him" (Gen 4:8). Rivalry establishes the communication and is its end. One should avoid thinking that the original tragedy is based on the stained character of Cain and the innocence of Abel. Once the communication begins, the pendulum of the murderer-victim relation can swing in either direction, so the story could have the opposite conclusion. But it happened this way: Cain killed Abel, since Cain directed the first word to Abel. Dialogue is the possibility of the impossible; it's the power to carry out the act that negates that possibility. The start of this dialogue makes its fulfillment impossible. What could Abel have said in response to Cain's invitation? We don't know even that much.

Death rises up between Abel and Cain. Death is the immediate realization of the desire for recognition, and at the same time, it's murder, the negation of that desire. What Cain couldn't tolerate, the reason his face fell, is not explained in the text. Abel's offering, his firstfruits, the fruit of his labor, pleased Yahweh, the other. Abel recognized himself in the desire of the sacred, and the sacred came to him, not from a part that didn't belong to him, but from himself feeling desired by the other. And in this case, that feeling is

---

[4] It's interesting to observe that the Hebrew text announces but omits these words. Perhaps these words were too strong or so innocent that the scribe didn't understand their ultimate power?

interchangeable with Cain himself. Yahweh's satisfaction with Abel's offering is the same as Cain's desire. Thus Abel doesn't need a word to address the other; he had the meat and blood of his offering. It is not coincidental that in the allegorical interpretations in the Judeo-Christian Haggadah, this narrative is read as the love story of two brothers for their sister, who, in this case, plays the role of the means, the instrument of desire.[5]

Cain did not feel desired, did not feel that his offering was the object of the other's desire. Cain is thus a betrayed lover who desires the desire of the other but finds himself alone. Abel is his disdain. Abel doesn't need Cain because he already has him bound by his desire. Abel has him already and therefore doesn't need him. Abel already has his story, his poem, his construction of a world in which he is recognized and doesn't need to announce it. His sacrificial cult is his culture. Cain has his culture only through Abel. Thus Cain needs to commune, to communicate with Abel, to see himself in Abel's face, to have his offering regarded as an object of pleasure, to see himself desired by Abel, the other. The decisive urgency is this: Cain wants Abel, wants his desire, invites him to go to the field, addresses him, and needs to commune and be recognized the way Abel is. Cain, the farmer, remakes the sacrifice that had been pleasing to Yahweh—not the offering of vegetables but the offering of flesh and blood, his brother's!

Before the first words directed by one human being to another, Yahweh says to Cain, "If you do well, will you not be accepted? And if you do not do well, sin is lurking at the door; its desire is for you."[6] The *desire of sin* is both a subjective genitive and an objective genitive. Cain desires to be the center of himself and at the same time desires the sin called Abel, the being who already was the center of himself. This desire turns against Cain because feeling this desire breaks the otherness, reducing the other to oneself, which is the radical realization and negation of recognition.[7]

---

5 See Gunkel, *Genesis*, 48.

6 Translator's note: Gen 4:7.

7 The most popular reconstruction of this narrative is found in the Hegelian myth of the lord and the slave. But Hegel's solution involves a mortal struggle yet

What serves as the basis for communication is also what makes it impossible. But what makes it impossible also demands it. This is the paradox of existence: what makes us human is a separation from the condition of solitude, but this rupture throws us immediately into the arena, which, while affirming, consumes the same humanity that it establishes.

This is what Konrad Lorenz tells us in his book about aggression: "It's a curious paradox that the greatest gift of the human being, the peculiar faculty of conceptual thought and verbal communication that raised the human being to a level above all the creatures and gave him dominion over the globe is not exactly a blessing. The great dangers that threaten humanity with extinction are direct consequences of conceptual thought and verbal communication."[8]

The myth of the brothers does not tell the story of some accident on the way; it's not the legend of a misunderstanding. It's a foundational narrative about our paradoxical ontological condition.

II. Two Faces

The two-sidedness of the human condition consists in this: what makes us human also threatens our very survival. The beauty of the paradox is that we create the narratives that confront us with our own inviability as creatures, and in so doing, rationally but in amazement, we encounter our own irrationality. The Yahwist myth of the two brothers who face off against each other is a motif repeated in numerous cultures and peoples and is a verdict on the human condition, on its tragic communicability. It is also the narrative that warns us about this same tragedy. It tells us a primordial story that reveals the very insanity of the present, of any attempt to communicate. The myth makes us accomplices. In it, we are simultaneously the victim and the assassin, simultaneously Abel and Cain. The myth knits us into

---

suspends the ending when an individual, out of love for life, accepts slavery and gives up his freedom, whereas the myth of the two brothers already opens with its radical ending. There is no compromise. Contrary to Hegel, here life is freedom, and the confrontation of freedoms is tragic. Cf. Georg Wilhelm Friedrich Hegel, *Phänomenologie des Geistes* (Frankfurt: Suhrkamp, 1977), 145–55.

[8] Konrad Lorenz, *On Aggression* (New York: Bantam, 1963), 230.

a web in which we become entangled, and thus entangled, we both protect ourselves and mutilate ourselves. Telling stories, as Christa Wolf reminds us, "is human and produces human effects, memory, sympathy, understanding—even when the story is . . . a lament over the destruction of our father's house, or the loss of memory, the collapse of sympathy, the lack of understanding."[9]

Today, Cain and Abel exist together because, or to the extent that, their story is told. Might that not be the reason for the faded quality of this myth: it survives as an unidentifiable narrative in which we, as accomplices, are at once Abel and Cain? What protects us is that this is the narrative of our own condemnation. This narrative rises up like the limit of our transgression. Between me and the other, there is the other story that protects me from communication and does not permit me to speak the genocidal word. This is the possible and permitted limit of civility: oblique communication, communication about the impossible community. The realization of the desire that leads to the life-and-death struggle, the struggle to be no longer a part but the whole, can never be satisfied except in words, in stories that relate their own impossibility. Cain and Abel can still live because, and to the extent that, between these two there exists the story of Cain, who killed Abel and wanted the other's immediate recognition.

The human is a teller of stories, a maker of myths that protect him from the fulfillment of his desires, from his own tragic capacity for direct verbal communication. Between silence and speech, between solitude and murder, emerges the myth, the first story that pulls us out of our silence and unbearable solitude. But myth does even more; it also protects us from the direct word, from horizontal and immediate communication, from the fatal blow. Through myth, Octavio Paz tells us, "every man and woman of the group feels like part of a totality that is at once natural and supernatural!"[10] Human beings recognize themselves in these stories because they offer an image of an unattainable totality, of the lost and painfully remembered dream of an impossible community.

---

[9] Christa Wolf, *Cassandra* (New York: Farrar, Straus and Giroux, 1984), 173.

[10] Octavio Paz, *La otra voz* (Barcelona: Seix Barral, 1990), 72.

Every civilization establishes itself and sustains itself in this narrative web that recounts, explores, and detects the paradox of the human condition. But every civilization, every culture, cultivates its possible story alongside other cultures and civilizations with their stories. Each one uses its story to justify the barbarity of the other. Myth always belongs to the tribe. Cain and Abel, protected as brothers by the story that unites them in the tribe, then battle it out with races and nations. The narrative that detects the tragic condition of human existence and arises like a means of protection in the brothers' struggle is still the story of the group—not a universal narrative. It is still the civilizing story of the West. What protects us from ourselves and puts a face on us also turns us into a wolf for the stranger, who doesn't have our story, our word—only his own. The murderous act is committed against this story, this word. What Cain kills is not only his brother but his cult, his culture, and in the process he becomes the very subject of the sacrificial act that belonged to Abel, who now is the very object of the offering.

III. The Americas

The conquest and colonization of the Americas is a long story of tragedy relived and of communication consummated. Much has already been said, in the remembering of the last five hundred years, about the conquest and its consequences. But I would like to pose the issue within the paradox of human communication. The conquest bears this mark: it was the great primordial effort at immediate communication. Cain and Abel again meet face-to-face. Now, protected from themselves, they recognize their equals but prefer what is distant and distinct.

Felipe Guamán Poma de Ayala, narrating the famous encounter of Pizarro and his men with Atahualpa of the Inca, tells of this clash between those who were so different from each other:

> And then Don Francisco Pizarro and Don Diego de Almagro began to speak to him through the interpreter, Felipe, a Gancabilca Indian. Pizarro told him that he was the messenger and ambassador of a great lord who wanted to be his (Atahualpa's) friend, and that he (Pizarro) had come for that reason.

> Atahualpa listened attentively to what Pizarro was saying and to what the Indian Felipe was saying. The Inca then replied with majesty and said that if it was true that Pizarro had come from so far way, then Atahualpa could believe that his lord was great but that he (Atahualpa) had no need to make friends because he also was a great lord in his kingdom.
>
> After this response, Frei Vicente entered, holding in his right hand a cross and in his left a breviary. He said to Atahualpa that he also was an ambassador and messenger of another lord, who was a close friend of God's, and that he wanted Atahualpa to be his friend, adore the cross, and believe in the gospel of God and not worship anything else because all the rest was to be mocked.
>
> Atahualpa answered and said that he didn't have to worship anything but the sun, which never dies, and that under his law there were no pottery objects of worship or gods: that was standard. And he asked Frei Vicente who had told him that. Frei Vicente said that the gospel, the book, had told him. Atahualpa said, "Give me the book so that it can speak to me." So they gave him the book, and he took it in his hands and began to turn the pages. Then Atahualpa replied that the book had said nothing to him and wasn't speaking to him. All this he said with majesty, while seated on the throne. Then he threw the book down. Frei Vicente gave this order to his men: "Quick! Come help, my soldiers! These gentile Indians are against our faith!" Then Don Francisco Pizarro and Don Diego de Almagro also gave an order, saying: "Attack, men, these infidels are against our Christendom and against our emperor and king. Let's have at them!"[11]

This text does not relate only a massacre. The massacre is only, once again, the result of the profound human effort to make oneself understood and loved. The two sides were Cain and Abel, each

[11] Miguel León-Portilla, *A conquista de América Latina* (Petrópolis: Vozes, 1987), 108–9.

with his distinct story and each desiring the desire of the other so as to achieve his totality. Death, massacre, is what fulfills that desire. Strangely (or perhaps logically?) the faded and forgotten story resurges in the encounter with the other.[12] Pizarro wanted a friend, but achieving that required that his firstfruits (the Crown and the church), his story, be loved by the other. This was a rerun of the original tragedy of the ontic rivalry that grounds human encounters, the effort to communicate, to commune with the other, to transform the part into the whole. As Tzvetan Todorov observes regarding the struggle between Cortez and Montezuma, "The Spanish win the war. They are indisputably superior to the Indians in inter-human communication . . . , and it's not surprising that the specialists in communication win."[13] The ships of the discoverers, their incursions, and their conquests are metaphors for the mythical words that Cain addresses to Abel.

Distinguishing human communication from communication with the world, Todorov points to the same distinction made earlier between the horizontal communication of Cain and Abel and the oblique communication mediated by the myth that integrates horizontal and vertical relations: "We are not accustomed to thinking of communication as something more than its inter-human aspect. Since the world is not a subject, dialogue with it is very asymmetrical (if one can even call it dialogue). . . . The concept would be more productive if communication were understood in such a way as to include, along with individual-to-individual interaction, the interaction that takes place between the person and his social group, between the person and the natural world, and between the person and the religious universe."[14]

---

[12] It is important to bear in mind the impact that the discovery of the Americas caused after the letters from Amerigo Vespucci, which contradicted Columbus's opinion and revealed that the lands discovered by the Europeans could not be understood from the viewpoint of European ecumenism. Here the term *discovered* is correct because the Europeans discovered that they were not recognized by the unusual other they encountered. Cf. Luis N. Rivera Pagan, *Evangelización y violencia: La conquista de América* (San Juan: Cemi, 1991), 12–14.

[13] Tzvetan Todorov, *La conquista de América: El problema del otro* (México: Siglo XXI, 1989), 105.

[14] Ibid., 75.

What Todorov proposes is that we understand the myth not as the message but as the medium within which communication can reestablish the impossible *communitas*. But this was not the inheritance from the conquest. The triumph of the conquest was the victory of horizontal communication, in which the medium is the message, as McLuhan put it in his famous expression.

The result was not only the massacre of peoples and nations; it was the destruction of the history of the peoples of the New World. The firstfruits of the people encountered, the gold with which they adorned representations of the sacred, are the medium that becomes the message. For this reason, these firstfruits also represent the medium that justifies the conquest. But it's the medium through which the other's desire is conquered. An engraving by Guamán Poma de Ayala represents Atahualpa and a conquistador. In his hand, the Inca has a golden plate. He is seated. Standing in front of him is the conquistador, eyeing the gold. From the Inca's mouth come these words: "Do you people eat this gold?" The conquistador responds, "We eat this gold." It's necessary to devour the totem. Eating it transforms the conquistador into the very object of desire.

This is the fascination of the conquest. It was not a simple act of exploration and subjugation; it was also an act of seduction, of making oneself desired. So that this may happen, it's always necessary to destroy the other's story, the one by which the other, like Abel, fulfills himself by himself and knows that his offering is pleasing in and of itself. Contrary to the image that people have of the conquistadors on the basis of the *leyenda negra* (black legend), José Vasconcelos reminds us that the conquistadors were "moved by surges of glory and appetite for contemplation, enchantment, and splendor."[15] Ruggiero Romano makes the following comment about the conquistadors: "Poor devils, they are [the] youngest sons of middle, minor, and very minor nobility (many times imaginary), who discovered in their homes the style of aristocratic life, with the myths, the ideals, and the ambitions that the land of Spain can no longer satisfy. . . . And, *nota*

[15] José Vasconcelos, "El pensamiento íberoamericano," in *Filosofía latinoamericana: Introducción al filosofar* (Bogotá: El Buho, 1984), 53.

bene, they want to deserve and not simply gain, since the problem is not only to find the gold that one cannot earn in the big city, but, more than that and principally, to affirm oneself socially, to make a place for oneself, to establish oneself in society."[16]

IV. The Meaning of Conquest

It is in this context that there emerges, as far as I can confirm, the word *conquer* or *conquest*, with the connotation of "winning someone's affection, sympathy or approval."[17] In the military context in which the term originally finds its use, the term easily oscillates between its most elementary meaning of acquiring through triumph and its etymological sense of bringing together, reuniting, communing, communicating, hence the always ambiguous connotations of this term. Through an imperial order, Carlos V ordered the terms *conquest* and *conquistador* suppressed from official discourse; in 1540, he substituted the terms *discovery* and *colonizer.*[18] Why might he have done that? Did he want to avoid the military connotation of the conquistadors' undertaking? Or did he want precisely to conceal the fact that in the conquest, the fear of not being pleasing, of not being "good enough," is covered up?

Around the beginning of the seventeenth century, the word *conquest*, made infamous by the *leyenda negra*, starts to be used to describe the act of sexual seduction. Would it be a surprise, then, to find in a poet and preacher like John Donne, who lived in this period, a description and an amorous seduction in his poem "To his damsel going to bed"?

---

[16] Ruggiero Romano, *Mecanismos da conquista colonial: Os conquistadores* (São Paulo: Perspectiva, 1973), 27. On this point, see also Alberto Flores Galindo, *Buscando un inca: Identidad y utopia en los Andes* (Havana: Casa de las Américas, 1986), 28–30. Todorov, in *Conquista de América*, reiterates this same position while speaking of the meaning of the plan that guided Columbus: "The need for money and the desire to impose the true God are not mutually exclusive, there even exists between them a relation of subordination: the first is a means; the second is an end" (20).

[17] Translator's note: "Conquistar": to win over to one's way of thinking. See *Simon and Schuster's International Dictionary English/Spanish, Spanish/English* (New York: Simon and Schuster, 1973), 1069.

[18] Romano, *Mecanismos*, 56.

> Permit my caressing hands and let them go
> Back, forward, up, down, and in the middle;
> Oh, my America, my newly discovered land,
> My kingdom, most secure when handled by a
> Man. My mine of precious stones, my empire.
> How blessed I am in discovering you.[19]

It is not difficult, then, to understand that Cain was truly the first lover. He was the conquistador. His desire was to be desired. In the words of Octavio Paz, "In love, we do not seek knowledge so much as we seek recognition; when we choose the object of our love, we want that person to choose us."[20] There, once again, is the paradox, which I present now in the words of a poem by John Donne: "But you will lose the conqueror's style / if I, your conquest, perish through your hate."[21] And here are the words that the other (God) says to Cain in the myth of the brothers: "Its desire is for you."[22]

Julio César Arana, a Peruvian rubber baron at the beginning of the twentieth century, was accused by the Select Committee of the House of Commons in England of torture and genocide of the indigenous peasantry through his exploitation of rubber. In reply to the committee, he justified his use of the term *conquest* with the following words: "This word conquest, which they tell me sounds very strong in English, we use it in Spanish to attract a person, to conquer his sympathies."[23] Old Cain would be happy with this explanation; it's all he wanted: to conquer sympathy. His urgency was that of a communicator. But for communication to happen, it was necessary to reduce the other to a condition of dependency. He needed to communicate his desire, but he could do it only by creating in the other

---

[19] John Carey, ed., *John Donne* (Oxford: Oxford University Press, 1990), 13. Translator's note: Westhelle translated Donne's poem into Portuguese, and I have translated it back into English from Portuguese.

[20] Octavio Paz, *Sor Juana, or the Traps of Faith* (Cambridge, MA: Belknap, 1988), 95.

[21] *The Compact Edition of the Oxford English Dictionary* (Oxford: Oxford University Press, 1980), s.v. "conquest," verb, 4b.

[22] Translator's note: Gen 4:7.

[23] Michael Taussig, *Shamanism, Colonialism, and the Wild Man* (Chicago: University of Chicago Press, 1987), 28.

the same need for communication, the same desire. But Abel, the other, is the being with the bestial and immediate self-recognition.

We must imagine that Abel was a happy person. He had that disdainful happiness that was simultaneously an object of love and hate. Hence we're not far from sixteenth-century representations of the native as both the good savage in paradise and the feared cannibal. Might this not also be the ambiguous image that Cain had of Abel? It was necessary to humanize Abel, to civilize him, to make him needy. This is the game of seduction, of conquest, which unites love and hate. The rule of this communicative conquest always functions in these two chords: the other is bestialized as the object of hate and at the same time infantilized to be the object of love.[24] The rule is to usurp the other's (hi)story, the construction of his subjectivity, his way of erecting a dwelling place in the world. This is the way death begins: Cain takes Abel into the field, which is Cain's dwelling place. Without a dwelling place, without his culture, without his (hi)story, Abel is reduced to silence. It is not by coincidence that in various reports of the conquest, from the Aztecs to the Yanomami,[25] the triumph of civilizing communication is presented as the death or silencing of the gods, of those representations that give meaning to history: "We are simple folks, we are perishable, we are mortal. So let us die, let us perish, since our gods are already dead."[26] Conquest as a communicative act is the imposition of a foreign (the conqueror's) language, the imposition of a heteronomy.

The result of this communicative encounter was the destruction of the collection of myths that were the mediating narrative in Latin America. As the Mayan report from Chilam Balam puts it, "They taught us fear. They came to make the flowers wilt. To make their flower bloom, they damaged our flower and swallowed it up."[27]

---

[24] From Cortez to Xuxa, the rule is the same (I'm not referring to Xuxa's relationship with children but to her magisterial infantilization of language in the seduction of children and, especially, adults): knowledge as a strategy of power implies the destruction of the other's knowledge.

[25] See the beautiful "Depoimento de DaviKopenawa Yanomami," in *Yanomami: A todos os povos da terra* (São Paulo: CCPY, Cedi, Cimi, NDI, 1990), 11–15.

[26] León-Portilla, *Conquista*, 20.

[27] Ibid., 60.

Among various American peoples, *flower* is a frequent metaphor for designating language.

V. Silencing

The victory of horizontal communication is in the imposition of silence and of the rule of inarticulate language. In the sixteenth century, António Vieira already understood all that when he said that the ill from which Brazil was suffering, its sickness, was having its voice silenced. Already, slightly before Vieira, at the beginning of the sixteenth century, this is the testimony we find in a writer who never visited America but whose intuition about the description of the continent is nothing short of genius. I speak of Shakespeare, who, in his late work *The Tempest*, describes the designs of the New World ("brave new world," as Shakespeare put it) as represented by the character Caliban (an anagram of "cannibal" and a corruption of "Caribbean").

Caliban is and remains a slave. He has no way out. But in Caliban's submission, Shakespeare suggests that the consummation of Prospero's dominion brings with it a seed of resistance and reaction. This element is communication in reverse: swearing and cursing. Let's look at one passage:

> Prospero: Shake it off. Come on. We will see Caliban, my slave who never gives us a kind answer.
>
> Miranda: 'Tis a villain, sir. I do not love to look on him.
>
> Prospero: But, as 'tis, we cannot miss him: he does make our fire, fetch in our wood, and serve in offices that profit us. What, ho! Slave! Caliban! Thou earth, thou! speak. He's the one who makes our fire, gathers the firewood, and serves us our meals. This is to our advantage. Hey, slave! Caliban! You over there, speak!
>
> Caliban: (*within*) There's wood enough within.
>
> Prospero: Come forth, I say! There's other business for thee. Come, thou tortoise! When? (*re-enter Ariel, like a water-nymph*) Fine apparition! My quaint Ariel, hark in thine ear.
>
> Ariel: It shall be done (*exit*).
>
> Prospero: Thou poisonous slave, got by the devil himself upon thy wicked dam, come forth! (*enter Caliban*)

Caliban: As wicked dew as e'er my mother brush'd with raven's feather from unwholesome fen drop on you both! A south-west blow on ye and blister you all o'er!

Prospero: For this, be sure, to-night thou shalt have cramps, side-stitches that shall pen thy breath up; urchins shall, for that vast of night that they may work, all exercise on thee; thou shalt be pinched as thick as honeycomb, each pinch more stinging than bees that made them.

Caliban: I must eat my dinner. This island's mine, by Sycorax my mother, which thou takest from me. When thou camest first, thou strokedst me, and madest much of me; wouldst give me water with berries in't; and teach me how to name the bigger light and how the less, that burn by day and night: and then I loved thee, and show'd thee all the qualities o' th' isle, the fresh springs, brine-pits, barren place and fertile: Cursed be I that did so! . . .

Prospero: Thou most lying slave . . .

Caliban: You taught me language, and my profit on't is, I know how to curse. The red plague rid you for teaching me your language!

Prospero: Hag-seed, hence! Fetch us fuel and be quick . . .

Caliban: No, pray thee. (*aside*) I must obey: his art is of such power, it would control my dam's god, Setebos, and make a vassal of him.[28]

Caliban had lost his history. He was no longer an island. He had succumbed to seduction. The curious part of these passages is that for Caliban, cursing has power precisely because it's expressed in the language of the dominator: "You taught me your language, and my profit on't is, I know how to curse." This language is, however, at the same time a way of resisting from the reverse side of the utopia, from the other side of communication: the language of swearing, which penetrates every last corner of the languages spoken in Latin America. As

[28] William Shakespeare, *The Tempest*, act 1, scene 2, 303–39. Translator's note: Westhelle used a Portuguese translation of this text.

Octavio Paz demonstrated,[29] this cursing is practically dogmatized in the legends about Malinche, Cortez's Aztec lover, who served him as translator, as *contrabandista* of words.

One might also add to this information its reverse. Latin American mothers are frequently slandered and serve as scapegoats for anything bad that happens. Yet they also are converted, as if in the reverse image of a camera obscura, into redemptive virgins, sempiternal immaculate mothers (Our Lady of Aparecida, Our Lady of Guadalupe, the women saints, the *mães de santo*) and are always treated with affection and familiarity. We frequently use (affectionate) diminutives in talking about them, as in the peculiarly Brazilian case of St. Terezinha[30] or of young *mães de santo* from the Candomblé in Bahia. Sérgio Buarque de Holanda holds up this trait as fundamental for defining the language of both Brazil and Spanish-speaking Latin America.[31]

In other words, the language that was imposed did two things. On the one hand, it destroyed the Latin American soul, and on the other, it bequeathed the language of a new articulation: damning, swearing, the language of resistance, the final and apocalyptic language that turns against itself. Simultaneously, on the reverse side of this (hi)story, in this devastated field, there arises its opposite. As Hermann Gunkel said, "Endzeit gleicht Urzeit."[32] This is the opposite of the *lhano* manner of speaking. It's courteous but unceremonial; it has a family feeling; it reestablishes elementary, organic links of friendship, brotherhood, relatedness, and companionship. It's the language of fundamental relations—not of relations that are bureaucratic, formal, rational, diplomatic, or power-related. Bestialization is followed by infantilization: the record of a successful communication.[33]

---

[29] Octavio Paz, *El laberinto dela soledad* (México: Fondo de Cultura Económica, 1959), 59–80.

[30] Translator's note: St. Thérèse de Lisieux.

[31] Sérgio Buarque de Holanda, *Raízes do Brasil* (Rio de Janeiro: José Olympio, 1982), 107–10.

[32] "The end-time is like the beginning-time."

[33] Translator's note: The apocalyptic language imposed by the conquest not only silenced the native population but produced its opposite: an informal, family-oriented communication far removed from power relations.

The communicative act that originated the conquest created a culture of silence and dissimulation that demarcates the space in which the oppressed can resist. Moreover, as Luigi Santrini comments, "Silence appears to be the sign of an epiphany for the poor, in the sense that silence is included in an order of truth—the historical truth of domination—while the word belongs to an order of power."[34] That's why the Latin American face commonly appears with an expression different from its actual emotion. Metaphor, concealment, dissimulation, and silence remain as the language that documents the persistence of the same violence that gave Latin America its origin.[35]

The history of the five hundred years of Latin America seen from the outside is like a report on the blind in their submerged and labyrinthine lives, as Ernesto Sábato brilliantly shows in his book *Sobre Heróis e Tumbas.*[36] He describes an observer who is obsessed and terrorized when he experiences the world of the blind, which is apparently chaotic but in fact terrifically organized. It's a world he is unable to penetrate. For him, vision, analytical clarity, and narrative reveal the impossibility of dominating the object of fear. This reality is at the same time fascinating, clearly pathological but terrorizing because the observer does not see himself being observed. Despite his knowledge of the situation, he is not recognized as someone capable of pointing out to the blind man that he is blind. He is profoundly disrespected by the blind man. The blind man is like a disdainful woman; a man can love her for being a woman but hate her if she ignores him. The history of communication in Latin America is, in this strange way, a history of seduction.[37] We are Abel and Cain, Cain and Abel.

VI. The Case of Latin America

Theological communication in Latin America cannot forget, under penalty of repeating the errors of the past, that Christianity's salvation

[34] José de Souza Martins, *Caminhada no chão da noite* (São Paulo: Hucitec, 1989), 116.

[35] Ibid.

[36] Ernesto Sábato, *Sobre héroes y tumbas* (Buenos Aires: Sudamericana, 1965), 247–376.

[37] Could it be by chance that a well-known Brazilian communicator today uses, as a password to the soul of the people, the phrase "Folks, don't leave me alone!"?

project was part of the same conquest that stole other people's history. José Carlos Mariátegui said quite appropriately that "the missionaries did not impose the gospel; they imposed the cult, the liturgy."[38] It's not that the Marxist Mariátegui had some special esteem for the gospel. What he meant was that instead of there being a religious encounter in which the Judeo-Christian myth was compared with the indigenous myths, there was the paradox of horizontal communication in which the means—that is, the cult/liturgy, the institutionalized word—became the end of mission and catechesis. Cain and Abel entered into dialogue so that there would be no dialogue. It was an act of seduction, an act by the lover who kills his brother to fulfill his desire to be desired. Between the two, there was no narrative, only direct discourse: the discourse of the conquistador, of the communicator.

Between narrative on the one hand and history and discourse on the other, there is a basic difference.[39] Narrative is the presentation of a phenomenon that occurred at a certain time and that does not require interference by the narrator. When this (hi)story is a narrative about the principle of the world or society and when this narrative unintentionally explains that (hi)story and detects and maps it, we have a myth. Discourse always supposes a direct relation between the one speaking and the one listening; it supposes an intention on the part of the speaker to influence the listener in some way. Narrative, unlike discourse, is an indirect, oblique communication. In discourse, its means is its own end, its message. These ideal types are mixed, but the imposition and violence in the predominance of the discourse always remain. Theological communication in Latin America can now be hit with this question: Which has priority, the history or the discourse?

On a continent of silence and unarticulated shouts, authentically oblique communication will take place based on the possibility that theology can articulate the (hi)stories in which the Christian myth is revealed and expressed, or is not. This myth is that the totally other,

[38] José Carlos Mariátegui, *7 ensayos de interpretación de la realidad peruana* (Lima: Amauta, 1979), 173.

[39] See Tzvetan Todorov, *The Poetics of Prose* (Oxford: Basil Blackwell, 1977), 25.

once upon a time and in space, in a strange gesture of love, delivered himself to a world that did not recognize him. It's the inverse of a conquest; it's a Cain who gives himself up to the disdain of Abel.

Just as the encounter of Cain and Abel assumed the form of myth, of foundational history, in order to protect Cain and Abel, it is conceivable to reestablish the bases of a possible intimacy by reconstructing the myth of the conquest and colonization, since yesterday and today, internally and externally, this myth extends throughout Latin America. I suggest that, on the basis of these exemplary (hi)stories and their paradoxes, it's possible to open an oblique communication. Theology has the responsibility to teach by opening up such a communication, and this is perhaps theology's most important task now. Perhaps, then, against this background, it again makes sense to tell the story of Christ, who is much more the second Cain than he is the second Adam, to tell stories of the one who also taught that "to you has been given the secret of the kingdom of God, but for those outside, everything comes in parables" (Mark 4:11). Theology is what is done between the silence of Abel and the direct word of Cain. Death dwells on the two extremes.

VII. Books

In *The Thousand and One Nights*, there are various stories that connect narrative with life and with its absence and that connect silence and direct speech with death. One of these is the story of Dr. Duban, whom the king threatens with death. In exchange for his life, he asks the king's permission to tell the story of the crocodile. Permission is not granted, and Duban is killed. But immediately before being decapitated, he offers to the impious king a book to read during Duban's execution, and this represents an incredible inversion of conquest within its own logic; it's the conquest of the conquered! The executioner does his job, and the head, now disconnected from the body, speaks: "Oh, king, you may look at the book." The king opens the book, whose pages are stuck together. Putting his finger in his mouth and wetting it with saliva, the king is able to turn the first page. Then he turns the second page and so forth. He continues in this way because the pages can be separated only with some difficulty, until he reaches the seventh page. He looks at it, and there's nothing written on it. "Doctor," he says, "I don't see anything on these pages." "Keep turning the pages," says the head. So the king turns more pages and finds nothing. After a few moments, the toxin has entered the king's body; the book was impregnated with poison. He takes a step, staggers, and falls to the floor.[40]

Like the breviary given to Atahualpa as a mute symbol of the truth to be imposed, the book that does not tell a story kills. A book that is imposed and a book that is blank are both poisoned books.

[40] Ibid., 74.

A FAITH IN SEARCH OF LANGUAGE
THE SEDITIOUS CHARM OF THEOLOGY IN THE EVANGELICAL CHURCH OF THE LUTHERAN CONFESSION IN BRAZIL

I. The Crisis of Faith in Modernity

Schleiermacher, considered the most important theologian of the nineteenth century, has the merit of having recovered the academic and cultural reputation of theology at a time in which the "monks of atheism" (Heine) witnessed and proclaimed the process of "putrefaction of the absolute" (Marx). The enlightened spirits of the age had defamed Christianity, calling it the opium of the people and, later, even the "vampire of humanity" (Bauer). They went so far as to set up an inverse relation between religion and humanity: the more religion there is, the less humanity (Feuerbach).

But only in a few cases did this criticism take aim at the very essence of the religious phenomenon. It was the dogmatic institution of religion that was being criticized. Proposals for a new religion, with or without the name *religion*, brought together great ecumenical projects called "the religion of humanity" or "natural religion." There was no necessary contradiction between this enlightened spirit and devotion to the goddess Reason or to the Supreme Being. The fundamental issue, the sore spot of the crisis, the stumbling block on the

---

This text was originally presented as the inaugural lecture of the second semester of 1991 at EST (Escola Superior de Teologia) on the occasion of the celebration of seventy years of theological education in the Evangelical Church of the Lutheran Confession in Brazil. Later, it was published in the journal *Estudos Teológicos* 32, no. 2 (1992): 68–82.

path, was the positivity of religion, the institutional form that clothed it and the dogmas that sustained it. This was the problem because, through the institution and through dogma, the infinite possibility of the autonomy of the individual was being limited.

In Kant's famous definition of the Enlightenment, positive religion played the role of the villain who created in the human being a feeling of dependency that led to the laziness and cowardice of whoever thought it was better to be tortured than to assume the consequences of an autonomous subject in control of his destiny.[1] Lessing, the great hero of the Enlightenment at the end of the eighteenth century, issued the definitive verdict on the contradiction between the convictions to which reason leads us and the necessity of accepting as truth historical facts such as miracles, prophecies, or the resurrection of Christ. Between the two, there is a "deep and disgusting trench" (*garstiger breiter Graben*) impossible to get over for anyone with intellectual integrity.[2] Only voluntary ignorance, not wanting to be educated, is what sustains positive religion, the church, and its dogmas. Revelation and education are synonyms. In Lessing's words, "Education is revelation coming to the individual; revelation is education that came and continues to come to the whole human race."[3] Christian education, in Lessing's view, is a contradiction in terms. Theology as an educational enterprise of the church is a sham, and theological production is rubbish. Pedagogy is to catechesis as light is to darkness.

What did Schleiermacher do? He took theology out of the business of defending dogma and the ecclesiastical institution, he stopped trying to make of theology the rationalization of the absurd, and he made it into a practical and positive science. His object turned out to be not revelation, whose content had been demolished by the Enlightenment, but empirically demonstrable faith. What interested Schleiermacher was the very thing that so many enlightened spirits

---

1 "Aufklärung ist der Ausgang des Menschen aus seiner selbstverschuldetenUnmündigkeit." Immanuel Kant, *Ausgewählte kleine Schriften* (Hamburg: Felix Meiner, 1965), 1.

2 Gotthold Lessing, *Lessing's Theological Writings*, ed. Henry Chadwick (Stanford: Stanford University), 55.

3 Ibid., 83.

of the age failed to recognize—namely, that the people lived out their religion and demonstrated it in a popular piety that expressed itself in the religious practices of communities of faith. That was what theology should talk about. Its object should be faith empirically demonstrated in piety or, as we would say today, in mysticism. Schleiermacher discovered in religious feeling something that neither practice nor theory could justify—the feeling of absolute or unconditional dependence, which is considered an irreducible component of anthropology, a kind of religious device (or order) in human anatomy. For this reason, theology is possible as a discourse of empirically verifiable faith. Theology is defined as the conception of the emotive disposition of Christian piety presented in the form of language.[4]

Hegel, who was Schleiermacher's colleague at the University of Berlin but in the Department of Philosophy, shared with him the same preoccupation with the possibility of doing theology. But unlike Schleiermacher, Hegel was not a Pietist or a Calvinist but a Lutheran absolutely convinced that the basis of religion was not in feeling or in spirituality but in God's very being, in the absolute idea that takes form in religion as a moment for the realization of its own freedom. Hegel said sarcastically that if Schleiermacher was right, then a dog would be a better Christian, since in dogs the feeling of unconditional dependency had been perfected. In religion, God is estranged from himself for the sake of achieving his design of being all in all. Religion is the report, the externally available documentation about the realization of God himself. Religion exists not through human feeling but through God's self-realization in history, and theology becomes this science that articulates, discerns, and examines these masks of God left in history in the form of religious language, the representations that populate the religious imagination of the people—their myths, rites, legends, and stories. In religion, says Hegel, "it is not thought that has priority; what prevails is myth. In all religions there is oscillation between the imaginary and reflective thought."[5]

---

[4] "Christliche Glaubenssätze sind Auffassungen der christlich frommen Gemütszustände in der Rede dargestellt." Friedrich Schleiermacher, *Schleiermacher-Auswahl* (München: Siebenstern, 1968), 40.

[5] Georg Wilhelm Friedrich Hegel, *Werke* (Frankfurt: Suhrkamp, 1971), 18:107.

II. The Theological Rearticulation

Both Schleiermacher and Hegel, despite their differences, agreed that theology is not the recording of or talking about God, about his attributes and qualities. They followed the *via negativa*, in which talking about God begins with what God is not—that is, not the feeling of dependency and not the historical record of the sacred. Speaking about God is first of all speaking about what points to the divine and simultaneously conceals it. According to Paul Ricoeur, the first naivete disappears, the first naivete being the capacity to accept immediately what was thought to be evidence of the divine—namely, the so-called proofs of Christianity, such as the fulfillment of prophecy, the miracles, and the spread of Christianity. What comes into awareness from this moment on is very well described by Castoriadis when he says that religious necessity "corresponds to the refusal by humans to recognize the absolute otherness, the limit of all established explanation, the inaccessible other side that is found everywhere we go, the death that dwells in all life, the non-sense that borders and penetrates all meaning."[6]

No matter where we go in the mapping of contemporary theological positions, from Barth to the theology of the death of God, from liberal theology to evangelicalism, from modern theology to *nouvelle théologie*, from religious socialism to liberation theology, from the theology of secularization to the theology of popular religiosity, we have the same fundamental disenchantment that grounds theological reflection. As Castoriadis puts it, "Religion supplies a name for the unnamable, a representation for the unrepresentable, a place for the unlocalizable, and achieves and satisfies at the same time the experience of the Abyss and the inability to accept it. . . . Religion is, par excellence, the presentation and concealment of Chaos. It constitutes the making of a compromise that simultaneously prepares the impossibility for humans to lock themselves into the here-and-now of their 'real existence' and the nearly equal impossibility of their accepting the experience of the Abyss."[7]

---

[6] Cornelius Castoriadis, *Os Destinos do Totalitarismo e Outros Escritos* (Porto Alegre: LPM, 1985), 113.

[7] Ibid.

The search for a way to formulate the language of faith is universal. In this sense, every person is a theologian and carries within himself or herself the dilemma of saying what cannot be expressed but nevertheless needs to be said. This awareness that theology is the limit of language, this recognition that its self-expression has already passed the horizon of what can be said, is the fundamental mark of theology in modern times. But what has to be said has to be said. Silence, the total refusal to name the unnamable, exposes one to what Luther called the *deus nudus*; it's the experience of the terror of terrors, of everything and nothing, of the huge black hole of existence. What saves us is also what ignores us.[8] Nothing is more central to the religious experience than abandonment and absence. It's the Job-like experience of abandonment and absence that all theology, starting with that of Job's friends, has been trying to fill. The awareness of the ambiguity that the one spoken of is not present in what was said and that the proclaimed presence is the announcement of an absence is the mark of the necessary theological dilemma.

If Heidegger was right in saying that language is the house of being, then religious language is the temple of the sacred, a temple that does not contain the sacred but that indicates and represents an absence that conceals the sacred but doesn't keep it wrapped up. Perhaps a better image than Heidegger's comes from an indigenous Latin America group, from whom we have the following story. When these natives were contacted, they were presented with a Bible. The contacting group tried in various ways to explain to these natives, who had no written language, what that book was. Finally, one native understood everything that there was to be understood when he called the Bible the skin of God, the clothes of God, in an analogy to the skin that God gave to Adam and Eve when they couldn't tolerate the sight of their own truth. This skin is what localizes the unlocalizable, gives form to what has none, contains what cannot be contained, and makes access to the inaccessible possible. All this for the purpose of situating us in the present as we are stretched like a hammock between the origin

---

[8] See Beiden C. Lane, "Fierce Landscapes and the Indifference of God," *Christian Century* 106, no. 29 (October 1989): 907–10.

and the final purpose of existence. This is not a fable or an imitation of reality. Rather, we call it myth: a narrative that reflects on the origin and ultimate purpose of contingent existence and establishes forms of action and thought by means of which we understand ourselves and situate ourselves in the world.

The reason for the existence of myth is not that it explains reality but that it detects it[9]—that is, myth functions not by mapping reality but by locating us in it and offering us a visible center in the daily experience of turbulence and chaos. Myth is revelatory but *sub contraria specie*. Hence theology is searching for myth and then explaining it but simultaneously affirming that the myth is not reality itself. Before theology is faith in search of reason, as Anselm argued; it's the search for a language, the language that engenders reason itself. Myth is the first form in which this language is articulated. The theologian says, "There it is, there! But it isn't there." Hence it's faith in search of language that confesses that what one has is still only language. We look at ourselves in it, but still only as if in a mirror, as Paul said.

Myth is alive, like language, and it moves, stretches, and contracts. But more than language, myth is not just any story. It's a foundational story, one through which we have access to the mysteries of existence but that also conceals them from us. Myth puts us back into primeval time, at the moment that something of importance happens for humans. Mircea Eliade says that when a myth dies, it becomes a legend, an exemplary story, a "case," thus losing its ability to present and simultaneously conceal the mystery.[10] The life of the myth is in its capacity to incorporate new experiences into its narrative web. This is the reason that theology not only discerns the myth but also reworks it. A case in point is baptism, which from cleansing in repentance becomes a passage to spiritual life and then an introduction to community life, and finally the cosmic water that renews all creation. It's the Reed Sea crossing that becomes the passage from death to life and finally from marginality to a life of freedom. It's Mary, who starts out as a young woman but is converted into a virgin to be finally thought of as immaculate.

---

9 Philip Hefner, "Myth and Morality," *Zygon* 26, no. 1 (March 1991): 126.
10 Mircea Eliade, *Mito e Realidade* (São Paulo: Perspectiva, 1972), 13–15.

The awareness of this organic relation between theology and myth is the distinctive element of Latin American theology, both in regard to the theologies that, in one way or another, adopt the method of demythologizing and in regard to covert fundamentalisms and confessionalisms. Demythologizing lays things bare, whereas fundamentalism makes the myth into a legend. The practice of rereading is what Tillich calls transmythization, which is a reworking of the myth to make it come alive and incorporate new experiences, thus making it better suited for detecting the ultimate relevance of daily experience.

III. The Theologian's Dilemma: Imagination versus Institution

I turn now to the dilemma of the theologian, which is saying things as they are but, at the same time, knowing that God is not really present in what is said. As for the institutional question, the theologian speaks for the benefit of the community of faith and with the community of faith as a starting point. But the theologian speaks in a way that both builds up and tears down the support of that community by constantly messing with the limits and contours of the myths that ground and sustain the community. The theologian is in part the priest who affirms and the prophet who denies, and this is so because theology is not only an ecclesial undertaking; its authorization to speak is sustained by the Word, which grounds the world and ends up being an accomplice of the world.

Therein lies the unhappiness of the theologian: the object of his discourse, religious language, the representations of the sacred, are and are not what they say they are. When Luther said that the theologian of the cross says things as they are, he meant that this theologian also says that things are not what they seem to be. This is the paradox of theology. In an article about the dilemma of the theologian, Van Harvey describes the problem: one can say that the theologian finds himself in the situation of Barrabas in the novel of the same name by Pär Lagerkvist.[11] Lagerkvist's Barrabas knows or thinks he knows that Jesus did not rise from the dead on the first Easter. Barrabas was near

[11] Van A. Harvey, "The Dilemma of the Unbelieving Theologian," *American Journal of Theology and Philosophy* 2, no. 2 (May 1981): 46–54.

the tomb on the morning of the first Easter and saw absolutely nothing. But he is deeply touched and attracted by the spirit of the young band of Christians, a spirit encapsulated in their motto: "Love one another." He is, however, persecuted by the thought that this spirit is present among them only by virtue of their fantastic beliefs. He is attracted to the community of those who preserve the myths even though he knows that he will always remain an outsider in this community. The dilemma of the theologian is that as long as he remains silent in this community, he is not a theologian, but if he speaks, he is still not a theologian, since he is not speaking to or from the community that sustains faith. Harvey's paradox exaggerates the question by radically separating the theologian from the community, but it points to the central problem, which is the relation between the imagination that sustains the faithful and the institutionality within which the theologian operates.

The issue is that the community in which theology is articulated is also an institution whose reason for being is the recognition and maintenance of its limits. This is the tension or dialectical polarization between what Castoriadis called the instituting society—namely, the "social imagination" that forms the mythical nucleus of society—and the instituted society, which is the fixity, the "inertia and mechanisms of self-perpetuation," of the instituted forms.[12] One is the cause, origin, and source of autonomy; the other is determinedness, the imposition of limits, the deceptive presence of heteronomy. The living out of faith as practiced and grounded in the founding center of the community, which is the revelation/concealment of the vital mystery with its fluid and movable limits, is just the opposite of what the institution does: it thinks on the basis of its limit—of what defines it over against what it is not. The person of faith thinks about the community on the basis of faith and assumes that the center of that community is justification by grace, the priesthood of all believers, the theology of the cross, and so on. But the institution thinks about attendance, numbers, limits, quotas, new areas, regions. Between these two poles theology oscillates.

---

[12] Cornelius Castoriadis, *A Istituição Imaginária da sociedade*, 3rd ed. (Rio de Janeiro: Paz e Terra, 1982), 414–18.

But in its oscillation, theology seeks to be faithful to what transcends both the imagination (without rejecting it) and the institution (while recognizing the inevitability of the institution). Between the autonomy of the imagination and the heteronomy of the institution lies the theonomy through which theology encounters its independence from institutional restraints and the freedom to encounter in the imagination the renewed source of its language.

Theology loses its freedom when it adjusts to the institution. It finds itself without a language. It gets enmeshed in what Luther called the Babylonian captivity. Yet without an institution, theology has the habit of being an exercise in the irrelevant. The institution is a necessary pole in the dialectic with the imagination. If you reject one, you lose the other. The institution not only restricts theology but also makes it viable. But theology and the institution move in opposite directions. Their criteria are different. The question is complex because an all-out war between theology and the institution destroys both of them, making one irrelevant and the other inane. Hence the compromise solution to maintain the marriage between theology and institution oscillates between the extremes of schism and adjustment, between prophetic disposition and priestly duty, between protest of the spirit and institutional conformity, between imagination and instituted society. The dilemma of theology is to keep measuring the tension between engagement with the imagination, on which the faith of the community rests, and the institutional commitment that sustains the theological task. In classical terms, it's the dilemma between the material cause of theologizing and its formal cause. This is the dilemma of theology in modernity, which has broken with the medieval identity between structure and content, between the positivity of dogma and the truth.

IV. Instituted Theology and Seditious Religion

This long digression on theology and institutionality serve only to permit us to speak about what I call the seditious charm of theology in the Evangelical Church of the Lutheran Confession in Brazil. The argument I'm developing is that theological education has been going on in this church for seventy years, but, until recently, the institutional principle was dominant. Theology was done on the basis of the demarcations of the ethnic and social limits of the communities of local German ethnicity. Dohms, who was both ecclesial director and theologian, worried in his 1934 article that "the church in general is not threatened and neither is the evangelical church in Brazil. But our church, the evangelical German church in Brazil is threatened. The ethno-national foundations of this church in this time and place are called into question."[13] What was Dohms afraid of? He refers to the Greece of the first Christian centuries to identify the danger and states that "the crisis of the religion of the Greeks was the crisis of their nationality; religious syncretism runs parallel to the mixture of races and nations."[14]

It's extremely revealing that, in this context, in which Catholic Germans in the south of Brazil were arguing with evangelicals over the spiritual territory of German ethnicity, Luther appears not primarily as a theologian but as the national hero of the ethnicity. On the Catholic side, since the nineteenth century, in connection with the event of the Muckers, the priesthood of all believers and the people's access to the Holy Scriptures have been held responsible for the seditious spirit of some colonists.[15] Sixty years later, we still hear from Dohms echoes of this accusation, to which he gives the following answer: "Luther is not the father of subjectivism but a father of his people and of the thinking of a national church."[16] On these subjects, we already have large amounts of collected material and heated discussions. Some people attribute to German ethnicity an eventual or conjunctural character in the self-understanding of the church.[17] Others say that the link between the gospel and German ethnicity is a pact between life and death.[18] Let us leave this discussion aside

---

13 Hermann Dohms, *Volk und Kirche* (Deutsche Evangelische Blätter für Brasilien, 1934), 125.

14 Ibid., 128.

15 See the master's thesis by João Guilherme Biehl, "Jammerthal—o Vale da Lamentação: Crítica à construção do messianismo Mucker" (MA thesis, Federal University of Santa Maria, 1991).

16 Dohms, *Volk und Kirche*, 127.

17 Martin N. Dreher, *Igreja e Germanidade* (São Leopoldo: Sinodal, 1984).

18 H.-J. Prien, "Kirche-Volkstum-Politik," *Estudos Teológicos* 11, no. 1, nova sequência (1971): 15/41.

while accepting a minimal version of it that maintains that whether for circumstantial or fundamental motives, there was such a linkage. I am suggesting that German ethnicity has been a variable. The constant, however, is the process of institutionalization, as a function of which German ethnicity was part of the struggle. What's important now is to ask about the implications of all this for theology.

I suggest the following hypothesis: as people thought of ethnic identity as a continuation or extension of the German nation on Brazilian territory, there was no theology organically linked to the churches. It was a theology that never touched the ground, because it assumed that the Germanic character of these churches was sustained by racial continuity, an assumption that confused ethnicity with biological roots. The environment in which theology evolved was not, then, the local congregation but the ecclesial structure, the synod. The legend of ethnic identity based on race was invented, while the living myth that the churches themselves were already creating and re-creating on Brazilian soil was lost. The inability to detect these myths, to get close to the imaginative world of the churches, still resounds in our midst when we read reports of pastoral activity that reflect a great commitment to the people but are also loaded with complaints about the magic meaning that rites and popular beliefs assume in our churches. The contextualization of theology is more of an institutional contextualization than a community contextualization, hence the tension between theologians and community. Prophetic posture serves to dissimulate the distancing between the ecclesial institution and the churches. This becomes clear when, in a similar context, "pastorcentrism" is denounced but theologians recommend that the gospel of salvation and liberation be announced to churches supposedly caught up in the web of consumerism. This tension between, on the one hand, the institution that sustains theology and, on the other, the churches is well described by Karl von Koseritz, a perceptive analyst of what was going on in the colony in the second half of the nineteenth century. When Koseritz evaluates the event of the Muckers, he assigns major responsibility for sedition in the colony to "orthodox evangelical pastors, who for a long time have been imported from Germany."[19] To these pastors, he says, "I looked in the mirror that our prophet set before you, of which you are the precursors and creators. Your miracle stories now turn against you. . . . Maurer is drawing the practical consequences from the theoretical premises of the clergy. Could a half-crazy con man, a person without education and almost illiterate, have succeeded in finding hundreds of followers in this colony if religious fanaticism had not kept the residents in ignorance and believing in miracles and superstition?"[20]

The accusation of ignorance comes from a learned man but correctly points to the gap between the clergy and the religion of the colony. What's more, when the clergy do not recognize themselves in the mirror of their context, in the language that gives texture to the living myth, they cannot be organically connected to that myth. But that material exists for a theology that was never developed is clear when Koseritz, echoing the Jesuits, issues the denunciation that leaving the people with the Bible is leaving them with "the most dangerous of all books": "All the lowest, cheapest horror novels that ruin fantasy and damage the palate are not so dangerous as certain books of the Bible, especially when the reader does not have the proper education for digesting the material in a reasonable manner."[21] What's interesting here is not quibbling about whether Koseritz was right in his assessment. The main point is that he correctly identifies the gap between the official theology and the practical theology of the colony. He points to the strained relations between the official/institutional theology and the living myth of the colony. The inability of the clergy to recognize themselves in the mirror of the colony becomes quite obvious in the reports of Pastor Hermann Borchard, who, a decade earlier, writes to Germany the following analysis of what he had seen in the colony: "Religiosity is not to be found in Brazil. The books of nonbelievers, like the Gospel of Nature, bad novels, rationalist writings, have found their way over the ocean. Novels are more widely read than the Bible, and the dance

---

[19] Karl von Koseritz, *Der Muckerschwindel auf der deutschen Colonie, Deutsche Volkskalender* (1875), 125.

[20] Karl von Koseritz, *Deutsche Zeitung*, May 17, 1873.

[21] Koseritz, *Muckerschwindel*, 126.

hall attracts more people than does the church. The observance of the Sabbath is unknown. A complete indifference dominates here. Religion is something that doesn't concern the majority of people; it's outside the range of their thinking."[22]

It seems that Borchard knew what he didn't want to find. He offers this explanation for the paganism of the colonists: "They were children of the poor working class in Germany and brought very little faith with them. But they still have the old family Bible that they brought with them, and it reminds them that they are evangelical Christians. They also heard that their parents walked miles to have them baptized, and for this reason, too, they want to baptize and confirm their children."[23]

He adds that these colonists erected beautiful churches whose aesthetic features set them apart from the parsimonious architecture of the colony. But if you're expecting a negative prognosis from this diagnosis, you're mistaken. Borchard deposits his hope in the fact that the German colonies have kept themselves racially pure, compared with the miscegenation that he had experienced in the United States, where he had been a missionary. He concludes, "As in no other place on earth, German ethnicity has a good future here. If, in some foreign land, it is possible to construct a pure German colony, then this is it."[24] The contribution that the church can make is to form a synod, an institution that organizes the limits of the institution and reconnects the links with the Mother Church.

Colonists whose immigration has cut them off from access to their mother are going to find in Borchard's proposal of a synod a substitute mother or a reattached umbilical cord that puts their anarchical and disorderly world back in order. For this reason, Borchard calls the

[22] Hermann Borchard, "Die Mission unter den evangelischen Deutschen in Suedbrasilien, Barmen," January 1, 1865, published by Friedrich Fabri, *Evangelisches Zentralarchiv in Berlin*, document 123989. A similar opinion is expressed, in the same period, by Pastor Wilhelm Kleingünther on the church of Porto Alegre. But in the latter case, the motive must be secularism. See Dreher, "O Papel de Hermann Dohms," 73n98. Translator's note: This statement, originally in German, was translated by Westhelle into Portuguese.

[23] Borchard, "Mission."

[24] Ibid.

church in Germany to its responsibility: sending clergy to Brazil. But it's interesting that he sets one condition: "I believe that trained missionaries will serve better here than persons trained in theology."[25] This recommendation, which sets the missionary against the theologian and understands the evangelical German colonies as a mission field, can mean only that Borchard's concern is to give a legitimate configuration to German ecclesiality. Theology as the critical construction of a language in the midst of living myths is put on hold.

In the period that follows the conquest of the Americas, we know of fantastic speculations about what it would mean to live south of the equator. In the same way that the seasons and the direction of water draining in the sink are inverted, it was suspected that all life suffered a similar inversion of structures and values. In this context, there arises the suspicion that sin does not exist beyond the equator (*ultra equinoxialem non peccavit*) or that the orders of values are reversed. The disorderliness that Borchard observes in the life of the colony has a similar origin. His cosmovision of what the South means is pointedly revealed in his report of his voyage by ship to Brazil, when he describes the passage over the equator: "We would not only exchange day for night, summer for winter, but would also enter into a totally new relation that would invert all of our conceptions of the world until now."[26] Borchard knew what he would encounter, and he found what he wanted: an evangelical populace on the other side of reality unprepared to keep the world upright. It was necessary to call for mama, who would make the son clean his room, hence the need for a synod and, then, for missionaries. As for theologians, they aren't necessary. There's already a sufficient number of them in the home office.

The dream of theological education in Brazil arises and becomes an incipient reality a century after the immigration, and almost sixty

[25] Ibid. The same opinion is expressed in his letter to the chief advisor of the Evangelical Church in Berlin on May 28, 1864, *Evangelisches Zentralarchiv in Berlin*, document 123989. In this letter, he assents to their sending one theologian but specifically to Porto Alegre, presumably to meet the challenge that rationalism represented in that city.

[26] Borchard, "Mission."

years after Borchard and his ideal, Rotermund,[27] will become a reality in 1886, after a failed attempt by Borchard himself. Dreher reports that in 1929, the Missouri Synod accused the Rio Grande Synod of not having a confessional base, to which the Rio Grande Synod responded that "confession" would mean a characteristic of distinction or a work program signifying that the distinct task of the Rio Grande Synod was to "limit itself to the population of German origin in [their] state."[28]

Dreher details various complaints that, at the end of the nineteenth century, are already being formulated, especially that the Portuguese language is taking over the colonies. The tension between the colonists and foreign pastors is interpreted as the presence of the "Prussian helmet,"[29] an indication that these communities, German as they were, resented not the alleged German ethnicity that the pastors brought with them but the fact that the pastor represented an institutionalizing order contrary to the experiences of the communities. In short, the issue was not Pan-Germanism but simply the proposal that the synod function as a substitute mother to whom the communities of an adolescent church reacted with simultaneous obedience and revolt, like any adolescent. This is what Pastor Kleingünther is referring to when he complains about an "unfounded fear of the Synod, on the part of the churches."[30]

V. The Art of Anchoring a Ship in Space

And the theology, what was it? I don't think it was anything more than the exercise of articulating a synodal identity that was surviving in Brazil while the German language offered to the churches themselves the religious identity by which they defined themselves. The need to define the Germanic character of the synod was no secret weapon of Pan-Germanism for conquering the territories south of

---

[27] Rotermund was a German immigrant who had the vision of a Lutheran church devoted to the preservation of German culture and language and sustained by agricultural cooperatives.

[28] Dreher, "O Papel de Hermann Dohms," 97.

[29] Ibid., 101.

[30] A letter from Wilhelm Kleingünther to chief advisor of the Evangelical Church in Berlin, Porto Alegre, December 28, 1968, *Evangelisches Zentralarchiv in Berlin*, document 123989.

the equator; it was the way the synod succeeded in keeping itself together and sustaining an autochthonous character for the churches it included. But this character was achieved only by maintaining two factors: the link with the Mother Church and the maintenance of the German language as the discourse of unity.

The recent theological crisis that the Evangelical Church of the Lutheran Confession in Brazil went through has everything to do with the doubly orphaned status that followed. The great merit of Rotermund and Dohms in maintaining the synod was to make it the space for theological organization as well. The great limitation was making the synod the *habitat* of theological reflection. It was not theology that made the connection between the institution and the local church; theology limited itself to being an articulation and linguistic repristination that no longer touched on or even helped reelaborate the living myths of the churches. The synod, in itself, was the presence of a mother that the country of origin had banned. Theological-ecclesiastical articulation in German was the way to keep present the ghost of an absent father. This was nothing less than an ingenious solution, thought up by Borchard, implemented by Rotermund, and consecrated by Dohms.

Everything was in order in the kingdom of theology, but it was an institutional theology, the theology of the synod, which was caressing the breasts of a distant mother and felt reassured by the linguistic phallus of an already absent father. The double crisis took shape in two stages. The first was the disappearance of the mother, the cutting off of the mother's milk that sustained and pacified seditious adolescents. The second was World War II. Mama went away. Elder brothers had to take care of the house. The paternal language was also banned for a time. Students of theology were sent back to their churches. The adolescent church started to administer the house. From that point on, the awareness grew that theological education would have to take place on Brazilian soil. The crisis was overcome because the father was still present. Let out of prison, the German language, the father's language, returned from the war like a father returning home after a crisis and solemnly declaring that the loss of their mother hadn't been so traumatic because, after all, she wasn't all that saintly anyway.

Before World War II, the struggle surrounding the Confessing Church in Germany had been met by dissonant voices in Brazil, but only from a minority. Barth's theology was presented as a modern thing, a new toy for doing theology, even though this was fifty years after the bombastic publication in Germany of his commentary on Romans.[31] Theological rearticulation and the growing influence of Barth and Barthians permitted theology to reorganize its space, having already been freed from the figure of a dominating and omnipresent mother. I'm not concerned by the fact that at that time there was no development of a Latin American theology. The Roman Catholic Church itself was only recently beginning attempts at theological formulations. What I emphasize is that the institutional fragility of the Lutheran synods was such that the Lutheran church in Brazil could do no more than maintain the synods themselves. Theology, on every side of the theological spectrum, continued to sustain the identity of the churches by the guarantee that linguistic unity furnished them, but without any organic connection with the myths and popular imagination of the churches.

But as Ana Cristina Cesar says, "It's always more difficult to anchor a ship in space." This became evident when the post–World War II generation not only went through the crisis of definitively losing the mother, whom the synod was artificially maintaining, but also came to reject the father, the linguistic phallus once imprisoned and now impotent. The change is brutal. In twenty years after the loss of the mother, theology in the Evangelical Church of the Lutheran Confession in Brazil has the task of not only finding a church and making it mature but also finding a new language. But where do you get a new language if theology not only was not anchored in the reality of the churches but even fomented the distancing of its language from the daily practice and imagination of the churches?

In 1959, Erich Fausel publishes a dictionary on the linguistic mixture found among German-Brazilians.[32] It includes three thousand

[31] Martin Dreher, "O Papel de Hermann Dohms na Criação e Consolidação da Faculdade de Teologia," in *Formação Teológica em Terra Brasileira*, ed. Lothar Hoch (São Leopoldo: Sinodal, 1986), 47–48.

[32] Erich Fausel, *Die deutschbrasilianische Sprachmischung* (Berlin: Erich Schmidt, 1959).

Portuguese words adopted into the lexicon and adapted to German syntax. In fact, this is a significant number that could justify the criticisms of an alleged German inculturation in Brazilian life. However, in regard to theology, we're going to be surprised to notice that 43 percent of the lexicon consists of entries that relate to agricultural and cattle-breeding issues within the colony; 25 percent to exclamations and expressions of sociability; 15 percent to urbanism, transportation, and commerce; 10 percent to bureaucracy and politics; and 7 percent to militarism and technology. It's interesting that expressions relating to religion do not exceed 0.6 percent, or eighteen words, all being identifiers but having nothing to do with relationships. Even more significant is that none of those eighteen words come from the Protestant milieu. Nine of them come from Spiritism or from Afro-Brazilian cults, and another nine come from Catholicism. According to Fausel, only four of these words are used frequently: nun, open-air mass, faith healer, and macumba.[33]

The postwar generation now reaches maturity. In the 1960s, theological education goes through a profound transformation. When we arrive at 1970, we're going to have a theological education administered totally in Portuguese. In fact, it is always more difficult to anchor a ship in space. The father was finally exiled. But what is to be done now? It's necessary to reconstruct the house of the sacred, to remake the language, to construct an identity. It's no longer enough to reject the father. We're living on the street. We adolescents of seventy years of theological education in our church need a house. We are behind the times. The ideal institution delayed our theological discussion, an incredible enterprise of anchoring ships in space, an enterprise that, once gone, left no traces. We are left with no foundation for reconstructing an old house. It was a chimera, and now we know that, all of us: conservatives, liberals, confessionalists, evangelicals, mystics, and sociopoliticians. I don't share the fear expressed by Jaci Maraschin in his contribution to the fortieth anniversary of the School of Theology, but he praises the emergence of the School of Theology in Brazilian life and culture and

---

[33] For a discussion of these data, see my article "Considerações sobre o Etno-Luteranismo Latino-Americano," *Estudos Teológicos* 18, no. 2 (1978): 77–94.

emphasizes the following: "It is certain that nothing is definitive and that there will be within Lutheranism people ready to return to the old homestead of the past with a longing for the traditions of their childhood and for things that, at a certain time in their life, meant more to them."[34]

No! Our problem is something else. The problem is that there is only one home to build on foundations as yet unknown to us. All we have are loose stones, fragments of stories and diverse, scattered myths that one person sticks here and the next person sticks somewhere else in a montage of various strange architectonic pieces. There's the charm, and there's the task of theology today. There's no turning back. There's no father waiting by the side of the road. It's right there in the pigsty that we'll construct a dwelling or fail to construct it.

The so-called crisis in theological education in the Evangelical Church of the Lutheran Confession in Brazil is nothing more than the devastated terrain on which we thought there was a house of the institutional imagination of the church. That's why we have this battle of brick and cement, this seditious practice in which everyone tries to make their models into reality. The criticism aimed at theological education in our church is the criticism of the construction of a language that may provide housing and criteria for the experience of the sacred in our churches. That's where the divergences lie. Therefore, the School of Theology, as a privileged space for the construction of this language, is also the prime target of criticism. Since the mid-1970s, groups of architects have come, one after the other, but they have not seen their projects represented in the theological spreadsheets of the School of Theology. And this criticism is radical because we're not talking about remodeling a few rooms; it's the entire house that's at stake. Never have the words of Carlos Drummond de Andrade rung truer: "The struggle with words is the most futile. Despite our struggling, morning barely comes."[35]

---

[34] Jacy Maraschin, "O Papel da Faculdade de Teologia no Contexto Sociopolítico, Económico e Religioso Brasileiro," in Hoch, *Formação Teológica em Terra Brasileira*, 195.

[35] Westhelle does not mention in what poem these lines are to be found.

I don't plan to offer my own architectural plan. I would only like to suggest that the basic issue in this project is the ground itself on which the new dwelling is built. The only error that we can commit, and thus repeat the past, is to propose another chimera—that is, a language without roots in our myths, even if these myths are fragmentary, because they exist and subsist in the life of the people where the gospel wants to be lived and proclaimed.

> Now it was some other dance,
> Other dreams and uncertainties.
> Other love under strange zodiacs—Other is the terror of constructing new mythologies.
>
> Mario Quintana

UNA SANCTA
THE UNITY OF THE CHURCH AMID SOCIAL DIVISION

I. Ecumenism: Unity or Totality

The relation between social stratum and religious affiliation is complex. This complexity is due to the absence of a direct causal connection between social status and religious systems articulated and practiced by ecclesiastical institutions. Social and economic differences and class relations do not extend into analogous relations either among churches (or similar religious systems) or even within churches. What divides or unites the churches are not ethical problems as such. That is, a situation of social class does not develop directly into a religious system. Religious systems are capable of including different social situations and, for this reason, are relatively resistant to specific ethico-social challenges. However, a certain relation exists. But because there is no direct causal relation, this relation must be described as asymmetrical.

This essay is an attempt to define what this asymmetry consists of and what constitutes its causality. We're facing one of the basic problems of ecumenism. On the one hand, understanding this relation would permit us to define the limits and possibilities of ecumenism. On the other hand, the ecumenical movement itself has been possible because the relation between social situation and religious involvement has been rather amorphous. It's impossible not to suspect that there might be a connection between the emergence of ecumenism

---

Originally published in *Estudos Teológicos* 31, no. 1 (1991): 29–46.

in the last century and the great historical marks that came after the two world wars (the International Missionary Council, the Life and Action movement, the Faith and Constitution movement, and finally, the World Council of Churches), including the concomitant expansion of international capitalism. Might it be that we are more ecumenical because capitalism became universal—that is, "catholic"? This, however, does not mean that one can apply a theory of reflex to explain the ecumenical movement on the basis of economic infrastructure. The very militancy of ecumenism in the cause of freedom and human development gives the lie to such an immediate association. But there remains, then, this inquiry: What are the limits and possibilities for the unity of Christians? In other words, what character does the ecumenical project of unity have, and where does it come down on ethical issues?

A correlate to the problem of ecumenism is the diversity and pulverization of the options offered by the new religious movements, whose multiplicity defies attempts to classify them by ethical criteria that suppose a direct relation between political, social, or economic criteria.[1]

From the "underside of history" (Gutiérrez)—that is, from the dependent nations of the world—a serious criticism has been aimed at the ecumenism of doctrinal consensus or of ecclesial rapprochement. Simultaneously, however, some of the most vigorous expressions of contemporary ecumenism appear in this same context. I'm not referring only to the cooperation among Christians and churches around social action and diakonia. Ecclesial practice itself has also been affected by this ecumenism, despite the total lack of doctrinal agreement. Presbyterians, Roman Catholics, Lutherans, and Methodists have not reached agreement on the Eucharist, to give one example. However, they celebrate the Eucharist in common, despite ecclesial resistance and the lack of confessional agreement that regulates such celebrations. These celebrations are possible, we must remember, only in certain social and political circumstances, which

---

1 On this question, see the synthesis offered by Oneide Bobsin, "Seitas e Igrejas," *Renovação*, April 1990, 7–11.

are the condition for their possibility. Such circumstances are ephemeral and not institutionalized. Above all, they are ambiguous. But they affect the ecclesial practice of those who share in the celebration.

Such ecumenical advances are rather circumstantial. Therein reside their strength and their limitation. Not only do they make more unity possible; they also cause divisions. The already consecrated distinction between ecumenism from the base and ecumenism from the top down does not offer much help in defining this phenomenon. Both the criticism and the ecumenical advances are framed by social and economic relations in the midst of conflicts and contradictions manifested at various historical junctures in which these criticisms and advances do not play an unequivocal role. This ecumenical process, with its advances and regressions, simultaneously affects the internal unity of an ecclesial institution and the relation among ecclesial bodies, both in practice and in theory.[2] What's important is recognizing that ecumenical practice is robed in many enigmas and is no less ambiguous at the base than at the top. As an illustration of this complexity, we have the curious correlation existing between the internationalization of capitalism and the development of the ecumenical movement.

Camilo Torres, the Columbian priest who died in guerrilla warfare in 1966, already presented the problem and proposed a solution: "I gave up my clerical duties and privileges, but I did not stop being a priest. I believe that I devoted myself to the revolution out of love for my neighbor. I stopped saying mass in order to practice love of neighbor in the economic and social sphere here and now. When my neighbor no longer has anything against me, when I have brought the revolution to its conclusion, then, if God permits, I will again celebrate mass."[3]

---

[2] See Julio de Santa Ana, *Ecumenismo e Libertação* (Petrópolis: Vozes, 1987), 116–21; and Gerhard Tiel, "O Processo Conciliar de Mútuo Compromisso para Justiça, Paz e Integridade da Criação," *Estudos Teológicos* 28, no. 2 (1988): 164–69.

[3] Camilo Torres, *Revolutionary Priest*, ed. John Gerassi (New York: Vintage, 1971), 368.

Torres's text continues with a commentary on Matthew 5:23–24. The criticism is clear. Celebrating communion is hypocritical in a context of injustice and class struggle. For this reason, he also censured the church for permitting such celebrations to conceal and harmonize existing conflicts through rites of alleged unity. Such has been the suspicion behind many ecumenical efforts.

Enrique Dussel took this discussion forward by suggesting that the problem does not reside only in the attempt to overcome social divisions in order to make viable a possible celebration of unity. For Dussel, the very attempt to celebrate unity already suppresses what is different and negates otherness. Social and economic inequality itself results from negating the other and reducing him to totality: "*Oekoumene* is the same as 'totality,' a highly abstract technical term. 'Totality' comes from 'total.' We say, 'the totality of meaning' of my daily world, because everything in this world has meaning. What's in my world makes sense for me but not necessarily for someone else. . . . Thus, the person who understands the meaning of everything that is happening is also the one who is at the center of the world. The person on the periphery of the world doesn't know what it's about."[4]

For Dussel, not even social and economic justice are sufficient conditions for unity, since such unity would represent the suppression of the other, of the distinctly different. However, the possible criticism of a total unity is not the same thing as the total criticism of a possible unity. The problem, then, is the following: What are the conditions for a possible unity—and not of a possible unity that suppresses all differences?

II. Social Classes and Religious Options

Max Weber gives us the classic formulation of the relation between social situation and religious demand: "The socially and economically privileged strata feel little need of salvation. Rather, they attribute to religion the function of 'legitimation' of their style of life. . . .

[4] Enrique Dussel, *Ethics and the Theology of Liberation* (Maryknoll, NY: Orbis, 1978), 4–5.

The situation of the unprivileged is the opposite. Their specific need consists in being saved from suffering."[5]

Weber's analysis of the relation between social structure and religious necessity is clear and perceptive and suggests a direct connection between socioeconomic stratum and religious articulation. Pierre Bourdieu comments on Weber's thesis and extracts some logical conclusions: "Religious demands tend to organize themselves around two main types, which correspond to two main types of social situations, that is, the privileged classes' particular demands for legitimation of the established order and the disfavored classes' particular demands for compensation."[6]

If such an interpretation of religious demands is applied to organized religious systems, we can observe, as Ernst Troeltsch has already noted, that this is the case of sects,[7] and only under special circumstances could we also include churches, as in the case of South Africa under apartheid. But such a direct relation between social stratum and religious affiliation is not so obvious or easy to recognize in the historical churches. Torres calls attention to this in his denunciation. Instead of expressing religious necessities in different religious organizations, these organizations are capable of being so inclusive that they mask religious options.

To clarify this issue, it's necessary to explain the role of religion within capitalism and its modern ideology. It's not possible to analyze the social structure of classes without considering the system that organizes that structure.

The emergence of the individual as an atomized entity and the creation of an ample ideological system on the basis of freedom and individuality are two correlated sides of modernity. This correlation brings with it implications for the role that the churches play in this system.

---

5 Max Weber, *Economia y sociedad: Esbozo de sociologia comprensiva* (México: FCE, 1969), 1:393–94; see also the commentary by José Ivo Follmann, *Igreja, Ideologia e Classes Sociais* (Petrópolis: Vozes, 1985), 31–32.

6 Pierre Bourdieu, *A Economia das Trocas Simbólicas* (São Paulo: Perspectiva, 1974), 87.

7 Ernst Troeltsch, *The Social Teaching of the Christian Churches* (Chicago: University of Chicago Press, 1931), 2:996.

III. The New Faith

Nietzsche's announcement of the death of God is known as one of the characteristic formulations of modern times. What's interesting, though, is the context in which Nietzsche makes this announcement for the first time. Zarathustra finds himself in a multitude in the public market, in which everyone was waiting for the spectacle of a high-wire artist dancing on a wire. There the superman is announced, and God is pronounced dead—dead because in the market, nothing else exists but individuals interacting. Individuals, says Nietzsche's Zarathustra, "are the most recent of creations."[8] The market reigns supreme. It's the space in which individuals exercise their most concrete freedom and define their identity and role. In truth, the emergence of the atomized individual who is differentiated from the exercise of his vocation, of his public role, begins with the Renaissance but culminates in the triumph of capitalism as an assumed ideology.[9]

The emergence of this individual who is already without an organic, perennial connection to his social role is what permits the radical affirmation of his freedom. So radical is this liberty that a negative formulation, such as in John Stuart Mill, is attributed to it: "The only liberty that deserves this name is seeking our own interests in our own way, while we deprive others of their freedom or impede their efforts to obtain it."[10] This formulation, which Western societies recite as prayers, places the whole problem of the limit of freedom outside the conscience of the individual and on the flexible terrain of human relations. But it is precisely in these relations that the relative realization of absolute freedom of the individual occurs. Such freedom becomes positive and is achieved only in the satisfaction of the concrete necessities that are always directed against one's neighbor. Conscience and reason become instruments of "insatiable desire directed against one's neighbor."[11] That's the reason Kant was able to identify the capacity of the individual to overcome cowardice and

---

[8] Friedrich Wilhelm Nietzsche, *Assim Falava Zaratustra* (São Paulo: Hemus, n.d.), 9–11, 46.
[9] Agnes Heller, *Renaissance Man* (New York: Schocken, 1978), 206.
[10] John Stuart Mill, *On Liberty* (Arlington Heights: AHM, 1947), 12.
[11] Heller, *Renaissance Man*, 450.

laziness as the fundamental characteristic of modern times.[12] The desire by which reason and conscience become instruments is the desire to concretize freedom in "unlimited accumulation" (Hobbes). It's the "desire for gain" (Locke). Human relations are mediated by an interest in realizing materially the absolute freedom of the individual while pretending that that freedom is somehow spiritual.

Human sociability did not disappear, but it was invested with a new character. Fraternity was, in fact, an ideal. But it's definition was not based on objective values or on an inventory of positive rights (a certain salary, housing, education, health, etc.). Fraternity was interpreted as a contractual arrangement designed to guarantee protection and mutual satisfaction of desires in a highly competitive situation. The associative ideal is realized in the corporation, in the machine—not in *communitas*—because the concretion of freedom is only the external side of the already conquered interior freedom. The u-topias of the Renaissance become topias. The "necessary truths of reason" (Lessing) are internal to reason itself and do not need historical demonstration. The liberal "mystique" is apophatic; it remains silent in the face of anything that cannot be positively expressed, as the neopositivist Wittgenstein assured us.[13] It guarantees the "divinity" of the individual by negating the value intrinsic to everything that transcends the individual.

Within this logic, the concept of property will receive an importance only comparable to the ideal of individuality. Property is nothing less than the external reward for the internal virtue of the individual: seeking gain, being creative and aggressive in the market. This is the way that the consciousness of the intrinsic and inalienable value of the atomized individual is expressed. Thus private property assumes a "sacramental function." It is the means by which the radical but abstract freedom of the individual is concretized. In religious

[12] Immanuel Kant, *Ausgewählte kleine Schriften* (Hamburg: Felix Meiner, 1965), 1.

[13] Ludwig Wittgenstein, *Tractatus logico-philosophicus/Logisch-philosophische Abhandlung* (Frankfurt: Suhrkamp, 1978), 115. "Es gibt allerdings Unaussprechliches. Dies zeigt sich, es ist da Mystische. Die richtige Methode der Philosophie wäre eigentlich die: Nichts zu sagen, als was sich sagen lässt, also Saetze der Naturwissenschaft . . . Wovon man nicht sprechen kann, darüber muss man schweigen."

language, private property becomes the sanctuary in which the self-realization of the individual is achieved.

The concept of the economic contract exemplifies these subtle but decisive changes that have marked modernity. If, in premodern times, there was a legal distinction between usury and tribute on one side and loans, interest rates, and fees on the other, this distinction is no longer so clearly defined.[14] Loans were considered a temporary renunciation of the right to property, for which reason interest could be charged. Usury and tribute implied social and political control over others without free agreement on their part. With modernity, tribute and usury apparently disappeared; these were morally denounced but recognized in practice. But what in fact really changed is the nature of the loans, which now are no longer understood as temporary renunciations of property. The loan is now the extension of the body of the individual lender (or association of individuals: corporations, states), who, counting on the gain-seeking of the debtor, will bargain for the greater portion of this gain.

Surprising in all this is the mysterious character with which this intrinsic meaning of the contract is clothed. In the market, which is where these contracts are made, there's an effective logic that possesses a profoundly theological meaning. Ironically, the very idea of freedom created its opposite, its negation. As Franz Hinkelammert demonstrated, the defense of liberty itself generated its reverse. Freedom cannot be assured for anyone who is opposed, either by action or by conscience, to this liberal definition of freedom.[15] As soon as property becomes the *res extensa* of individual freedom, it's necessary to declare all-out war on those who attack private property, whether it's those who steal it or those who ally themselves with a political project that prioritizes communitarian or social values at the expense of individual values.

Let's consider, for example, how this is articulated by Adam Smith, who does so with a language borrowed from theodicies and

---

[14] Benjamin N. Nelson, *The Idea of Usury* (Princeton: Princeton University Press, 1949), 20–28.

[15] Franz Hinkelammert, "Democracia, estrutura económico-social y formación del mundo mítico-religioso," *Pasos* 3, no. 8: 1–28.

who assures everyone that faith is "the conviction of things not seen" (Heb 11:1): "The individual uses his capital in such a way that it produces the greatest value possible. While doing it, he does not seek to favor the public interest and doesn't even know how much he is favoring it; the only thing he seeks is his own security, his own benefit. And in this there is an 'invisible hand' that leads him to serve an end that was not in his intentions. When the individual pursues his own interests, many times he favors the interest of society with greater efficacy than 'if he had done it intentionally.'"[16]

The "invisible hand" is capable of transforming egotism into charity and altruism. "For this reason," concludes Hinkelammert, "the bourgeoisie no longer needs any ethic beyond the demand for the most absolute respect for their social relations of production, i.e., for private property and the fulfillment of contracts."[17]

In this context, a new role is attributed to organized religious systems (churches and sects). Weber's thesis, according to which religion has a legitimating function for the privileged social strata, here reveals its limitation. The religious character of the modern "testament" does not require explicit ecclesial or doctrinal support. Wittgenstein perceived as much when, in his *Tractatus logico-philosophicus*, he put religion (*das Mystische*) and ethics under the heading of the ineffable.[18] In fact, in a certain sense, this is the case. Religion does not enter into public discourse. That's what the popular expression means when it says, "There's no discussing religion." But that doesn't mean that the systems and institutions that articulate the religious are superfluous. To the churches is attributed a double role: (1) in practice, the churches are called upon to assist those who are systematically marginalized, and (2) in matters of doctrine, the churches must elaborate an ideological system that guarantees to the members a sense of psycho-social integration. Let's consider these two aspects.

---

[16] Adam Smith, in Franz Hinkelammert, "Economia y teologia: Las leyes del mercado y de la fe," mimeo, March 1989, 7.

[17] Hinkelammert, "Economia y teologia," 7.

[18] Wittgenstein, *Tractatus logico-philosophicus*, 112–15.

The Safety Net

The mystic of the "invisible hand" is not powerful enough in capitalism, as the economic system of modernity, to prevent people from falling off the high wire they're trying to walk. The intensification of the internationalization of capitalism since World War II revealed its tragic side south of the equator. But not only south of the equator—where, for colonialism, sin does not exist—do we find people who cannot maintain their equilibrium. In his electoral campaign for his second term as president of the United States, Ronald Reagan proposed that the churches fulfill the function of "safety nets" for those who fall from the high wire of the "newest testament." If safety nets are necessary in the United States, the center of the capitalist system, how much more are they necessary in the dependent world, where the accident rate in the circus of the market is much higher?

In practical terms, such safety nets guarantee the credibility of the circus and the maintenance of the spectacle. The possibility of a radical rupture with the existing order has been frequently provoked and sustained by the masses who are not functionally integrated into the economy, especially small landowners and farm workers, even if these people don't organize themselves into political movements (as is the case with industrial workers).[19]

The growth in the numbers of the excluded demands a unified effort on the part of ecclesial missions and development agencies to keep this social anomie administrable. This strategy of integrative exclusion of subordinate groups offers an interpretation of the motto of the ecumenical movement since the beginning of the twentieth century: "Doctrine divides, service unites."

Since the arrival of the Seventh-Day Adventists in Latin America around the turn of the twentieth century, hospitals, schools, clinics, infirmaries, and senior citizen homes have multiplied through missions and social and medical assistance.[20] And the future promises

---

[19] Octavio Ianni, *Dialética e Capitalismo* (Petrópolis: Vozes, 1988), 101–12; José de Souza Martins, *Caminhada no chão da noite* (São Paulo: Hucitec, 1989), 97–110.

[20] Délcio Monteiro de Lima, *Os Demônios Descem do Norte* (Rio de Janeiro: Francisco Alves, 1987).

even greater efforts in view of the cyclical crisis into which Latin American economies have entered, a crisis aggravated by the weight of an unpayable foreign debt.

In such a situation, ecclesial philanthropy is no exception. Through agencies and entities, the churches have been able to provide humanitarian services to the excluded. Such services, besides fulfilling the function of "safety net," permit the churches to make Christian ethical responsibility impersonal.[21] Grace is proclaimed through the same channel (the church) that exempts people from a personal confrontation with ethics. Those benefited by the assistance that sustains them socially and biologically also will understand that the same grace preached is linked to the possibility of their survival in the system. In fact, there the medium is the message. And the churches, relieved of the task of fulfilling the public function of religion, can serve like Martha, though they serve not Jesus but instead the capitalist "testament" and, even so, without knowing what's really important.

Let us now observe the other process in which religion is involved by asking about the relation between the doctrinal articulation of a church and the "metaphysics of the market" (Hinkelammert).

Religion: Ideological Support or Disguise

I was saying that there is no direct relation between social stratum and religious expression. Except for exceptions that prove the rule, one does not find in the doctrinal corpus of the churches a defense of the bourgeois order or of the capitalist system. Neither will one find a theological translation of *The Communist Manifesto* as the doctrinal affirmation of a "proletarian church." In extreme cases, one will find the defense of a certain political state of affairs (as happened in Nazi Germany, Pinochet's Chile, or South Africa). Even so, one still does not have ecclesial confessions as articulated ideological systems. In truth, when ideological elements are explicitly introduced into doctrine, these are promptly denounced as false and incoherent.

---

[21] It's worth recalling the indignation of Chrysostom against the asylums (*xenodokeia*) created by the Constantinian Church, because they made responsibility toward one's neighbor impersonal. See Hinkelammert, "Economia y teologia," 8.

Establishing this incoherence was, for example, what marked the strength of the Barmen Declaration (especially thesis 3).

In the attempt to explain the asymmetry between doctrinal articulation and the dominant ideology, Pedro Ribeiro de Oliveira, in a seminal study of Brazilian Catholicism, showed that the content of religious representations is always conditioned by the religious system from which they emerge. According to the author, this conditioning imposes structural limits on innovation. A religious system possesses only a relative capacity for adaptation to the demands of a social and economic system. Innovations "cannot exceed determined structural limits imposed by the religious system, under penalty of losing their religious identity."[22]

For two combined reasons, the symbolic complex of Christianity cannot function as a direct legitimation of capitalism: first, because its symbolic structure arose in a different mode of production and, second, because capitalism does not require such legitimation.

Religious representations of Christianity can be useful to capitalism but are not essential.[23] In fact, capitalism has what Otto Maduro, using a concept from Althusser, calls a "relative autonomy" from the religious sphere.[24]

However, if a systematic legitimation of the ruling order does not exist, an indirect legitimation does exist. This indirect legitimation happens when religion is presented as a symbolic and doctrinal inventory that offers individuals psycho-social sustenance, thus harmonizing the structural conflicts in society. In other words, the objective of organized religion is to reach the atomized individual within the folds of the market. This can occur in both large-group encounters and pastoral visitation.

One of the presuppositions of the ecumenical movement is that what unites Christians is stronger than what divides them. Juan Luis Segundo offers a reflection that allows us to understand the connection that exists between late, internationalized capitalism and the

---

22 Pedro Ribeiro de Oliveira, *Religião e Dominação de Classe* (Petrópolis: Vozes, 1985), 325.

23 Ibid., 18.

24 Otto Maduro, *Religião e Luta de Classe* (Petrópolis: Vozes, 1981), 113–49.

ecumenical movement. This connection presents the other side of the sixteenth-century Reform movement that split the Western Church in the initial phase of capitalism, when plurality was a requirement for overcoming the moral and doctrinal objectivism of the Middle Ages. Defining ideology as a disguise that conceals contradictions, Segundo writes, "The much publicized 'Christian unity,' with its pastoral consequences, constitutes a clear ideological element. The ideal of unity for liberation was transformed into an ideal of unity to conceal conflicts, to minimize them compared to something else declared to be more important, and, in this indirect way, to maintain the status quo. . . . The ideology that puts the superstructure to work for the existing order is not a conscious maneuver in most cases; it's an unconscious slippage of ideas through channels where they won't shock the existing order."[25]

The real doctrinal conflict does not coincide with social and political conflict, and neither is doctrinal convergence the expression of overcoming what divides the people socially. Antonio Gramsci called attention to this when he observed that "regarding the origin of the Holy Spirit, it would be ridiculous to look at the social structure of Eastern Europe to explain that the Holy Spirit proceeds only from the Father, or to look at Western Europe to explain that it proceeds from the Father and the Son."[26] Flags do not explain or generate conflicts; they symbolize them. Taking the symbol for the reality to which it points is religious idolatry. Explaining the reality from which conflicts emerge on the basis of the conflicts themselves is philosophical idealism. Symbols illuminate participation in reality and acquire meaning in this participation.

However, the question remains why religion has a utopic strength, why its myths and rites are capable of moving the masses and even of breaking down the structure of systems. Such a storehouse of motivation is not to be found in the capacity that a doctrinal corpus has for systematic articulation. On the contrary, it's within the capacity

---

[25] Juan Luis Segundo, "As Elites Latino-Americanas," in *Fé Cristã e Transformação Social na América Latina*, ed. Instituto Fe y Secularidad (Petrópolis: Vozes, 1977), 186.

[26] Antonio Gramsci, *Prison Notebooks* (New York: International, 1971), 409.

of anachronistic symbols to emerge as metaphors that offer the possibility of expanding the linguistic world and even attribute completely new meanings to the world that the people experience. "The strength of revolutionaries is not in their knowledge," said Mariátegui, "it's in their faith, their passion, their will. . . . It's the power of myth."[27] The experience of rereading the Bible in Latin America has its importance not so much in exegetical articulation as in the empowerment of people to name their world with unusual meanings. Symbols (Pharaoh, reign, city, cross, resurrection, kingdom, Babylon, temple) become metaphors that amplify possibilities of interpretation that transcend orderly and inoffensive systems of representation. This is possible only because these symbols become metaphors for particular realities and shake up the categories.[28] To call a big landowner Pharaoh can be a systematic absurdity, but it is a powerful metaphor for locating the meaning of the oppression that exists in rural areas. Social conflict, injustices in economic relations, will appear as dissonant and unusual on the level of religious discourse in the conflict between an ordered doctrinal system and particular representations. Only in this sense do conflicts and social contradictions progress and develop in the religious sphere. For this reason, we said that the relation between participation in a religious system and in the social situation is asymmetrical.

IV. Religious Systems and Functionality

In Latin American countries in particular, the emergence of Pentecostalism is linked to the social conditions of the population rather than to economic conditions. The expansion of Pentecostalism in the 1930s is intimately connected to the penetration of capitalism, to the social effects that capitalism generated—especially the uprooting of populations.[29] Where there still exists a sense of being located, a

[27] José Carlos Mariátegui, *El alma matinal* (Lima: Amauta, 1960), 22.

[28] On the role of metaphor in religious experience in Latin America, see Ulrich Schoenborn, *Migalhas Exegéticas* (São Leopoldo: Sinodal, 1982), 126–30. For an exemplification in a case study, see Virgilio Elizondo, "La Virgen de Guadalupe como símbolo cultural," in *Raíces de la teologia latino-americana*, ed. Pablo Richard (San José: Cehila, 1985), 393–400.

[29] Oneide Bobsin, "Surgimento e Expansão do Pentecostalismo no Brasil," *Ceca-Informação, Formação, Experiência* 1, no. 3 (1989): 11–12.

sense of belonging, the people remain tied to the traditional churches without direct correlation with a social stratum. The demand for new religious options is the result of the search for meaning in a world experienced as unstable and lacking in existential reference points. The traditional churches presuppose these reference points. Thus their search is not for meaning. It is rather the attempt to provide some order and to organize the significant experiences of their members: "From the church, we expect more rational explanations than we do solutions."[30] Only in this way can we speak of a correlation between a social stratum and a religious option.

In capitalism, in the midst of the spirit of modernity, a religion is functional when it forms an institution that offers a self-sustainable system of doctrines and practices that foment the creation of a psychosocial space in which a person finds himself. "Self-sustainable" means that this system, in order to establish its identity, does not require explicit ideological support for or from any social class in civil society, not even from the state. (Religious) "system" means a structured order of religious representations with ultimate significance for human existence. Order and significance are the two poles of the same phenomenon, and emphasis on one or the other will depend on the experience of stability and social organization.

An illustrative example shows how religion can structure existence in a self-sustainable way. This example comes from the Germanic communities in Brazil. If in the beginning these communities were a cultural and social enclave, after World War II one can observe their progressive integration into Brazilian society, first through the market and then through social organizations.[31] But until the 1960s, this integration did not occur at the expense of ecclesial identity because the churches (the Lutheran and, to a lesser extent, also the Catholic) succeeded in guaranteeing their group identity. Erich Fausel's 1959 study of a dictionary of three thousand Portuguese words inserted

[30] Gerd Uwe Kliewer, "Estratificação Social e Filiação Religiosa," *Estudos Teológicos* 1, no. 29 (1989): 48.

[31] Martin N. Dreher, *Igreja e Comunidade* (São Leopoldo: Sinodal, 1984), 245–54. The year 1984 marks the beginning of the theological and missional reorientation of the IECLB (Evangelical Church of the Lutheran Confession in Brazil).

into current usage in German (as spoken in these communities) corroborates this interpretation. If it's true that the limit of our language is also the limit of our world, the following numbers reveal those lim its: 43 percent of the three thousand words in this dictionary refer to farm life; 25 percent are expressions of sociability; 15 percent come from urban and commercial life; and 10 percent from politics and bureaucracy. Those are the most frequent references. References to religious life, however, constitute only 0.3 percent, a figure that permits us to recognize the self-sustainability of the religious system and its relative autonomy.[32]

A religious system (whether ecclesial or similar), if it wants to be functional, will also be essentially conservative, not for any explicit defense of the socioeconomic system, but to protect the structure and significance of socioeconomic relations through the religious system's own representations and symbols that offer space for significantly structuring individual existence. Such structuring acts upon the human will by turning into a virtue whatever the social structure of relations absolutely demands. Pedro Ribeiro de Oliveira offers this commentary: "Religious representations serve the social function of hegemony precisely because they act upon people's will and lead individuals and groups to think of the social practices imposed upon them as voluntary acts."[33] Within this basically conservative nucleus, innovations can appear. But when controlled by the ecclesiastical center of power or by the institution that systematizes doctrine, such innovations will have an adaptive nature, as required either by external factors (secularization, for example) or by internal factors (maintenance or growth in membership).[34] The fundamental characteristic of this religious functionality is its universality. Concepts like grace, justification, gospel, liberation, and so on are, in principle, applicable to any and all situations, and as long as these concepts are not contextualized or particularized, functionality will be maintained. As for methodology, universality (being in principle applicable to everything) is

[32] Vítor Westhelle, "Considerações sobre o Etno-Luteranismo Latino-Americano," *Estudos Teológicos* 18, no. 2 (1978): 85–86.

[33] Oliveira, *Religião*, 320.

[34] Maduro, *Religião*, 143.

the requirement for functionality, which Segundo formulates in the following clever way: "If it occurred to us . . . to ask to what extent existence would change if ecclesiastical authority declared that Jesus is God only analogically . . . the answers would show that Christians become aware of dogmatic change without experiencing any disruption in their lives. But something very different might happen if it were decided that the practical translation of 'grace' is 'popular unity,' or if 'sin' meant not collaborating with popular unity."[35]

V. The Scandal of Particularity

The scandal of particularity is (1) that it turns against the rationality of a religious system, interrupting its ordered course by inserting particular elements of a contextual character, and (2) that it turns against an established and domesticated existential meaning, since particularity provokes constant slippage in meaning. To say that one's neighbor is a Samaritan, that it is necessary to hate one's own family, that a usurer cannot be a Christian, that God is Black or that she is compassionate, and so on creates dissonance, invades the systematic universality, and compromises functionality.[36]

For this reason, religious representations are not always functional. There is prophecy. There are words, concepts, shouts, acclamations, denunciations, rites, and gestures that come from beyond the walls of functionality. There is the charism that embarrasses power.[37]

All institutions, systems, and structures possess the endemic tendency to occupy power to guarantee their own preservation. But not all possess the same concentration of power. Not all are functional in the same way in their task of preserving the social structure. Not all are hegemonic. That is, not all possess moral and intellectual control. Not all share leadership or exercise dominion over all of society. Hegemony is the moral and intellectual nucleus around which the rest of the system orbits and on which it depends, being socially acceptable

35 Segundo, "As Elites Latino-Americanas," 186.

36 For an application of this thesis to the theology of Luther, see Vítor Westhelle, "O Desencontro entre a Teologia Luterana e a Teologia da Libertação," *Estudos Teológicos* 1, no. 26 (1986): 37–58.

37 Leonardo Boff, *Igreja, Carisma e Poder* (Petrópolis: Vozes, 1981), 234–49.

as such.[38] To define the degree of functionality of a religious system, it is necessary to recognize the center of the social, economic, political, and cultural system: its "sun."

Every period, context, and socioeconomic system locates its hegemonic center in its own way. For example, the Jesus of Mark's Gospel locates it in the dominant religious ethos. Paul counsels the community in Rome to be flexible on ethical questions, discerning what is a priority (Rom 14) and breaking with the moral rationality of the organizing philosophical system of the dominant ethos (Stoicism). And in the reign of Domitian, the visionary of Patmos locates the hegemonic center in the imperial politics of Rome. But whether Babel, Egypt, kingship, Babylon, the Temple, imperial Rome, the Vatican, or Moscow, the prophetic voice of dissonance reveals its efficacy through its ability to locate hegemony.

With modernity and the system that organizes it socially and economically—that is, capitalism—the hegemonic center is no longer a place (though Washington, DC, serves as a symbol) but a ubiquitous class that, in the market system, controls social relations and dominates the forces that produce wealth. That's the strength of this system; it's not localizable. It has centers but has no geographically locatable nucleus. This characteristic of modern times also determines the form in which religion expresses its prophetic elements. Religion will no longer express its prophetic elements with a new code of social organization.

The religious struggle against hegemony takes the form of nonadaptation, of nonconformity. The effectiveness of this struggle is not in any imagined capacity to offer an alternative system that could replace the dominant one. By their very nature, religious representations do not offer that possibility to modernity. A theocracy is unthinkable. Religion, while it possesses values that transcend market relations, is not and cannot be hegemonic. This is the reason that in a church, there can be and almost certainly will be dysfunctional elements. Social, economic, and political conflict will invade the ecclesial space through this dysfunctionality rather than through any

[38] Oliveira, *Religião*, 18.

proposed alternative system. In the ecclesial environment, the choice is not between capitalism and socialism but between conformity and rupture, between adaptation and dissonance, between functionality and anomie, between adjustment and liberation, between system and utopia. What is at stake in these antinomies, on the level of discourse and religious practice, is the relation between the universal and the particular—that is, between, on the one hand, a discourse that promotes functionality by being applicable to all people and all things without relation to production and the reproduction of life and, on the other hand, a discourse that expresses the symbols and metaphors that anchor transcendent values in daily experience.

Dissonance and Utopia

The relation between the universal and the particular in a religious system is determined by two correlated factors that we will now discuss.

First, the hegemony of a system has as its objective a totality of meaning and an ideological harmony. Consonance is the goal to be achieved so that a consensus will result. Apologies are not required. Capitalism doesn't do its own propaganda. What it does do is make profits. And for that reason, capitalism cannot be called conservative. Neither can one, in a strict sense, speak of a status quo in capitalism. The following observation comes from *The Communist Manifesto*: "Constant transformation of production, uninterrupted disturbance of all social conditions, and perennial uncertainty and mobility distinguish the bourgeois era from all preceding eras."[39] The truth is that the market reigns supreme. Only dissonance in regard to the system as such needs to be suppressed. Whatever is not in consonance with its "catholicity" must be reduced to silence or inarticulate expressions. But this silence and these inarticulate expressions are precisely the signs of protest and resistance: "The dominant classes, even in the apparently most stable phase of consolidation of their hegemony, never achieve absolute control of collective life. There always

[39] Karl Marx, *Seleção e introdução Franz Borkenau* (Frankfurt: Buecherei, 1956), 101.

remains (even in the form of mutism, glossolalia, hysteria, apathy, or merely destructive terror) a certain resistance on the part of the dominated."[40]

These elements of resistance and protest deserve our attention because they are a type of demonstration and subversion by those people who, socially and economically, are placed on the margins of the system. If this is a fundamental characteristic of the biblical faith—demonstrated in the biblical literature through the God who hears the cry of his people and the cry of Jesus in his exorcisms—it is still today a requirement for understanding the negations of the system in dissimulated expressions. Those who were obliged to speak the language of the dominator, to assimilate his culture, conceal within that language and culture the resistance of the dominated. Caliban, the dominated in Shakespeare's *The Tempest*, makes the following comment: "You taught me your language, and my profit from it is knowing how to curse."[41]

But the protest of those who have no voice is not simply disorganized. It already possesses the seed of the new codified as the subversion of the system to which it does not adapt. We're talking about the old new, the utopia in the "topos," the capacity to contradict what has been said by using an ironic gesture, a laugh, or feigned madness: "Metaphor, concealment, dissimulation, silence remain as the language that documents the persistence of the same violence that gave birth to them."[42] That's where one finds the revolutionary possibilities for what cannot be harmonized and instead remains as the cosmetic makeup of a dream that engenders the new.[43]

The critique that Latin American theology makes of ecumenism does not undo the ecumenical practice that has achieved notable advances precisely through ecumenical pastoral activities and advisory bodies. Its primordial function has been to permit the

[40] Maduro, *Religião*, 110.

[41] William Shakespeare, *The Tempest* (New York: Penguin, 1959), 46. On the question of dissimulation of language in popular culture, see Martins, *Caminhada no chão da noite*, 110–22.

[42] Martins, *Caminhada no chão da noite*, 116.

[43] Ianni, *Dialética e Capitalismo*, 133–35.

decoding of the cries and silences of the people and thus to sensitize the mission of the churches to the evangelical task of permitting formal "catholicity" to be invaded by the protest of particularity. In the formulation of Pedro Casaldáliga, "The universal word speaks only dialect."[44]

Syncretism

If dissonance is a form through which the dialectical relation between the universal and the particular can offer utopian perspectives for those who are on the margins of the system, syncretism constitutes the strategy of an ecumenism that will offer the possibility of the unity of the church. Using Tillich's formulation, such a strategy consists in uniting the Catholic substance to the Protestant principle.[45] A functional religiosity does precisely the contrary; it has the Catholic form (the system) and the Protestant substance (freedom), but the freedom never gets realized.

Hermann Brandt, in an article on syncretism from a Latin American theological perspective, argues that ecumenism and mission are together realized in syncretism. The consequence of the incarnation—being open to the particular—will demand an option "for a new syncretism or, in other words, the disposition for reform of the church."[46] Syncretism is defined as a missional necessity for a church that is open to the particular so that the spiritual principle of protest can rise up against a formalized universality. In this sense, syncretism should not be interpreted as eclecticism. It should be understood as the contrary of harmonization, thus implying permanent openness to the scandal of particularity and permitting dissonance to appear as what it is.[47] Only in this way will the disorganized cry or the silence

---

[44] Quoted in Hermann Brandt, "Teologia Contextual como Sincretism?," *Estudos Teológicos* 2, no. 27 (1987): 114.

[45] Paul Tillich, *Systematic Theology* (Chicago: University of Chicago Press, 1963), 3:245.

[46] Brandt, "Teologia Contextual," 115.

[47] For the different meanings that syncretism has assumed, see Boff, *Igreja, Carisma e Poder*, 147–49; Leonardo Boff, "Avaliação teológico-crítica do sincretismo," *Vozes* 71, no. 7 (1977): 53/68; and André Droogers, "Sincretismo," *Estudos Teológicos* 21, no. 3 (1981): 139–50.

of the marginalized find the possibility of expression and articulation as a utopia, as a prophetic voice.

Syncretism implies "openness to the presence of the liberating Spirit of God among the poor and oppressed,"[48] and I mean precisely among the poor and oppressed, since they are the ones who have been exiled and made inferior by the socioeconomic system itself. These are the people who seek a meaning to existence, a meaning that is authentic for them. In the ambiguity of the religious experience that they have, they express this meaning through the most varied practices and symbols. These are the people who are virtually alienated from the ordered social system (the cosmos) and don't even belong to it (John 17:14).

Rebellion from the Underside

As we approach the conclusion of this discussion, we affirm that the problem of the relation between social and economic conflict and the unity of the church should be formulated as follows: In the face of an unjust socioeconomic structure, what is the possible unity of the church? Two responses were tested. One possible, though always relative, unity can be achieved through the adjustment of a religious system to the hegemonic system. This does not mean that only the privileged classes would constitute the social group of a church that positioned itself in this manner. Rather, it means that such unity would be achieved only through the obliteration of the conflicts and contradictions that determine structural injustice. Inevitably, such an ecumenical program would lead the church to fulfill its dual role of safety net and ideological disguise (see section III above).

Another possible unity can be sought through a dysfunctional syncretism that opens space for the scandal of particularity. This doesn't mean that only the economically poor and the socially marginalized would constitute the profile of the community. But it does mean that the church as an institutional space would understand its mission as an opening, in practice and discourse, to the cries, silences, and utopias of those who find themselves in a system to which they

[48] Brandt, "Teologia Contextual," 115.

do not belong. Such a community would be the space where what cannot be said outside can be said—that is, a transparent space and, in this sense, a sacred space. Paradoxically, such ecumenism is practiced when doctrinal consensus is destabilized.

The question of unity in a divided world is thus a question of neither doctrine nor practice. It's a question of adjustment or justice, of conformity or revolt. Among the options offered above, we have to decide what we are prepared to share for the sake of the unity we think it's important to achieve.

The choice among these options still lacks a criterion, and I don't think that this criterion is at all obvious or that it can be elaborated here, except in broad outline.

The incarnation has been suggested as a possible criterion.[49] Another possibility would be to work with the theology of the cross, using the arguments of Paul in 1 Corinthians 1.[50] A formal criterion could also be explored in the way Dussel does with the category of "otherness."[51] Without entering into a discussion of these proposals, it is possible to recognize a biblical motif that nourishes Christians in their option to live a liberating faith.

Ernst Käsemann published an article in which he seeks to respond to the question of whether the canon of the New Testament serves as a basis for the unity of the church. He argues that "the canon of the New Testament is not the foundation, as such, for the unity of the church. Rather, it's the foundation . . . for a multiplicity of confessions."[52] The diversity of the message of primitive Christianity is such that "we will observe not only considerable tensions but also, not rarely, incompatible theological contradictions."[53] For Käsemann, we will find the basis for the unity of the church in the gospel, which

---

[49] Hermann Brandt, "Die Inkarnation der Befreiung—die Befreiung der Inkarnation," *Materialdienst des Konfessionskundlichen Instituts* 34 (1989): 8.

[50] Taking Luther as a point of departure, this is what Martin N. Dreher does. See his article "A *theologia crucis* de Lutero e o tema da teologia da libertação," *Estudos Teológicos* 2, no. 28 (1988): 137–52.

[51] Enrique Dussel, *Método para una filosofia de la liberación* (Salamanca: Vandenhoeck and Ruprecht, 1964), 1:225.

[52] Ernst Käsemann, *Exegetische Versuche und Besinnungen* (Göttingen: Vandenhoeck Ruprecht, 1964), 1:221.

[53] Ibid., 218.

stands in relation to the canon as the Spirit stands in relation to the letter. The Spirit does not contradict the letter, but neither is it identical to the letter. The Spirit "manifests itself in the letter."[54]

What this manifestation implies is not explained. It could be a simple abstraction. But the importance of the argument is that it points to the fact that harmonization of the canon is a task that, exegetically, is both useless and irresponsible. The spiritual principle foments the unity of that which is different without reducing the differentness. "The Spirit," Tillich observes, "does not produce new and refined letters. . . . The Spirit judges all letters."[55] The "letter" kills when, alone or in unity with other "letters," it imposes the totality of meaning. The Spirit of life will always repeat for the "letter": "Again it is written . . ." (Matt 4). The manifestation of the Spirit is always an insurgency in the system.

This has implications for ecclesiology. As an institution, the church shares in the structure of power. But since the Reformation and, decisively, since the French Revolution, institutions like the church have not been hegemonic, and their faintly marginal character makes for a certain institutional ambivalence. As religious systems, the churches became aware, first in practice and then in theory, of their own relativity, which made possible their vulnerability to novelty. The churches have also opened themselves to rebellion from the underside. In Latin America, in particular, they have even articulated that rebellion. Ecclesial hierarchies, with their preoccupation with self-preservation, seek to block such openings, and this is the case not only with the Roman Catholic Church but with the Protestant churches too. Risk-taking, however, has always been the raw material of the spiritual presence.

The relation between institutional conformity and the protest of the spirit remains as the ongoing ambivalence of the church. Gerd Theissen, informed by the theory of evolution, called attention to the antievolutionary characteristics of the church throughout history—that is, nonadaptive characteristics such as vulnerability, asceticism,

54 Ibid., 223.
55 Tillich, *Systematic Theology*, 3:268.

martyrdom, love of one's enemy, and so on. With respect to evolution, these are self-destructive tendencies. But precisely these characteristics favor ethical responses that transcend cultures and even common sense, and in various periods, through the church's foolish stubbornness in opting for the way of nonadaptation, these characteristics place the church beyond the limits of its time.[56]

[56] Gerd Theissen, *Biblical Faith* (Philadelphia: Fortress, 1985), 158–63. See also the analogous argument developed by Juan Luis Segundo, *Evolução e Culpa*, Teologia Aberta para o Leigo Adulto, vol. 5 (São Paulo: Loyola, 1977).

PRESUPPOSITIONS AND IMPLICATIONS OF THE CONCEPT OF PRAXIS IN HUGO ASSMANN

> I'd like to understand fear, courage, and the urge that pushes people to do so much, to put their own flesh into making things happen.
>
> —João Guimarães Rosa

I.

In 1971, the year in which the first systematic manifesto of liberation theology was published in Lima under the authorship of Gustavo Gutiérrez, a book of comparable importance appeared in Montevideo with the title *Opresión-liberación: Desafio a los cristianos*. Its author was the (at that time) priest Hugo Assmann, a Brazilian. Along with Juan Luis Segundo, who has to be considered the precursor of Latin American liberation theology and its best-known exponent, and with Gutiérrez, who, as mentioned, made the first attempt to systematize what had been percolating in Latin American theology for about a decade, Assmann made an equally important contribution to the program of liberation theology.

In an attempt to explain exactly what Assmann's contribution was, we have to emphasize two points in particular.

The first point is that Assmann helped establish a substantive connection between theology and the social sciences in Latin America.

Originally published in *Estudos Teológicos* 21, no. 1 (1981): 7–31.

He considered the social sciences to be the true partner of theology and rejected the traditional view that philosophy, especially metaphysics, should be the point of departure for theology and particularly for fundamental theology. In this sense, Assmann and liberation theology repeat the rupture that the Neo-Orthodox movement had already made with natural theology at the beginning of the twentieth century. Instead of isolating theology from the historical and social sciences and turning theology into something that flowed straight from revelation, Latin American liberation theology reestablished fundamental theology as social theology, postliberal and post-Neo-Orthodox![1] If in Segundo the methodological presupposition begins to be developed, in Assmann the content of the social sciences becomes incorporated and applied practically to theological analysis.

Assmann attributes two central motives for the necessity of his methodological procedure. The first motive is the critique, however incipient, aimed at theology by the social sciences in Latin America; this critique constitutes the historical purgatory through which theology must pass to specify its historical place and to become responsive to the social, political, and economic problems that emerge in this place.[2] The second motive is that interdisciplinarity offers to theology the companionship of the most committed theoretical undertaking in Latin America. Situating himself within the Marxist tradition, Assmann values the social sciences in Latin America as the most successful effort to unite theory and praxis[3] to the point that one can consider these sciences, owing to their political impact, as "rebel sciences"—that is, sciences that emerge from and respond to a revolutionary situation.[4]

---

1 Methodologically, it was Juan Luis Segundo who first established the primacy of social data for theological reflection. See his book *De la sociedad a la teologia* (Buenos Aires, 1970). Its very title reflects his method, which was already implicit in his book *Función de la Iglesia en la realidad rioplatense* (Montevideo, 1962) (and please note that early date!).

2 Hugo Assmann, *Teología desde la praxis de la liberación: Ensayo teológico desde la América dependiente*, 2nd ed. (Salamanca, 1976), 108ff., 116–17.

3 Hugo Assmann, "Die Situation der unterenwickelt gehaltenen Laender als Ort einer Theologie der Revolution," in *Diskussion zur "Theologie der Revolution,"* ed. Ernst Feil and Rudolf Weth (Munich, 1969), 218–48, 220.

4 Ibid. See also Assmann, *Teología*, 112, 118–19. For Assmann, the interdisciplinary relationship with the social sciences avoids the danger or temptation for theology to create a totalizing or metaphysical horizon and reminds theology of

The second point in regard to Assmann's contribution to the program of Latin American theology is intimately related to the first and is what immediately interests us—namely, the concept of praxis in Assmann, who, along with the emerging theological tradition of which he was a part, bequeathed more defined content to the term.

The vast amount of study done on the relation between theory and praxis in the last decades[5] illuminates the problem, which Marx placed at the center of the theory of knowledge and, by extension, at the center of philosophy and "science." The relation between and among *praxis*, *poiesis*, and *theoria* in Aristotle has been restudied in light of the influence that these categories have had (1) on the formation of Hegel's thought (specifically, the relation between and among ethical or intersubjective interaction, interaction between spirit and nature, and "scientific" or philosophical conceptualization) and (2) on the determination of the relations between and among "forces of production," "relations of production" (or "interaction" as in German ideology), and "superstructure" in Marx.

For Christian theology, this problematic is implicit in its tradition and emerges, on the one hand, with the Marxist critique of religion and the rejection of the broader epistemological base elaborated by Christian theology, expressed invariably by one or another interpretation of Anselm's *via negativa*, and, on the other hand, with the rejection of the *unio mistica*, which goes back to the Neoplatonism of Plotinus. That tradition was criticized either in terms of a rationalization of the mechanism of inverted projection (Feuerbach) or as an expression of an unhappy, alienated conscience (Hegel).

---

its historical character (see the foreword by Assmann as editor of *Pueblo oprimido, sector de la história* [Montevideo, 1972], 15). When Assmann refers to the social sciences in Latin America, what he has in mind especially is the theory of dependency, which has been his most characteristic and original element. See Assmann, *Teología*, 108ff.

5 For example, Nicholas Lobkowícz, *Theory and Practice: History of a Concept from Aristotle to Marx* (South Bend, 1967); Hannah Arendt, *The Human Condition* (New York, 1959); Juergen Habermas, *Theorie und Praxis* (Berlin: Neuwied am Rhein, 1963); Matthew Lamb, "The Theory-Praxis Relationship in Contemporary Christian Theologies," *CTSA Proceedings* 31 (1976): 149–78; Richard Bernstein, *Praxis and Action: Contemporary Philosophies of Human Activity* (Philadelphia, 1971); and John Hoffmann, *Marxism and the Theory of Praxis* (New York, 1975).

Let us recall that, for Aristotle, an approximate analogy for explaining the theory-praxis relationship is drawn from the example of a market in antiquity. The individual observing the life and artistic spectacles that took place there was the typical case of the theoretical man who, on the basis of daily observation, elevated his thought to the point of conceptualizing the universal, the divine (*nofis*). The artist performing the spectacle was the practical man, whereas the person working behind the scenes to construct the tents, build the infrastructure, and produce a material result was the poetic man. If, in Aristotle, the contemplative life extended in a logical continuum from observation of daily life to the contemplation of the divine being, in Plotinus, these two theoretical extremes are dissociated, granting to the Christian tradition a theoretical model in which praxis (in both its meanings) would come into play, generally speaking, as a secondary problem. Contemplation (*theoria* or *gnosis*) of God, of the Divine One, does not maintain the same relation between subject and object that exists in the observation of things through the senses (*episteme*). Even in High Scholasticism, with its "rationalization of the irrational" (Lukács), that theoretical rupture remains expressed in the inaccessible essence of God, even though he is manifest in his existence. Even so, the Reformation corrected this speculative "slip." With the help of Nominalism, the sphere of reason was limited to the particular, to things immediately experienced as real, thus maintaining theoretical reason in external relationship to the experience of faith—that is, separating reality from the reality of revelation (Occam). Only in Marx—but in a certain way already in Fichte and in the Left Hegelians—the problem of praxis was rescued from its marginality, and, for the first time in the history of human thought, the problem of praxis became the starting point for theory itself, its fundamental datum.

Thanks to the efforts of the Frankfurt School on the question of theory, the problem of the theory-praxis relation once again came to be considered explicitly as a central problem of Western thought and went on to influence thinking in theology, which drank from its springs. The difference between the two meanings of praxis—which in Hegel and Marx had been understood (1) as part of the man-nature relationship, which goes back to the Greek *poiesis*, and (2) as part of the interhuman relationship, which is the approximate meaning of the Greek *praxis*—was assumed by the Frankfurt School, especially by Habermas, but in a way that is the inverse of Marx, while formally maintaining the same model. Habermas made the inversion of the relation between forces of production and relations of production (in Habermas, the system of human communication) into the central point of his "Para-Marxism" (Assmann). Though recognizing that Marx was correct in his analysis of the liberal phase of capitalism, Habermas argues that late capitalism is characterized by its inverting of the mode of relation between forces of production and relations of production in such a way that relations of production have primacy. Without getting into the manner in which Habermas justifies turning Marx upside down, it's important to note that as a result of Habermas's position, at the end of the day, politics determines economics. Free human interaction—not nonalienated production—becomes the factor that generates a society able to overcome the contradictions of capitalist society. Hence it is easy to understand how the intellectual, whose primary function is communicative praxis, takes the place of the proletariat as the subject of a new society.

Although Habermas is not at all sympathetic to theological discourse, thus distinguishing himself from his famous predecessors (e.g., Horkheimer, Benjamin, Adorno), his position has opened a breach in theology, and J. Metz, H. Peukert, M. Lamb, W. Post, and others have eagerly leaped into it. The point of entry for theology is the transcendent dimension present in human intercommunication, symbolized by the irreducible relation of man with the experience of death. Only in interhuman relations does death have any meaning, and meaning, by the way, is never exhaustible but is transcendent. Death is the subjectivist basis that evokes the Christian concept of love to account for the mystery that death—especially the death of an innocent person or of six million Jews, to locate the historical background in which political theology is trying to express itself—breaks with every possibility of finding an immanent meaning for human life. Which is to say, with an intention different from P. Freire's when he coined the term, that theology is fundamentally "necrophiliac." Lamb even suggested that deaths are the subject of history, thus transcending both Marx and Habermas. Joking aside, this transcendent element attributed to the intersubjective relation constitutes the cornerstone of what Peukert, in his book *Wissenschaftstheorie-Handlungstheorie-Fundamentale Theologie*, recognized as fundamental theology.

That factor of nonidentity present in the intersubjective relation is, then, the basis for defining the concept of praxis, with which political theology has struggled so much. The Marxist concept of praxis is rejected because it defines *praxis* on the basis of the production of the means of subsistence. The focal point becomes communicative, political praxis, which is the general way in which praxis is understood within the theology that has been produced under the auspices of critical theory.

Thus it is not difficult to grasp the problems that arise when, as we shall see, the term *praxis* is understood in diverse ways without that fact always being explicit. Both political theology and Latin American liberation theology define themselves conceptually as praxeologies, affirming the priority of praxis—that is, the truth that is done (John 3:21). Despite that nominal concordance, we will see that there exists a basic difference already in the point of departure—that is, in the definition of the term *praxis*. Given this lack of clarity, the result is either an ingenuous typological identification between those distinct theologies[6] or a not-so-ingenuous attempt by political theology to co-opt Latin American theology.[7]

Our attempt is to define the concept of praxis in Assmann to the extent possible and necessary, Assmann being the Latin American theologian who most used and developed the concept. That task is, above all, a contribution internal to liberation theology itself, in the search for precise methodological elements, and is only marginally an attempt to divide the waters between that theology and the one developed in the light of critical theory. It is our conviction that the time has already come for recognizing that the controversy between liberation theology and critical theory should not be exaggerated. If

---

6 David Tracy, *Blessed Rage for Order: The New Pluralism in Theology* (New York, 1975), 64–87, 172–236.

7 Lamb, "Theory-Praxis Relationship," 171ff.; and Matthew Lamb, "Dogma, Experience, and Political Theology," *Concilium* 113 (1979): 79–90.

the discussion here begins with this introductory note, it's only as a response to the persistent attempt by the North Atlantic world to treat these two theologies as identical.

II.

The emphasis that Assmann puts on the concept of praxis is evident throughout his writings. The way he uses the term reveals, from the outset, a Marxist influence, even when there is no specific reference to Marx. Assmann admits no separation between theology as a theoretical activity and sociopolitical praxis. By the way, he accuses Metz and political theology of making that separation. According to Assmann, the reason that North American political theology established a barrier between political theology and political praxis, thus casting theology outside the "concrete context of praxis," is that North American political theology "did not pay sufficient attention to Marxism."[8]

Before we move on to the discussion of the way Assmann understands the term *praxis*, it's important to refer to what he understands by the term *Marxism*, since Marxism is the source for the central elements of his use of the concept of praxis. Besides the fact that he considered himself to be a Marxist, his knowledge of Marxism involved a qualitative improvement in the treatment of the subject and its appropriation by liberation theology.[9]

Along with Reyes-Mate, Assmann edited two volumes (of a planned three) of an anthology that analyzes the treatment of the question of religion in the most representative Marxist literature. Each volume is accompanied by a long introduction by the editors. The first volume is dedicated to Marx and Engels and contains more material on religion than do the anthologies of Marx and Engels, which are already published in many languages. The second volume

[8] Assmann, *Teología*, 17–18.

[9] Segundo personally assured me of what an accurate reading of the history of liberation theology would confirm: Assmann did not participate in the first moment of liberation theology (which goes from the meeting of theologians in 1966 in Santiago, where the central theme was the relation between salvation and historical emancipation, and in Medellín in 1968), but his contribution starting in 1968 gave liberation theology a more accurate knowledge of Marxism.

is a quite original undertaking that consists of selections from what are, in the opinion of the editors, the most representative Marxist texts.[10] What interests us in particular is the choice of names that were considered worthy of sharing the almost seven hundred pages of the second volume of the anthology. The twenty-two Marxists selected are as follows: Bebel, Plekhanov, Lafargue, Dietzgen, Jaurés, Sorel, Kautsky, Labriola, Rosa de Luxembourg, Liebknecht, Lenin, Trotsky, Bukharin, Lunacharski, Stalin, Pannekoek, Korsch, Gramsci, Lukács, Thorez, Togliatti, and Mao. In a nonexhaustive typology, the editors present three basic positions regarding the treatment of religion in the theoretical systems of the Marxists. The first posture in this typology is the "Leninist," in which the editors include theorists as different as Plekhanov, Kautsky, Trotsky, Stalin, Bukharin, and Mao, as well as Lenin himself. The second posture consists of those whom Assmann and Reyes-Mate call "heterodox practitioners," a group that includes Rosa de Luxembourg, Liebknecht, Thorez, and Togliatti. A third and final group (though, as mentioned, the typology does not pretend to be exhaustive) is made up of "critical theorists," including Lunacharski, Pannekoek, Korsch, Lukács, and, more in line with the second group, Labriola and Gramsci. Assmann and Reyes-Mate do not identify explicitly with any of the above. They try to see positive elements and critical aspects in each of the three postures. They also recognize that, in regard to the theme of religion, the internal differences among these groups are fewer than the similarities that unite them: "It seems that the basic position with respect to religion does not vary much from Lenin to Lukács: no one expects much from religion." However, "if, in all these theoreticians, the conclusion is equally condemnatory, it doesn't appear that, in all of them, it's equally logical."[11] Hence there exists sympathy for the position of the "heterodox practitioners" (especially, it seems to me, Rosa de

[10] Cf. Marx and Engels, *Sobre la Religión II*, ed. Hugo Assmann and Reyes-Mate (Salamanca, 1975), 11. The editors are conscious of the arbitrary character of the selection they have made but consider the attempt necessary. A third volume was promised and was to be dedicated to the treatment of religion among Latin American Marxist thinkers.

[11] Ibid., 41 (introduction).

Luxembourg), since the way this group derives logical thinking from praxis opens space for an eventual liberating praxis among Christians. For similar motives, one can detect in the editors a sympathy for Labriola and Gramsci in relation to their profound considerations on the sociocultural dimension of religion in Italian Catholicism. Probably influenced by Gramsci, Assmann proposed that the common arena in which the contact between theology and the social sciences should be developed was the social datum that he labeled "the Christian element." In our understanding, this would be the central category for what is above called "social theology," which is the fundamental theology of Assmann.

The names that Assmann and Reyes-Mate included in the second volume of the anthology are important, but so are those theorists who were excluded. Among the various names that can be recalled, what stands out is the consistent exclusion of any thinker linked to the history of the Frankfurt School, which has offered the most influential interpretation of Marx in the twentieth century.[12] This exclusion looks to me like a conscious decision on the part of the editors. Assmann, at least, seems not to consider the Frankfurt School to be Marxist in the strict sense of the term; he refers to it somewhere as "Para-Marxist."[13] It is certainly accurate to say that Assmann is no more sympathetic to critical theory than he is to political theology.

In a general way, we will attempt, in what follows, to summarize Assmann's position with regard to Marxism. In his opinion, in Marx and Engels there is an ambiguity concerning the critique of religion. That ambiguity can be seen in what relates to the negation

---

[12] Some names left out are Bernstein, Bloch (whom Assmann considered an example of biblical rereading, *Teología*, 174), Garaudy, and Althusser, but these last two are more recent.

[13] See the critique of Habermas's (and Horkheimer's) instrumental or technological rationality. According to Assmann ("Tecnologia y poder en la perspectiva de la teologia de la liberacion," *Estúdios Ecuménicos*, no. 37 [1979]: 27–36), the notion of technology with which Habermas works becomes reified, and the important point, which is the relation between technology and power, stays in the background. However, Assmann gets cozier with critical theory when he criticizes the presence of a metaphysics in Marxist orthodoxy. But that is a central element in so-called Western Marxism, even if this is one of its least clear points.

of religion. A consistent Marxist position would have to take the particular negation of religion to its logical conclusion, just as any ideology is particularly negated.[14] That is, the essence of any ideology, its universal aspect, must be sought in the mode of production, and that is the case with religious ideology too. However, Assmann argues, there is a tendency in Marxism (present with more emphasis in Engels and in the Leninist position) to critique an absolute essence abstracted from the mode of production but within the phenomenon of religion. According to Assmann, the weakness of this critique is that it loses sight of or disdains the concrete historical situation in which a religious phenomenon emerges in its particularity and that it launches into metaphysical speculations even though these are intentionally antimetaphysical. And this is exactly the attitude of the bourgeois critique of religion.

Although it's not our task to evaluate Assmann's critique of Marxism, it's appropriate to say that Assmann's argument is consistent with Marxism. However, what appears to be lacking is the distinction between the critique of metaphysics and the metaphysics of critique. Any particular negation of religious ideology (and Assmann agrees) assumes the reduction to the particular of the absolute demands that that ideology makes. This business of determining the absolute and reducing it to the particular is nothing more than a negation, if I may speak like Spinoza, with whom Marx agreed on that point. Thus the critique of a transcendent essence of religion is the presupposition by which religion or ideology can be recognized and approached in its particularity. And the truth is that that critique can simply replace one absolute with another, as in the case of Bruno Bauer and self-consciousness. But not every critique of absolute essence assumes a transcendent alternative.

What really interests us, however, is not the small details. What's important is to see the conclusions that Assmann draws from his

---

[14] Marx and Engels, *Sobre la Religión I*, ed. Assmann and Reyes-Mate (Salamanca, 1974), 31ff. Here Assmann and Reyes-Mate suggest that, given the fact that Marx, in his critique of religion, rarely refers to the Church, Marx identified Church with religion. Thus one can assume that when Marx speaks of religion, what he has in mind is the Church in its historical particularity.

evaluation of Marxist ambiguity regarding the critique of religion. From that evaluation, he explains the presence of different approaches to the religious phenomenon within the Marxist tradition. By avoiding the problematic interpretation of the relation between particular and universal, we are able to say that the pertinent distinction in what Assmann wants to develop is established between the posture that elaborates an internal critique of religion and the critique that restricts itself to the external aspect—that is, the critique that analyzes religion in its historical and social aspects. Assmann concludes that if the ideological superstructure has the capacity, in a revolutionary situation, to carry forward the critique of the capitalist mode of production, then religion, as a part of that superstructure, has a priori that same capacity. No one can really deny, by way of dogmatism, that this can occur, once one has agreed that the point of departure is a reflection on the historical and material reality in the midst of the struggle for liberation. Given the fact that Christians (or even a small minority of them) have participated in that struggle in Latin America, Assmann argues, it's logical to conclude that one can find, in Christian circles in Latin America, evidence of participation in historical praxis for liberation. And he concludes, "In that case, a qualitatively new situation is produced: from that critical praxis there can arise a Christian theory, i.e., an ideology that doesn't necessarily have to be ideological. That is precisely what is occurring today in Latin America."[15] This, then, is the basis and the criterion for defining what theology is as liberation theology: a "critical reflection on faith as praxis."[16] Just as Assmann rejects the critique of the essence of religion, he also says nothing about the essence or the nature of faith. Thus the question remains open as to whether faith is the same as praxis or whether faith is its source. That question will appear later on in Assmann's discussion of the "mysterious dimension of love."[17] But before that, we have to elucidate some central characteristics of the place of praxis—that is, the

---

[15] Ibid., 34.

[16] Hugo Assmann, José Blanes, and Luís Bach, "Cristianos por el socialismo: Exigencias de una opción," *Cristianismo y Sociedad* 33, no. 34 (1972): 19–70, especially 63.

[17] Cf. Assmann, "Tecnologia y poder," 28.

historical Latin American context, the place in which faith is embodied. For this purpose, it's important to consider the choice of thinkers included in the anthology mentioned above, which, by the standards of "Western Marxism," can be considered a bit orthodox. The search for theoretical presuppositions can have a rather exotic aroma, but it's important, since Assmann doesn't see himself in the position of having to explain them, and for his purposes, he doesn't need to. But for our concerns, this is an important point.

In his article "Political Commitment in a Context of Class Struggle,"[18] Assmann describes the historical context of Latin America as being characterized by the phenomenon of class struggle. Referring to Marx, he shows that class struggle is a historical category that "is explicitly connected to particular stages of the development of production." Latin America finds itself at a particular moment in which class struggle is quite intense. Following the theory of Marx, Assmann assumes that this situation, such as it is currently, was not always this way and will not continue this way in the future. If this is the situation that characterizes the present moment in Latin America, it seems indisputable that those committed to the praxis of liberation need to take up this struggle on all economic, political, and other levels on which it is happening. The origin of that commitment to the praxis of liberation is found in the analytical presuppositions that describe the situation such as it is and then call for an ethical commitment. This commitment must be obedient and "disciplined," invested in "praxis with the proletariat."[19] The praxis of the working class also becomes normative for the Christian who injects himself into the struggle for liberation.

The elements mentioned above, which are found in Assmann's short essay, are not easy to combine systematically unless we presuppose some basic elements from historical materialism. For Marx (and also for Engels), human actions share two basic characteristics. The first corresponds to the relation between man and nature, from

---

[18] Assmann, "Political Commitment in a Context of Class Struggle," *Concilium* 84, no. 4 (1973): 473–81.

[19] Assmann, *Teología*, 105.

which productive activity par excellence can be derived. The second follows the first but is distinct from it in the sense that it refers specifically to the interhuman relation and, basically, to intercommunication: "Production appears only with the growth of population. This, in turn, presupposes the intercourse of individuals with each other."[20] These are the two aspects of praxis that Marx will later conceptualize as "force of production" and "relation of production" or "relation of property"—that is, the relation of classes according to material goods produced and appropriated.

From these inadequacies—namely, the tensions between the historical stage of development by the forces of production and the dominant social intercourse, which is determined by the power to appropriate the means of production—social revolutions emerge: "All the collisions in history have their origin . . . in the contradiction between the forces of production and the forms of intercourse."[21] The tension between the forces of production and the relations of production, or more precisely, the diachronic development of these two, needs to be justified. The question immediately arises, Why isn't there an identification—that is, a match—between the historical development of the two praxes, which, together and in their dialectical relation, constitute the "mode of production"? Marx explains this phenomenon by saying that above the mode of production, "social and political superstructures emerge."[22] In Marx, these superstructures are designated by the general term *ideological superstructure*, which functions basically as a legitimizing instance of the dominant social intercourse with regard to the productive process. This superstructure tends to stabilize the tense relation between the two dimensions of a mode of production. At the same time, the productive process continues to

---

[20] Karl Marx and Friedrich Engels, *The German Ideology* (Moscow, 1964), 37. Or, as Engels formulated it in *Dialectics of Nature* (Moscow, 1972), "first labor, after it and then with it speech—these are the two most essential stimuli under which the brain of the ape changed into that of man" (174).

[21] Marx and Engels, *German Ideology*, 83. The same thesis was reaffirmed by Marx fourteen years later. Cf. Marx, *A Contribution to the Critique of Political Economy* (New York, 1970), 20–21.

[22] Marx and Engels, *German Ideology*, 83; cf. also Karl Marx, *Das Kapital: Kritik der politischen Okonomie I* (Frankfurt, 1976), 96n33.

develop technologically, resulting in the absolute implementation of the social conditions of life. According to Marx, in the capitalist mode of production—and this is important for understanding political praxis in Assmann—the absolute increase in the material conditions of life is unequally distributed between the two basic social classes that this mode of production permits and demands: one class that carries out the productive process and the other that establishes property relations. As a result of this situation, we have a relative decrease of control over the means of production on the part of the producers (workers) while production is increasing. This situation develops into a growing separation between the two basic classes and eventually will result in the collapse of the social order—that is, of prevailing property relations.

That conflict becomes viable, however, only because the ideological superstructure mediates the two dimensions of human praxis, thus creating a third: political praxis, which uses juridical, political, and military institutions and theoretical and ideological discourse. As we said, that political praxis tends to legitimize a given relation between social intercourse and the forces of production. Since the relation of these elements is dynamic and historical, the dominant social intercourse in a given historical period resists—with the help of the ideological superstructure, up to a certain point—the contradictions in a mode of production. That intercourse becomes obsolete and goes into collapse when the cumulative advance of the means of production and of the goods produced becomes so contradictory with respect to the mode of production that it exceeds the resources mobilized for that purpose by the dominant class. Obviously, we shouldn't reify the power of contradiction to which we are referring. For Marx, that power is historically manifest in the interests of the working class.

We can now say that within a capitalist system, the ideas and institutions (the ideological superstructure) that function as an instance of legitimation also serve as a mediation between the mode of social interaction and the productive forces—that is, between the interests of the capitalist class and the interests of the workers. But in the historical moment at which the maladjustment between production (worker) and distribution (capitalist) reaches a critical point, as is the case in Latin America, we are going to find, in that same ideological structure, the mediation of revolutionary praxis as its dominant or soon-to-be dominant component. Instead of promoting harmonization, institutional and ideological mediation begins to help transform the mode of social distribution of property. While maintaining this explanation on a schematic and formal level, we can say that when the resources of the old model of legitimation are exhausted because of the low level of adjustment between production and distribution, a new and revolutionary ideology begins to occupy the space abandoned by the old one and helps articulate the new mode of distribution that emerges. But that can never happen unless the conflict that emerges between the interests of the two economic classes rises to the level of an ideological conflict, which is the dialectical and necessary consequence of that first and more general conflict. The anarchist, by the way, is someone who tends to do without institutional and ideological mediation.

In Assmann, the conflict of ideologies becomes the framework for the conflict of theologies. He clearly recognizes the two dimensions of a mode of production—that is, the two dimensions to which we have been referring.[23] Given the fact that in Latin America, the contradiction between the mode of production and the relations of production has reached an advanced stage of maladjustment, "harmony" can be maintained only by imposition, and in the case of Latin America, that means military imposition.[24] Since we are arriving at that conclusion, or rather while the analysis of reality is moving in that direction (since reality is dynamic, one never "arrives" at a conclusion in positivist terms), an ethical decision becomes imperative. However, in Assmann, an ambiguous question remains: the question of whether that "imperative" is interpreted as a Kantian a priori or as an objective

[23] See Assmann, *Teología*, 67, where the pertinent distinction is made between praxis in humanizing, social sentiment, and reproductive praxis; and Assmann, Blanes, and Bach, "Cristianos por el socialismo," 60.

[24] This point is developed through the "theory of dependency," to which Assmann subscribes. The theory of dependency is represented by a movement with a wide spectrum of theoretical variations, but there is fundamental unity with respect to the proposed socioeconomic theses.

contingency immanent in history. What's certain is that that decision is made in the face of the demand to align the stage of production with the mode of distribution. But the necessity for revolutionary change has its source in the social class that obviously has something to gain by becoming conscious of its condition on the basis of its own productive praxis, which it has been materially.

Just as in Marx, praxis is defined first of all as human work with its teleological aspect (the concept that the craftsman has in mind before doing his work).[25] This human work is, in turn, influenced by historical and material conditions.[26] In a situation of extreme contradiction between production and distribution, what happens, in reality, is that the activity of constructing a new social order—made possible, in principle, by the relatively advanced stage of the material conditions available—is obstructed. Perhaps an example will help simplify: If a mode of distribution or of property relations denies certain goods to a social class while these same goods are produced by the same class that has no access to them, then the material conditions are present for that class to demand its share of the result of its own production. If that is not achieved, the fundamental right of the human being is denied—that is, the right to work, the right to that which, for Marx, is the primary characteristic of the human species, the right to produce its means of subsistence. If one cancels the most properly human aspect of this production—that is, its teleological aspect—a fundamental human right is wiped out. As a result, the teleological moment of human production, when negated, also tends to be ideologically capitalized in a form of religious alienation, in an illusory projection. Linked to the negation of the right to work is a series of factors related to it: limitation of the productive process, unemployment, political domination by technology (technocracy), and so forth. In general terms, that situation serves as the backdrop to Assmann's condemnation of all international aid for Latin America, aid that puts the right to bread ahead of the right to work, if the latter ever appears.

---

25 Marx, *Das Kapital*, 193.

26 "Men make their own history—but under circumstances directly encountered, given, and transmitted from the past." Karl Marx, *The Eighteenth Brumaire of Louis Bonaparte* (New York, 1963), 15.

On the list of basic human rights, the first one Assmann mentions is the right to work: "First the right to work and through it all the other rights." This is "the only acceptable . . . hierarchization of priorities."[27] Only by taking into consideration the analysis of this situation and its objective definition as revolutionary can the concept of praxis be concretely understood as "the real struggle on a horizon of effective possibilities for the liberation of our oppressed peoples."[28]

The political implementation of the analytical considerations mentioned above leads to a commitment, an alliance with all those who engage in that praxis, starting with the workers.[29] In this sense, Assmann's position is clear and radical: a liberating praxis is that which seeks to establish a socialist mode of social intercourse. The so-called third way is a false alternative,[30] which doesn't mean that a Third Way doesn't exist; it's simply false as an alternative. Through the ideology of Catholic Action and also through the fruitful incorporation of the thought of Maritain, the politics of the third way received considerable support from the Catholic Church and from the people during a period in which dissatisfaction with the status quo was tempered by Cold War ideology. Assmann considers the ineffectiveness of the third way model in achieving any radical transformation to be a problem endemic to the model itself. Moreover, its ideological motives, coming from Christian sources, left little doubt, for an attentive theologian, as to their nature. For that reason, it is also not surprising that liberation theology, which emerged historically as a reaction to the theology of Catholic Action, makes anticlericalism one of its most fundamental, characteristic, and public elements. It is worth noting that that posture dates from before 1972, when the Christian Democrats abandoned the leftist front in Chile and opened

---

[27] Hugo Assmann, "Breves consideraciones al margen del informe final del encuentro de Oaxtepec," *Estúdios Ecuménicos* 38 (1979): 50–52. This point is elaborated together with the critique of the ideology of the eradication of critical poverty defended by the Trilateral Commission. Cf. Hugo Assmann et al., *A Trilateral: Nova Fase do Capitalismo Mundial* (Petrópolis, 1979).

[28] Cf. Assmann, Blanes, and Bach, "Cristianos por el socialismo," 34; also Assmann, *Pueblo oprimido*, 13.

[29] Assmann, Blanes, and Bach, "Cristianos por el socialismo," 43–45.

[30] Assmann, *Teología*, 173.

the door for the coup d'état that took place the following year. That coup served as the tragic proof of what liberation theology, then becoming influential, was affirming.

Assmann is not saying—and he even specifically denies—that the struggle against the third way implies reproducing the Soviet socialist model in Latin America; neither does the dependent capitalism in Latin America reproduce the capitalist model that operates in the North Atlantic world. Those historical types to which we refer certainly represent two models of production that, as such, constitute the option for Latin America. But to think about a simple historical repetition would be an abstraction from the very dynamic of history. The socialist revolution in Latin America fits into a framework of possibilities that are different from those that accompanied other socialist revolutions, a fact that conditions the result. One should suppose that that result will have its spectrum of variations even within Latin America, which, after all, cannot be considered a homogeneous continent.[31]

In the process of liberation, the future of Christianity is also at stake. On this point, Assmann is categorical: "We are the only viable alternative for meaningful Christianity in the future. . . . We are the Christianities that have already inaugurated the future of Christianity."[32] Judgment on Christianity has to be weighed in the balance of praxis. What remains to be seen is how capable Christians are of entering into an alliance, on a strategic-tactical level, with those who historically have been engaged in a liberating praxis.

Thus far, we have described the basic elements of the first part of Assmann's definition of theology: critical reflection . . . on faith as praxis. He himself summarizes his method by dividing the process of critical reflection of historical praxis into three levels of articulation: (1) the level of social, economic, and political analysis, which will reveal the character of sociopolitical and economic organization and the relation of forces in the present moment of class struggle; (2) the level of concrete political options, which unfolds side by side with

[31] Ibid., 93, 162.

[32] Hugo Assmann, "The common task of the social sciences and of theology in unmasking the necrophilia of capitalism," in *Capitalismo: Violencia y antivida I*, ed. Elsa Tamez and Saúl Trinidad (San José, 1978), 21–37.

the first option; and (3) the strategic-tactical level, which is that of the planned implementation of the political theses.[33] It is at this third level that the task of breaking up the ideological blocks within Christianity and recovering the dialectical character of Christian symbols will be developed.[34]

III.

As we have seen, Assmann goes from analysis of the historical situation of Latin America to the comprehension of economic praxis, and from there, he explains the specifically political character of that praxis in the midst of a revolutionary situation. That political praxis also includes the ideological struggle that takes place within religion and is aimed at breaking up the ideological blocks in the religious sphere by bringing class struggle into the church but without restricting it to an intraecclesial perspective.[35]

If we frame the problem of the theory-praxis relation in the way just discussed, we can affirm that Assmann's posture falls within the Marxist interpretation of that relation and, in this sense, is distinct from the understanding of praxis in critical theory. Assmann speaks of the "primacy of the political," but that's not the same as political theology's understanding of that term.[36] Political praxis, for Assmann, is an ethical consequence of a political decision made on the basis of social analysis, which, in turn, finds its fundamental element and most basic necessity in the right to work. Political praxis is the culmination of economic praxis (production) and social praxis (human

---

[33] He discusses the three levels of critical reflection many times in his writings: Assmann, "Tecnologia y poder," 104ff.; Assmann, *Pueblo oprimido*, 14; and so on. One of the best expositions of the subject, however, is found in Assmann, "Cristianos por el socialsimo," 34ff.

[34] Assmann compares the creation of symbols (as human values) with the creation of value in the material process of production. Thus since capitalism alienates the material surplus value in the productive process, it also alienates the ideological surplus value in the process of the production of symbols. This analogy between ideological production and material production, which Assmann systematizes, was suggested by Marx (*Das Kapital*, 86). Socialism gives back to the producer (worker) not only the economic surplus value but also the ideological (see Assmann, *Teología*, 171–202, esp. 194).

[35] Assmann, *Teologia*, 186.

[36] Ibid., 93.

interaction determined by the division of classes). That is, political praxis aims to overcome the contradictions of a society by liberating economic praxis from the unemployment endemic to capitalism and by liberating social praxis from the limits imposed upon it by class, race, and sex.

Since Assmann understands praxis on all its levels as "the embodiment of faith," critical reflection on praxis (as faith) is the proper task of theology. The reality in which praxis is encapsulated is the first "text" on which the Christian must reflect.[37] Since this reflection can be articulated only on the ideological level (both discursive in theology and institutional in ecclesial practice), it itself becomes an element of praxis. And as history is transformed through praxis, the "text" itself is transformed, so that reflection never loses its dynamic and creative aspect. Assmann does not deny that the process can be truncated, institutionalized. That's the point at which a revolution becomes a "religion."[38]

Thus far, if the argument indicates the frame of reference of the concept of praxis in Assmann, another question comes up: Is theology nothing more than a mode of reflecting on social reality as far as its specifically religious datum (that which is Christian) is concerned? Is theology's objective nothing more than serving as a strategic-tactical instrument for mobilizing the religious masses in Latin America? The words "nothing more" lend a pejorative tone to these questions. In truth, there isn't much that's excluded from these questions. The answer to them certainly cannot be given without, at least, offering a detailed qualification. But that qualification would transcend Assmann's theological scope, especially since the need for such a question does not emerge from a "praxiological" demand. Basically, Assmann refuses to respond in theoretical terms to the problem of Christian specificity. The only specific element is the very negation of this specificity—that is, the self-emptying (*kenosis*) of Christianity in giving itself over to the praxis of love.[39]

---

37 Ibid., 24 passim. This is the "sociological Bible" of which Assmann speaks; ibid., 48.

38 Ibid., 155.

39 Ibid., 117, 136.

This problematic, however, is not entirely abstract. Even if Assmann has not explicitly formulated it, it emerges here and there in his writings. The concrete problem is that if theology must carry forward the ideological struggle in the theological arena, it can't indefinitely escape those questions, especially when they are used as reactionary weapons. The ideological blockages to be broken up are built on defamatory critiques of liberation theology.

The first difficulty that we encounter in this context and that inserts itself into the center of the problematic discussed above regards the relation, for Assmann, between praxis and faith. There is no doubt that, as his first priority, he intends to make this matter clear: on the basis of his logical starting point, historical praxis, there is no way to demand any type of *analysis fidei* abstracted from the historical context, which constitutes the "text" on which the Christian is to reflect critically.[40] Any speculative attempt to abstract historical circumstances means falling into an ideological trap by the simple fact that that abstraction involves the rupture of the union between theory and praxis. Thus faith itself must be submitted to the critical reflection that emerges from praxis. Consequently, faith becomes subject to scrutiny when it is embodied in historical events. At the same time, however, Assmann does not want to classify faith in a secondary category. As I understand it, the way he resolves the problem is, on the one hand, to equate faith and praxis but, on the other, to leave faith as a formal category of praxis, which is the very substance of history.[41]

One could draw many theological implications from the equation that Assmann tries to establish between faith and praxis, especially if we seek to compare it with some classical definitions of faith in the history of Christian theology. But such comparing becomes unimportant once we consider the concept of tradition in Assmann. For him, the only tradition that matters, as far as Christianity is concerned, is the cultural evolution of Christian symbols and their reproduction in the course of the historical reality that, in Latin America,

[40] Ibid., 71.
[41] Ibid., 22–23.

generated the sociological datum recognized as "what's Christian."[42] Thus we can say that nothing resembling a history of dogma exists as a positive expression of the revelatory datum received in faith. Faith can achieve positive ("dogmatic") expression only in terms of the concrete historical relation between the human being as the subject of the praxis and a given historical reality, which both conditions that praxis and offers the raw material for it. What was said about nature during the Renaissance (that it doesn't make leaps and bounds) is now said about history and also about faith, except that the dialectical movement reserves for itself the right to accomplish qualitative transformations by escaping from a mechanistic linearity. In this way, faith itself cannot be thought of as the result of a revelatory, suprahistorical datum. The "civilizing" process (Don Ribeiro) is an expression of the "revelatory" (Bauer) process. Truth itself, in its ontological meaning, is a historical becoming, as Assmann affirms in recalling the words of Rubem Alves: "Truth is the name given by the historical community to those historical acts that were, are, and will be efficacious for the liberation of man."[43] Assmann himself describes this "becoming true" with the notion of historical process, which, in turn, is the category that can best describe the kingdom of God:

> The kingdom of God is never identical to the structures of the world but rather inserts itself into them as a process in which it develops. The notion of process represents perhaps one of

[42] "What's Christian" (which can also be called "sociological Christianity" or simply "Christianity"; ibid., 174) has two dimensions: the apparent level and the deep or essential level. On the apparent level are found the symbols and the Christian institutions as they reveal themselves positively in the tradition by carrying out an ideological function. On the essential level, one finds the essence of those symbols in their creative and revolutionary value as manifestations of the worthiest human aspirations. Assmann, in this distinction between the essential and the apparent, follows the methodology of Marx, in which the function of science is to bring to its essence what in ideology is revealed in appearance. Once this is achieved, one turns to the apparent level in revealing the alienating function and the contradictions of the ideological superstructure. This describes the ideological struggle; cf. Karl Marx, *Grundrisse* (New York, 1973), 100ff. For a practical application of this method of unmasking and ideological subversion, see Assmann, "La actuación histórica del poder de Cristo," *Cristianismo y Sociedad* 43, no. 44 (1975): 43–54.

[43] Assmann, *Teología*, 65.

> the categories to be introduced into theological vocabulary for speaking about the kingdom of God, because, besides its socioanalytic validity for setting forth problems of structural change, it contains the two poles of the eschatological tension in their intersection in history: the "already" and the "not yet." . . . It is a process that connects with the guiding thread of the constant dynamic of the historical process.[44]

The question now is to find out if Assmann does or does not postulate a limit to this concept of truth immanent in history (in which the element of transcendence is only the historical "not yet"), in which faith appears exclusively as conditioned to what historically assumes bodily form. In our view, the way Assmann approaches that problematic gives rise to a double interpretation. In his writings that date to the end of 1971 and the beginning of 1972, we find an approach that in a certain way differs from that which, in general, is found in his writings published after that.

The characteristic of the first period is the explicit presence of a mysterious sphere, of a detailed and inaccessible reality. If Assmann were then asked if his position involved a historical reductionism, his response certainly would be similar to what follows: "There is, evidently, a radical dimension of mystery in love that has entered history, and that dimension escapes any adequate criterion of classification and qualification. Only art, poetry, and mystic symbols achieve an allusive language close to what we experience as the mysterious density of self-giving in love."[45]

At this point in his theology, Assmann thinks about an aprioristic moment that, by at least three levels of critical reflection, precedes what we referred to above. That a priori moment is conversion, metanoia, "launching oneself into risk and insecurity." Two other moments follow metanoia and are characterized as *krisis* (interpreting and

---

[44] Ibid., 164.

[45] Ibid., 117; however, the text goes on to say, "But that represents no justification for theology to remain light years away from the concrete globularity of the historical praxis of love, because many of the components of that concretion can in fact be named and analyzed."

judging reality) and "as the gesture or action of the in-breaking and creation of the new (praxis)."[46] The first moment cannot be reduced to the two that follow—that is, *krisis* and praxis, which, in turn, work themselves out on three levels of critical reflection and action. In this context, God appears as a transcendental category that explains the exteriorization of faith in the praxis of love manifest materially in history: God is the one who provokes. Thus faith is not exhausted in praxis because faith is the formal cause of that praxis: "Faith in that provocative God and in his liberating action confers on the action of the Christian a more audacious hope and a more valiant intensity."[47] Therefore, though Assmann denies any specificity that is not kenosis, self-emptying, he reserves for theology and for Christianity an irreducible *proprium*, a "trans" that is not immanent even in the process of the kingdom in history: "The Christian utopia of the Kingdom of God is structurally transprocessual and does not allow itself to be reduced even to the process of liberation."[48]

As we can see, there are problems that emerge from Assmann's position. How can he have recourse to a radical dimension of mystery and, with it, justify a certain Christian audacity when, at the same time, praxis, in its self-sufficiency, must be defined on the basis of the praxis of the exploited and oppressed? Assmann certainly appears to locate that audacity on the limits of the "auxiliary vanguard"—that is, the place of superstructural struggle where most Christians perform their praxis. On that level, a polarization becomes more imperative.[49] But that does not resolve the problem, because then God would be a "provocateur" of nothing more than a superstructural aid in the process of liberation. The workers, the exploited, the oppressed, as the ultimate subjects of the process of liberation, necessarily assume, in Assmann's praxis, that mysterious dimension, unless Assmann wanted to universalize (à la Rahner) his concept of *Christian*. But

---

[46] Ibid., 152.
[47] Ibid., 156.
[48] Ibid., 154.
[49] Ibid., 132ff. On the tendency for radicalization found in groups of leftist Christians, who thus lose sight of political mediations and relax in social analysis, see the interview with the Chilean exile José Zalaquett in *Christianity and Crisis* 36, no. 11 (1976): 152–57.

that seems to be far from all of his various intentions. Might it not be a self-contradiction for Assmann to affirm that "transprocessual" dimension (even if it's merely formal) as long as, by his own criteria, the transcendental elements lend themselves to ideological exploitation? Again, one solution might be to adopt (in the manner of the Frankfurt School) a "negative" concept of praxis and locate, in the power of negativity, the transcendental dimension we talked about. But that would in various ways contradict fundamental elements of his definition of praxis as the historical production of truth, and in the political sphere, it would imply a third way–ism, which he unforgivingly blames on political theology. There is no doubt that Assmann emphasizes the positive character of the concept of praxis as "doing the truth."[50] It's worth mentioning that he in no way rejects the negative element. He wants his position to be dialectic by distancing himself, in this sense, from positivism and empiricism. For him, the unity of cross and resurrection manifests in the historical power of Christ "implies fighting wherever one finds in history the defeat that prepares the way for victory, and the victory that requires a new defeat to continue being a victory."[51] Beyond any doubt, Assmann has affirmed that the struggle in Latin America is the struggle for socialism.

If the problem we are presenting does not find a solution in Assmann's writings up to the beginning of 1972, we can affirm that the situation changes a bit after that date. Since then, we no longer find that radical dimension of mystery either as a prerational ethical moment or as a formal category that serves as a methodological resource.[52] Whether Assmann was or was not conscious of that problematic and then advanced in the direction of supplanting it is a

---

[50] Assmann, *Teología*, 63.

[51] Assmann, "Actuación histórica," 54.

[52] It seems exaggerated to affirm that there is a "rupture" in Assmann's thought. It's even dubious that there's been a conscious change of position. Perhaps it's more correct to speak of a thematic dislocation that, as it develops, suppresses resorting to the transcendental or mysterious datum. For a deeper discussion of the problematic, there's an unpublished article by James Savolainen, "Theology in the Shadow of Marx: The Theory-Practice Relationship in Liberation Theology and the status of the Christian Specificum." Savolainen rejects the hypothesis of a change of position by Assmann and points out the problems in adopting an

question that does not interest us and that we cannot properly answer. If we analyzed some points in Assmann's theological development, we would be abstracting his thought from the historical context in which it developed in order then to create static judgments about a theoretical moment. Our intention, rather, is to show that there exists a constant "improving of the questions," as Assmann likes to say, so that the answers always emerge as more concrete, more encrusted with new historical circumstances.

Although it's only in 1976 that Assmann began to speak explicitly about a second phase of liberation theology,[53] the characteristics he attributes to that second phase are found, in programmatic form, in a very important article called "The ideological surplus value of Christianity."[54] In our view, this article establishes a methodological "place" for theology that, at least potentially, dispenses with the recourse to that "transprocessual" dimension that we spoke of above and locates theology decidedly in the "milieu" of those social sciences that are committed to the struggle against capitalism. Praxis is affirmed as the "first and foundational" element, and at least the ambiguity between praxis and conversion is gone.[55] Contrary to what we saw above when theology was situated in an undefined area between metanoia, *krisis*, and praxis, now its task is sharply defined as the function of unmasking the transcendental elements recruited by the capitalist system for the purpose of legitimating itself in its crises—that is, for harmonizing the contradiction between the relation of production and the forces of production: "Idolatrous religion is indispensable for the oppressor."[56] The social sciences now interact with theology in a decidedly internal way. Theology includes the social sciences. Theological reflection emerges in a moment of social analysis: "The place

---

aprioristic moment to safeguard the specific character of Christianity, even if that a priori is merely formal.

53 Assmann, "Tecnologia y poder," 34: "In this sense, one arrives at affirming that liberation theology has entered a second stage of its process of maturation—analytically centered on the true necrophiliac essence of the capitalist system; theologically centered on the effort to produce an anti-fetishist theology."

54 This article was first published in April 1972 and is part of Assmann's book *Teología*, 171–202.

55 Assmann, "Tecnologia y poder," 30.

56 Assmann, "La tarea común," 2.

of theology in the social sciences is the place of the legitimations of transcendental character that both normally accompany social theories and also are, definitively, their communication hub, though almost always implicitly. The explanation for those transcendental ties is usually given only as defensive-offensive ideology in times of crisis. The structural interconnections on that plane can and must be analyzed scientifically."[57]

The place of theology as a moment of social analysis—and not social analysis as a moment of theology, external to itself[58]—requires an even greater consideration of the contemporaneous situation of capitalism, especially with regard to its form of ideological articulation, the ideology of the Trilateral Commission, which involves immediately "theological" elements. As Juan Luis Segundo has already taught us, theology has an iconoclastic function. This function manifests itself negatively in the unmasking of the appropriation of religious symbols by the dominant power and positively in the recovery of the original liberating character of those symbols, thus leading to their socialization. The analysis that Assmann makes of ideological surplus value follows, on the level of superstructure, the same mechanism as is used for the creation of economic surplus value (which constitutes one of Marx's most ingenious discoveries) for complementary purposes. But we should let Assmann speak for himself:

> It's sufficient, then, to summarize by saying that a first and negative meaning of ideological surplus value applicable to sociological Christianity refers to the sociocultural excess of myths used as internationalizing channels for domination. A second meaning, which, being positive, is transferred to socialist goals, is applied to that which, in symbolic and mythic universes, is worth more than all the perversions. It is

---

[57] Ibid., 59.

[58] That posture is not unusual in Latin American, principally among theologians linked to the Neo-Orthodox movement, in which a separation between "heaven and earth" (Barth) or the adoption of a "methodological atheism" (Bonhoeffer) is justified. Cf. José Miguez Bonino, *Doing Theology in a Revolutionary Situation* (Philadelphia: Fortress, 1975), 95ff.

> also applied to what continues to be available to its liberal parcels, with its point of rebellion still intact. On this deep plane of symbols and myths, a socialist Christianity will be able to act vigorously in favor of the social ownership of those symbols and myths, in faithfulness to the original intentions of the Christian sources, and coincident with the original practical purposes of the myths.[59]

This rupture with the theological tradition is profound, comparable and analogous to that which Marx effected in the philosophical tradition by establishing the priority of the production and reproduction of real life for the theoretical interpretation of the world. If Marx, with his subversion of the theory-praxis relation, predicted the suppression of philosophy and its concomitant preservation on a higher level (*Aufliebung*), it is our opinion that Assmann intends to complete the same program in regard to theology. That means negating any theology built upon the negation of the "original theology"—that is, the one that manifests, in symbols, the experience of liberation—by exploiting it ideologically. What Assmann intends to do, in our view, is to achieve the negation of the negation, to use Hegelian-Marxist terminology. For Assmann, as we have said, a theological tradition as such does not exist, in the same way as for Marx (contra Hegel), there is no history of philosophy as such. What exists is a tradition of symbolic production situated historically in social and economic modes of production. Criticizing Assmann for his posture in regard to the theological tradition makes no sense unless one assumes the critique of his starting point: the praxis of production and reproduction of real life. It is only from that perspective that one can formulate a criticism about the absence of a dogmatic concept of God or about the polarization of the transcendent dimension. As a counterweight, a critical posture of that type would have a difficult time finding a theoretical frame of reference except in idealism or irrationalism. Hence before Assmann's theology becomes the desired object of criticism,

[59] Assmann, *Teología*, 193.

his theoretical offensive emerges as an implacable accuser of the ideological machinations of idealism.

We should remember that a critique of Assmann can and must be done from a point of view internal to his own articulation of his theology, a perspective that accepts his "praxiological"[60] starting point and proceeds to the examination of his argument. In this context, considerations will arise about the possibility of sustaining, by analogy to economic production, an ideological production from which one can infer the existence of a mechanism of ideological surplus value, or about the original revolutionary character of Christian symbols, and so on. That examination of his theology will take place, but contrary to the idealist critique, it will contribute to the very definition and development of the ideological struggle, both within the Christian dimension of that struggle and outside of it. It's worth mentioning that the emergence of those issues does not depend on a simple academic examination of the "letter" of liberation theology. Rather, it depends on the power that the symbols of liberation have for historical actualization "in the real concretions of the kingdom of God on earth, in the tangible anticipations of the future *new*."[61]

---

[60] Though we have used this concept, it's important to remember that it is defined according to Assmann's concept of praxis and thus involves a different meaning from that attributed to the term and spread by political theology.

[61] Assmann, "La tarea común," 32.

CONSIDERATIONS OF LATIN AMERICAN ETHNO-LUTHERANISM

Almost all (96 percent) of Latin American Lutherans live in the Southern Cone of South America. With few exceptions, they are of German extraction and join together in religious communities characterized as "German churches." Most notable among these churches are the Igreja Evangélica de Confissão Luterana no Brasil, the Iglesia Evangélica del Rio da la Plata in Argentina, and the former Iglesia Evangélica Luterana en Chile. Until the schism in Chilean Lutheranism, these church bodies enrolled 80 percent of the Lutherans in the Southern Cone. (The problem of Missouri Synod Lutherans will not be discussed in this essay.) According to terminology previously adopted, these three church bodies can be considered transplants. They were not firmly planted in their new reality and were, to a certain extent, impenetrable, closed in, tending to reelaborate the ecclesiastical model of origin with an intrinsically "catholic" character, which is, moreover, a notable feature of the Lutheran Reformation, which was "catholic" in the principalities in which it was adopted. This character contributed to the creation of an unwholesome attitude in the new land, especially where German immigrants were a minority. It also involved the typical consequences of an anachronistic Reformation, landing here three centuries after the Counter-Reformation. But as I will attempt to show, these consequences did not constitute the crucial issues that make us question our history, our heritage, our memory. In fact, the churches came in

---

Originally published in *Estudos Teológicos* 18, no. 2 (1978): 77–94.

a second moment, built on the level of determinants of a sociological order. In the first part of this essay, we will look at these determinants. In the second part, we will attempt to draw critical conclusions and open up some perspectives for these transplanted churches, which, now more than ever, reveal themselves to be churches in anguish. The Igreja Evangélica de Confissão Luterana no Brasil will be our principal concern, while the Iglesia Evangélica del Rio de la Plata and the Iglesia Evangélica Luterana en Chile will appear as useful parameters. The Chilean example, particularly the schism of the church, will appear as the most complete paradigm for locating the tendencies of these churches to the extent that it is possible to trace parallel commonalities among the three denominations.

The questions raised here and the evidence presented will take up again the problematic proposed by two letters from the six theology students who suspended their studies at the Superior School of Theology (EST) in the middle of the second semester of 1977. Though not explicitly, this essay is a commentary on these letters.[1] At the very least, we will attempt to rediscuss a theme that urgently needs to be remembered. Finally, we agree with A. Buendig in his study on a community of the Iglesia Evangélica del Rio de la Plata (1973): "There is no reason to doubt that true respect for the tradition consists in vivifying it and projecting it dynamically forward. . . . It's important to know how to pour old wine into new wineskins, a task that always imposes a challenge for lucidity and creative imagination."[2]

I. The Church as a Creature of Society: The Politico-Economic Determinant

The analysis of transplanted Lutheranism in the Southern Cone should begin with the basic, concrete fact that generates the entire later complex and in which the transplanted churches are all involved—namely,

---

1 The hypothesis presented here for interpreting ethno-Lutheranism only brings together glimpses of a widespread debate that preceded and followed the departure of these six students from the School of Theology. Thus these will be nothing new for those who participated in that discussion. They will find their contributions in this text.

2 A. Buendig, *La Iglesia Evangélica del Rio da la Mata (IERP) y la Congregación Evangélica de Esperanza*, 187.

immigration. And the motive that caused it was socioeconomic in character. Immigration from Europe in the nineteenth century is estimated at forty million. It resulted from a demographic explosion in Europe.

These immigrants were well received in Latin America, which they had selected as an oasis of peace where they could seek a standard of living that had already become prohibitive in their societies of origin. In the case of Brazil, the immigrants arrived in a country whose economic organization, based on the exploitation of slave labor, was running on empty because of the unsustainable position of the rural hierarchy on the one hand and of the slaves on the other. Just at the moment in which the social revolution required an intermediate stratum in society, where Blacks, on the basis of previous conquests, would go on to assume a role of ascendancy, the immigrant appeared and occupied that intermediate space, irremediably displacing the Blacks.

The position the immigrants assumed is due not only to the privileges that they had, if one compares them with the Blacks, but also to their heritage as a human group coming from technologically more capable peoples. The distribution of land, though it happened in a worse way than hoped for, guaranteed a minimum of conditions for the socioeconomic organization of these immigrants. It should be emphasized that the Germans in the Southern Cone ended up occupying the best land, near the littoral regions of the continent, both in Brazil and in Argentina and Chile. Before becoming an external proletariat ("agricultural laborers"), these immigrants grew as a people (ethnic group) and tended to develop an isolated replica of the European society from which they had come.[3] This explains the sociopolitical marginality of these groups in their early years, a fact that does not contradict the voices that in the past century considered the economic situation of the Protestants to be excellent.[4] That more or less homogeneous situation for the immigrants and their descendants persisted up to the twentieth century, when, in 1940, it is said of the German Brazilians engaged in agriculture that only a very

---

3 Darcy Ribeiro, *As Américas e a Civilização* (1977), 414ff.
4 Tschudi in 1860, Boanerges Ribeiro, *Protestantismo no Brasil Monárquico* (1973), 102.

few of them were big landowners or salaried employees.[5] In Chile, the situation is clearer. There the Germans are originally all evangelicals and defined by extension as an "aristocratic group."[6]

The economic development of the immigrants in the Brazilian scenario took place at the same pace as the process of socio-economic stratification that the entire society was going through, especially since the beginning of industrialization, which, in the decade of the 1930s, replaced imports. This industrialization coincided with the sedimentation of an intermediate layer in Brazilian society. At that time, agricultural lands were going through a process of subdivision, becoming small properties. That process generated more manpower available for other immigrants, who then assumed an increasingly prominent position in the still incipient industry. That process of elitization began with the sellers of supplies for the clearing of land and passed through the wholesalers, eventually reaching the headquarters of firms in the main cities. A similar process occurred with salaried employees in agriculture.

There is no reason to believe in the unity of immigrants as the cause of the privileged situation that they achieved. Already at the beginning of the nineteenth century, the Jesuit Amstadt[7] observed the great difficulties that existed in disseminating a cooperativist mentality among the Germans, especially the evangelicals, despite the fact that they were small farmers, with every prospect for gaining success in cooperativism. The cohesion of the immigrants was more the result than the cause of their economic situation. Group consciousness was mediated by a "consciousness" of class.

It does not seem to us, for example, that the immigrants who formed large enterprises felt any embarrassment about paying their compatriots as wage employees (see the case of sales and the role that owners played). Class tension was introduced among German immigrants as the result of the inevitable economic development in a

---

5 E. Willems, *Assimilação e Populações Marginais no Brasil*, Estudo Sociológico dos Imigrantes Germânicos e seus Descendentes (1940), 267.

6 Karle, *Vom deutschen Volkstum am Letzten Winkel der Welt* (1939), 57.

7 Translator's note: This was an attempt to organize German immigrant farmers into agricultural cooperatives.

precapitalist system in the absence of a sufficiently abundant native population to serve as an army of less qualified laborers. It is notable that in regions where the immigrants had less of a presence in the evolving society, such as in Chile or in the Rio de Janeiro–São Paulo axis, the schism of classes took place on the margins of the group that could maintain itself as elite.

Nevertheless, on an ideological level, the class schism did not become as obvious and noticeable as it was in reality because of the short time that the immigrants were in this situation; they still had not created a historical memory. That also explains why, among the subaltern classes, Kliewer's research observed an ideology of social harmony.[8] Evangelical German Argentinians appear, in the research of A. Buendig, as bearers of the same ideology.[9] That would also explain the absence of a strong workers' tradition in working-class cities colonized by Germans (Blumenau, Joinville, and in part, São Leopoldo). It's understandable that someone who has just taken a loss caused by a process of socioeconomic change might have good reasons for being conservative. The question here is analyzing what we could call the "trauma of proletarization," which would have a subversive effect on class consciousness. In this way, German immigrants, as a group, represent the defense of the class interests of their elite. Consequently, this defense is not contested even by Latin Americans of German extraction who were marginalized in the process of stratification in the areas of greatest German presence.

Not all Latin Americans of German extraction belong to a transplanted church, but all transplanted Lutheranism is composed of immigrants and their descendants. Thus it's appropriate to ask how those churches expressed themselves in relation to those interests that were represented practically by only one class. To quote J. Held, "Lutheranism in Latin America is not only traditional and liberal but rests on the premises and ideals of one social class."[10]

---

8 Cf. Gerd Uwe Kliewer, "Uma Comunidade Evangélica frente aos Problemas Sociais e à Atuação Sociopolítica da Igreja," *Estudos Teológicos* 17, no. 1 (1977): 16.

9 Buendig, *Iglesia Evangélica*, 132ff.

10 J. Held, "La Contribución Luterana a la Misión de la Iglesia en América Latina," in *Cuadernos de Teologia*, 1974, notebook 2, p. 100ff.

The Chilean episode is highly instructive for interpreting the situation of those transplanted churches. In a certain way, it's an ideal case. In Chile, there was a political change surpassed in importance only by what happened in Cuba. In that sociopolitical explosion, the Iglesia Evangélica Luterana en Chile took paradigmatic positions. Suddenly, the political situation was subverted, and for the first time in Chilean history, the bourgeoisie lost its rights. German Chileans were part of that bourgeoisie. After the election of Allende in 1970, Frenz, who had been elected president of the Iglesia Evangélica Luterana en Chile that same month, with similar electoral difficulties, predicted that the Marxist government would be a catastrophe for German Chileans, a fact that was confirmed in the Allende period with the emigration of 10 percent of them, as a result of the agrarian reform. After two and a half years of the Marxist government, a period that a member of Iglesia Evangélica Luterana en Chile called the "night of nightmares," the position of the church would reveal itself to be unequivocal. By the way, that same member of the Iglesia Evangélica Luterana en Chile later became president of the dissident Iglesia Luterana en Chile. Frenz correctly interpreted the spirit of the parishioners in Santiago when he told them in a sermon, in that fateful September of 1973, the month of the coup d'état against Allende, "I know that most of you are feeling good, that you're full of joy, because there's a new hope for the future. . . . For many of you it seems that a new day has exuberantly dawned."[11] Through the military, the bourgeoisie took back the reins of the situation and was in no mood to let go. Hence the involvement of the pastors of the Iglesia Evangélica Luterana en Chile with exiles, the unemployed, prisoners, and their families was enough to cause the members to break with their pastors, who were led by Frenz. Within a complex process, the schism revealed itself clearly: pastors versus laypeople. However, this schism concealed the true struggle taking place between the interests of the working class and those of the bourgeoisie. At the time, of the fifteen pastors of the Iglesia Evangélica Luterana en Chile, none came from the churches they

[11] Translator's note: Frenz was well aware that many of his parishioners opposed Allende and favored a military coup.

served. This characterizes the separation of these pastors from certain obligations, given that they were almost all foreigners. Their interests were not directly tied to any social class. Frenz summarizes, "We pastors are not affected by these current measures. We have almost nothing to lose." They were, therefore, so unconstrained that they could, at a given historical moment, make a gesture of solidarity with the people persecuted by the coup d'état. That small gesture, mediated by the Iglesia Evangélica Luterana en Chile, produced within that church body a class struggle so heated that, bizarrely, it occurred between pastors and laypeople. Let us now consider two texts that masterfully clarify the two positions. The first text is from Schaper, a layperson and future president of the dissident group:

> While the Popular Unity government was in power, Lutheran families were living with great anxiety and bitterness. The work of generations . . . was lost through violent and illegal occupations . . . tolerated and even endorsed by the authorities. . . . In those years, terrible for us, there were many violent deaths . . . suicides and emigration, with loss of all material possessions. It was in this period that we saw Mr. Frenz and many of our foreign pastors accompanying and sharing amicably and ostentatiously with the authorities and forgetting to attend to the necessities of the Lutheran communities that they had come to serve in Chile. . . . When our night of nightmares ended with the disappearance of the Marxist government and the return to order, discipline, and the respect for human rights and property rights in Chile, our foreign pastors, with Mr. Frenz at their head, launched themselves, with all the freedom that their status as pastors and churchmen gave them, into helping their friends from the former regime, forming Committees for Refugees and Committees for Peace. . . . Only a government of such high Christian and humanitarian inspiration as that presided over by General Pinochet could remain silent out of respect for the ecclesiastical investiture of those from whom the criticisms came.

The second text is from Frenz, in the sermon that he gave in the month of the coup d'état: "How can you be so happy when hundreds of thousands of Chileans are losing all the hopes they envisioned? Don't you realize that they will construct a future for themselves on ruins and tears, on the hopes and yearnings of the workers?"

Up to a certain point, these two texts are similar. They denounce similar facts and exalt a social class. The basic difference is that they refer to classes with opposing interests. These class interests were so strong that 93 percent of church members left the Iglesia Evangélica Luterana en Chile and formed new church bodies. Therefore, in the declaration of the principles of incorporation that brought together 85 percent of the members of the former church, when it is stated that the church must be composed of laypeople, it is specifically saying that the church must be of and for the Chilean bourgeoisie.

If the parallels that we establish between the transplanted Lutheran churches of the Southern Cone are valid, we will find the same tendency in Brazil and in Argentina, with a few particularities. In Brazil, the more accentuated stratification among German Brazilians disguises the clarity of the opposition of interests, also because there isn't the same kind of break between laypeople and pastors. But at the same time, the difficulty the church has in accompanying the process of proletarization of the (German) colonist is transparent. The mission to the outskirts of the cities is both an effort in that direction and a confession of incompetence in carrying out that work by a church that, for example, has its sanctuary in the center of the city and has its members on file. Other efforts run up against parochial structures and stubborn ministerial uniformity (which is different from ministerial unity). Such structures and uniformity are what determines for whom and where ministry is to be done.

II. The Ethnocultural Determinant

As we have observed, Latin Americans of German origin in the Southern Cone passed through a stage of political marginality but went on to occupy a central place in this dependent capitalist society. Their ascendancy is due to an economic factor. That the economic determines the political is an old lesson of capitalist society.

That economic—and therefore political—influence cutting through Latin American society determined the church's shape to a certain extent; the church developed in a way that favored class interests, represented by the dominant ideology. However, that divisive influence did not lead German Brazilians historically into ethnocultural dissolution in the same proportion in which its integration, on the level of class, occurred in economics and politics. There is no cultural melting pot. But why?

It seems possible to establish an inverse relation between these two elements: economic division is inversely proportional to cultural isolation. As we shall see later, this isolation is more noticeable as the group becomes more elitized. Formulating this idea programmatically, we can repeat H. Dohms's definition of the ideal of Germanism: "The more Brazilian these German Brazilians are on political issues, the more ethnic they are on German issues." If that were not true, how could one interpret the obvious abandonment of cultural elements on the part of marginalized German Brazilians? How could one interpret the disappearance of the mother tongue or its complete transmutation through the assimilation of the Portuguese lexicon within German grammatical structure on the part of marginalized groups in comparison with the zealous preservation of the German language among the elite? Both in Brazil (the Twenty-Fifth of July Society) and in Chile (the Chilean-German League), German societies catalyzed the elites around the maintenance of ethnocultural elements. For example, among German Brazilians in Bela Hu or in Chácara da Prefeitura [poor neighborhoods], one does not observe the same tendency. In this way, as we previously asked about how the church behaves in the face of the demands of class, it's appropriate to ask here, What is its position in the face of the ethnocultural component presented above?

In Esperanza, Argentina, a community of immigrants was formed in 1856. Its ethnocultural development followed almost perfectly that of all transplanted Protestantism—namely, the pastors came later, and the great motivation for their coming was education. School was confused with church. The conditions for the coming of one of those pastors were clear: he had to serve the local inhabitants; he had to construct a German-language school, where he would teach two hours per day; and he had to learn Spanish "in case it proved necessary." In Buendig's study, he summarizes the function of the church as an ethnic group's preservation of a cultural essential united by language and bringing an ideology into the faith. And if we want to know what ideology, let us allow a representative member of that community to express himself: "The function of the church is to maintain order; when the children go to church, they obey more."[12]

In Brazil, it wasn't much different when the tradition and language became almost "signs of the Church."[13] Once again, school came together with immigration, and ecclesiastical structures were built only on the level of education in the culture of origin, with their functions already established by their foundations. Education came to exercise upon development an influence that would be the envy of the church's slow or nonexistent growth. In RS (Rio Grande do Sul) alone, during the 1920s, the German-language schools experienced a growth of 75 percent, while other schools grew by only 20 percent. The first attempts at ecclesiastical formation in RS didn't even worry about concealing their ethnocultural function. While the Roman Catholic Church was becoming the "gravedigger of Germanism in Brazil,"[14] the opposite was happening with transplanted Lutheranism. Although the confessional bases were defined only by 1922, already half a century earlier there were ethnocultural definitions for the future Riograndense Synod, such as "Church and Germanism are linked to each other by life and by death." The formation of the synod, in another opinion, responded to the necessity for "strengthening of the German elements regarding custom and language."

The first unsuccessful attempt among non-Germans, dating from 1901, caused a tremendous fight.[15] Moreover, this would become quite understandable on the basis of a definition of mission that came out of this failure: "The mission of the church is directed to the soul of the

[12] Buendig, *Iglesia Evangélica*, 142.

[13] Cf. Martin N. Dreher, *Kirche und Deutschtum in der Entwicklung der Evangelischen Kirche Lutherischen Bekentnisses in Brasilien* (1975), 4.

[14] Willems, *Assimilação*, 243.

[15] Dreher, *Kirche und Deutschtum*, 106.

people (the German people, of course)."[16] And the task of the church is "the struggle for the maintenance of Germanism and its essence."[17] Whether an exaggeration or not, the fact is that those elements were constitutive in the formation of the synods that resulted in the Igreja Evangélica de Confissão Luterana no Brasil. In reality, that thought is not so strange even today, even after World War II with its undeniable consequences. According to research done in 1966 in the communities of Porto Alegre, Vera Cruz, and Blumenau, of the 210 members who were asked if they belonged to a Brazilian church or a German church, 86 opted for the first choice, but 81, an almost equal number, affirmed that they were members of a German church. Talk of a "consular church" is therefore not a cliché. The same researcher was surprised that the reasons given for alienation from the church were, first, the dogmas and, second, the worship service, contrary to his expectation that the reason would be the tradition.[18]

If the ecclesiastical tradition was created as a function of Germanism, it's fitting to ask, along with R. Alves, about the function of the perpetuation of the institution. And the response can only be "Try to maintain Germanism." Another question is also appropriate here. What marked the transplanted churches was the independent spirit of the communities. The institution came second. In the beginning, pastors were no more than functionaries looking for a meal, given that they didn't even participate in the meetings of church councils.[19] Could it be that the creation of the "church of pastors" did not serve well as a revitalizing apparatus for Germanism in the upper strata of the culture? And might it make more sense to get advice from ecclesiastical functionaries who had been initiated in reactivating Germanism? The Superior School of Theology also comes into the discussion. From its perspective, one can speak, with some certainty, about a "church of pastors." But the question remains.

---

16 Ibid.

17 Ibid.

18 Cf. Luetzow, "Was denken Sie ueber die Kirche?," *Estudos Teológicos* 7, no. 2 (1967): 74ff.

19 Dreher, *Kirche und Deutschtum*, 52.

We are thinking that the ecclesiastical institution became the catalyst of culture while this culture was threatened by the politico-economic incision that German Latin Americans were making in the surrounding society. In this way, in other words, the church took on the function of a social tumor. There's an interesting example that we'd like to present. It's well known that language constituted one of the basic bonds of culture. In Brazil, E. Fausel made an inventory of three thousand Portuguese words/expressions that German Brazilians had assimilated into German grammatical structure.[20] It's possible to verify the degree of assimilation of the Brazilian element in the various dimensions of the life of groups of German Brazilians based on the quantity of words assimilated in those dimensions. In a survey that we did of these three thousand words, we found the following approximate data: 43 percent of the words refer to matters in the immigrant colony; 25 percent correspond to exclamations and expressions of sociability; 15 percent refer to urbanism, transportation, and commerce; 10 percent to bureaucracy and politics; and 7 percent to the military and technology. This is what stands out. The surprising thing is that the proportion of words referring to religion does not exceed 0.6 percent, or eighteen words, all of which are nouns not involving relationships. And what is even more significant, we did not find any words drawn from Protestantism. Nine of them refer to Spiritism and another nine to Catholicism. According to Fausel, only four words were used frequently: "mother," "outdoor mass," "faith healer," and "macumba." The only possible conclusion is that the Lutheran church presented itself as the last cultural redoubt. *Culture* is thus no longer the term, since culture assumes a dynamic process of the intersection of two individuals, with their beliefs and values in a concrete material reality. The maintenance of that German folklore/culture, in a European frame of reference, on the one hand, is incongruent with Brazilian culture, and on the other, it fulfills a function of ideological justification for a social class that gets wrapped in this folklore/culture.

---

[20] Erich Fausel, *Die deutschbrasilianische Sprachmischung* (Berlin: Erich Schmidt, 1959).

The case of Chile is more drastic. Both in Brazil and in Chile, school motivated the church and required the presence of the first pastor "so that the children may receive Christian teaching and not grow up like the pagans" (Philippi). Thus the first community was founded in Osorno in 1863 under the auspices of the German society, which had preceded it. As the facts demonstrate, Frenz's formulation was not exaggerated when he said that German Chileans "were Lutheran, first because they were German, and second because they needed to preserve their Germanness." In the beginning, the church was not necessary except for maintaining the schools. Valparaiso had an evangelical community in 1857, and its high school marked the beginning of its existence. But despite the community's existence, the first worship service was celebrated there only in 1866, a decade later. The community of Concepción was happier. Founded in 1867, it had, from its inception, not only a school but pastoral services, though these were suspended from 1879 to 1889. During that time, however, the school functioned without interruption. The first ecclesiastical corporation, bringing communities together, was created in 1888 with the following express purposes: support for the formation of congregations in Chile, the calling of pastors and teachers from Germany, social assistance for orphans of German Chileans, and publication of the German Bible and books of hymns and devotions.

Only in 1968, after more than a century, was the first Spanish-speaking community accepted into the Iglesia Evangélica Luterana en Chile as the fruit of increased missionary and diaconal concern starting in 1965. When the coup occurred and sent the Iglesia Evangélica Luterana en Chile into crisis, there were already three Spanish-speaking communities, which, together with their pastors, became the focus of German Chilean hatred accumulated during the Allende years. A more accurate verification will show, in the case of Chile, how the struggle of races became intelligible as a parallel to class struggle, though in no way could those Spanish-speaking communities be considered Marxist strongholds. But they represented a permanently open canal for bloodletting by German Chileans, given that the Spanish-speaking communities were poor and had no reason to agree necessarily with the interests of the bourgeoisie. In short, it's sufficient to say the following: in the middle of 1974, the German Chilean newspaper *El Condor* published an invitation from the German Chilean League (!) to laypeople (read bourgeoisie) of the Iglesia Evangélica Luterana en Chile to discuss the role of pastors, to decide on the conditions for receiving Lutheran communities of "other languages" (the invitation was in German), and to evaluate the need to reestablish in the church its character as a German church body. In fact, all the German-language communities but one separated themselves from dissident activity. This one community was the church of Pastor Frenz, who played a pivotal role in the crisis; this community also engaged in relatively advanced ecumenical and diaconal work in which services in Spanish were slowly being introduced.

The ethnocultural aspect defines the Germanic character, which attributes status to those who already have class. Therefore, the tendency of the transplanted churches as the last cultural redoubt is to be self-isolating, and since this isolation tends to become ruptured, thus requiring a position of solidarity with the subaltern classes, the result is schism and purification. That explains the inevitable frustration of any attempt to change the church on the basis of the galvanizing symbols of its culture/folklore (liturgies, hymns, new ways to worship, vestments, etc.). In this way, the old dream of the transplanted churches, expressly manifest in the fourth Latin American Lutheran Congress in 1965 in Lima, comes completely undone. This dream, constantly revived, is that of offering to Latin America Lutheranism's rich theology, its liturgical heritage, and its historical position as the facilitator of ecumenism. In truth, this is far from the facts, which show that those elements, especially the liturgy, serve not as an opening but rather, on the contrary, as self-isolation. Lutheranism's contribution will be even less when the class interests at its heart are clarified. Höferkamp called attention to the profound theological alienation of the Lutheran churches, whose heritage was totally lost amid its European raiment and could not be reflected upon because it was accompanied by a banker's pedagogy, which is always intrinsic to that feeling of theological superiority.[21]

[21] Höferkamp, in a lecture given at EST in January 1977 on the occasion of the Regional Consultation of the Lutheran World Federation.

Therefore, the ethnocultural dimension is complementary to class divisions. The politico-economic and ethnocultural aspects constitute the trees that anchor the mangrove swamp in which the transplanted churches find themselves.

II. The Church as a Creature of the Word of God: Reevaluation of the Doctrine of the Two Kingdoms

Thus far, we have seen the way the transplanted churches reproduce (with)in themselves the demands of society and are thus creatures of society. Given our tradition, which defines the church as a creature of the word of God, how are we to understand that state of affairs? It's interesting to turn to the author of that formulation, who is none other than a monk named Luther, who, understanding the church of his time as contradicting that same definition, became the leading spokesman for one of the most violent ecclesiastical schisms. He wasn't motivated by purism, since he recognized that there would always be two churches within the necessary catholicity—one of God and the other of the devil—and that only Christ could distinguish them.[22] However, that fact does not exempt the Christian from trying to discern exactly what "leads to Christ" by defining the place of the church. In order to have this discernment and make the very concept of the church more practical, one must try to situate this concept within Luther's system of the two governances. From that starting point, the clarity of Luther's ecclesiological positions becomes quite understandable. This approach should also shed some light on the situation we are dealing with. We're going to attempt to present a Lutheran reevaluation of the two kingdoms (governances) with regard to what is important for defining the church.

Reality presents two dimensions or competencies. An earthly one includes reason, justice, equity, the sword, institutionality, laws, order, and so on. The other dimension includes revelation, justification, the Word, faith, eruption, grace, and so on. Those two competencies, known as governances, make up the theological order of reality and of history. Whereas the first dimension describes

[22] Cf. WA 38, 545.

the material and massive (Segundo), social and empirical (Tillich) aspects, the second dimension imposes the essential (Tillich), minoritarian (Segundo), and spiritual (Luther) aspects. God is Lord of both governances through the mediation of Christ, though it is in the spiritual, according to Luther, that Christ is "expressly known." To the first dimension belongs the "sociological" attribute, and to the second, the "psycho-logical," if we take the latter term in its etymological and contradictory sense, though we could also think of it as "theo-logical" in a more restricted sense. Luther considered the clear distinction between those governances to be decisive while nevertheless emphasizing their independence. For example, in 1523, he wrote the following: "Therefore, we must carefully separate those two governances and maintain both. . . . In this world, one doesn't exist without the other." The spiritual governance is the pneumatic-anthropological and essential domain, where it possesses the directing act of the Spirit (and the spirit), whereas the earthly governance deals with things referring to the second table of the law: organization and maintenance of social, political, and economic life (the empirical level). However, if one is concerned about methodological dualism, Luther does not admit any moral antagonizing, since, in the perspective of the kingdom of God, both dimensions are included.

Now, if the church understands itself correctly, it does not identify with the spiritual governance but instead occupies a position of intermediation. I find that the church was well defined by Tillich as "the form of grace," which involves two aspects: the sociological and the theological.[23] As the "form of grace," it is not proper for the church to assume functions of the state, as happened in the Constantinian era. That confusion of governances was the central error that Luther pointed out with respect to papal Rome, and he found the same seed of confusion in the enthusiasts.[24]

---

[23] Paul Tillich, *Für und wider der Sozialismus*, 57; Tillich, *Systematic Theology* (Chicago: University of Chicago Press, 1963), 3:165.

[24] Here we would have to enter into another discussion. I think that Luther correctly interpreted, theologically, the confusion of governances, but he considered only its social effects and did not identify it at its origins.

Maintaining the methodological distinction of the governances was as important for Luther as was the creative situation of the encounter between the two. In that context, the church defines its mediating function with specificity, though that wasn't the only mediating instance (there is still the individual and eschatology). While not being identical to spiritual governance, the church is the representation or service dimension of spiritual governance. Therefore, in Luther's view, the church does not constitute power or authority. Service to the world is also service to God (*Gottesdienst*), and the Christian must not, in any way, fail to participate in worship/service of God, since "everything must be of service; where it is not of service, it amounts to robbery."[25] In its conformity to the world, the *societas ecclesia* is part of earthly governance (together with political and economic institutions and the family) in the material and sociological order. That incarnation, or that linking of governances, exists only as a function of the very separation of the two governances. That takes place under the threat that a distorted spirituality might want to put the world inside a chapel (the enthusiasts) and also under the risk that the material governance might award itself a supernatural power, tyrannically impeding the people from making their own history. Moreover, it is Luther himself who says, "Any tyranny on earth is always a transcendent reality."[26] Hence the church has a task to perform. Again we cite Luther: "Preachers who don't tell the princes and lords about their errors are corrupt and useless, are not with Christ, and are not faithful to him." And Luther adds, with regard to those who are supposed to make such denunciations, that they would not be acting subversively. On the contrary, "it's much more subversive when a preacher does not denounce the errors of the authorities. It has the effect of making the people angry and indignant and also strengthens the evil of the tyrants. In this way, the preacher himself becomes an accomplice."[27]

The church reconstitutes itself in the critical moment of the "copulation" of the two governances. This moment erupts like a *kairos*,

[25] WA 12, 470.
[26] Ibid.
[27] WA 31/1, 197f.

qualifying the sociological development as evolutionary and massive. Therein also lies the definition of the continuity of the church, as well as its sacramentality. For this reason, the Confessio Augustana VII can define the church as perpetual in the continuity of its sacramentality, this latter term being understood as the presence of the sacraments and the Word. Thus the church is a means of spiritual presence in material reality.

Our theological heritage demands from us a profound theological respect, a consideration for matter in its relative autonomy in historical development and in the laws that move it. One must take into account that "everything happens necessarily," as the author of *Servo Arbitrio*[28] put it. The history of salvation occurs out of absolute internal necessity but not by coercion or external obligation. This leads to a series of consequences for the church. The first of these, and the most general, is the one that Tillich points out—namely, that no ecclesiological analysis can be self-sufficient, disdaining the social aspect, and neither can a social analysis be reduced to itself, denying the sacramental dimension of the church, that dimension being sociologically impossible to tabulate. This is the quality that the spiritual governance attributes to the church and that defines the church as a creature of the word of God[29]—that is, as the *logos* incarnate.

III. The Confusions of Governances

The church is the dynamic environment through which flows the creative and minoritarian spiritual essence, describing the world in the form of a Word of announcement and denunciation (P. Freire), in anticipation of the kingdom of God. As a consequence, the church materializes in an institutional form. On the basis of this concept, we can understand the role of the distorted church in the confusion of the governances. If the church can be the copulative moment of conception, it can also be the opposite, prostituting and degrading itself. In the first case, love emanates from it; in the second case, egotism and tyranny. The form in both cases remains the same, but the

---

[28] Translator's note: Westhelle is referring to Luther's *On the Bondage of the Will.*
[29] WA 2, 430.

essence is the opposite. Within the interpretations that we adopt, the church is the cause of the confusion when it permits form to ideologize its substance—contrary to what occurs with the Church of Christ when its essence demands a form.

It was this confusion that Luther identified in Rome, which was more concerned with coercion and administration than with opening itself for that creative and essentially ecclesial contact between the people of God and the Word. It's the same theologian who brought the Bible to the people and established it as the place of the church, the creature of the Word: "Since the Word cannot exist without the People of God, neither can the People of God exist without the Word of God."[30] There the church is formed, and there arises the need for the institution. The institution, however, does not always remain faithful to its original configuration but assumes an autonomous formation or, at times, is designed for other motives. There are three classic types of ecclesiastical interpretations in the history of Protestantism. One is liberalism, with its support for two moralities, one political and the other religious, which is nothing less than displacing the church from its position of mediation to a position of separation. The second type is Pietism, which establishes the contacts and the responsibilities of the governances but does not take into due consideration the implications of earthly governance and its social continuity; instead, it falls into the privatism of the God-individual relation. A third type is the theocratic, which defends the prevalence of the church over the state so that the church becomes the conscience of the state, a situation that leads to eschatological haste.

Those positions are repeated, in a certain way, in Latin American ethno-Lutheranism, though with certain distortions. One of these distortions comes from the pastors-laypeople relationship. Thus far, we have referred to that relationship only in the case of Chile at a specific historical moment. That relationship can present itself as a fissure only in very particular situations, since pastors are not the ones who maintain the church of the pastors ideologically, administratively, or financially. It is maintained, on the one hand, by the

[30] WA 50, 659.

members, locked into an ideology, and on the other, by the churches in the First World. The pastors move in the narrow space between these two interests. These interests, moreover, are not really in conflict. But this character of bilateral dependence is also responsible for the sometimes brutal rupture between members and ecclesiastical functionalism, a phenomenon that has its origin in the formation of the ecclesiastical institution, which happened long after the founding of the communities (often without pastors) and that even today has not succeeded in imposing a character of catholicity but instead remains like an archipelago of isolated islands—that is, the churches.

Thus far, we have observed the way the German Latin Americans of the transplanted churches defended their interests in the ecclesiastical structure. The first part of this essay tried to show how Lutheranism performed a transplant that had strong symptoms of rejection and avoided incarnation, the result being a confusion of the governances. The church shaped itself according to its social form—that is, according to politico-economic and ethnocultural factors. Its form, while obeying those factors, did not result from their nature. That means that the Word-people encounter was obstructed, and the ecclesiastical structure, starting with the communities, served to promote an ideology of race and class. And we, ecclesiastical servants (pastors), cannot escape from this process. In a certain way, we are an "elite service" that succeeds in improving upon this ethnocultural self-isolation and in justifying, perhaps even with angry criticisms, a social class that is privileged and well represented in the Igreja Evangélica de Confissão Luterana no Brasil. It appears that exactly this analysis of the politico-economic and ethnocultural determinants needs to be considered by the groups of laypeople and pastors who have not considered it.

There is one other position, represented almost exclusively by ecclesiastical functionaries, without support from laypeople. It's true that in this position, an understanding of the problem discussed above does exist and that there is support for a theology of incarnation (or reincarnation). This position is similar to the one taken by almost all the pastors in Chile. It becomes possible exactly because of that fissure that exists between the ecclesiastical cadres and the German

Latin American communities (members). This is a schismatic symptom. But schism still doesn't mean that an ecclesial alternative exists. If it's true that this schism caused the rupture of the Iglesia Evangélica Luterana en Chile, it's even more true that the rupture didn't consist of a simple purge of pastors, because a few years before, some communities started doing popular ministry (i.e., outreach to the poor). This was the stay and support for the continuity of the church. And if it is true that the church as an ecclesiastical institution encouraged that new ministry, it's also true that the church could do so only within a favorable political framework that restricted the power of the bourgeoisie. When the government fell, the church also fell. But the popular ministry that the church was doing preceded all that and did not stop with the coup. In saying this, we are not attempting to emphasize anything except the fact that *the church, as an institution, develops within its own walls the relations of domination existing in society*. This tendency, involving the interests that assert themselves in the church, has already been described above. The result of this tendency is to render innocuous any attempt to transform ecclesiastical structure without the consent of the ruling politico-economic order. In the same way, equally innocuous is any attempt to make a cultural revolution in the church with the plan of transforming it through the galvanized symbols of cultural elements like liturgy, vestments, hymns, and so on. Such elements, being the last stronghold of culture/folklore, become an effect and not a cause. The critique of this position (dealt with in this paragraph) can also be compared with the system of the two governances.

The incarnation of the Word in the people defines the configuration of the institutional church. This is what we call popular ministry. Whenever ecclesiastical policy/politics puts itself ahead of pastoral ministry, rather than being a consequence of it, a confusion of competencies results, even if it is done with the purest motives and the most enlightened analyses. An ecclesiastical policy/politics as a principal action leads to confusion, since it does not take into consideration that the institution in which this policy/politics is being done is a mere detail of the political and economic system. Therefore, any political militancy must be directed toward the center of the system, and this becomes the task of a church supported by its pastoral ministry. In short, pastoral ministry and politics occupy different places and cannot be confused, unless one believes that the tail wags the dog. The institutional church remains determined by concrete reasons and will change as a reflex of the way the people of God act on earth. It is not as an institution that the church anticipates the kingdom of God, and neither is it as a state based on law. There remains the question formulated by the Lutheran bishop of Soweto, M. Buthelezi, who is Black: "How can the Church be free if its people are slaves?" My answer is that ecclesiastical politics is a concept that needs to be reduced, even in this electoral year, to secondary importance. Pastoral ministry needs to be carried out in the church as the service-worship dimension of spiritual governance.

We wouldn't want to close with this deprecatory evaluation, even if a new perspective arises from it. This is not an *orienting* theology but, rather, a theology *oriented* by the signs of the church that emerges at our margins and even beyond our rigid limits. The decisive point really is that this church that is being born is *not worried about respecting* these limits and is instead establishing other limits. It's appropriate to refer once more to those communities of the Iglesia Evangélica Luterana en Chile that guaranteed their continuity and were the fruit of popular ministry. But it's also fitting to recall examples from the Igreja Evangélica de Confissão Luterana no Brasil. Some have been mentioned on other occasions. And finally, we recall those signs that don't fit within the limits of the Igreja Evangélica de Confissão Luterana no Brasil. They are, after all, the places where the Word incarnates the people and where the sacrament happens—where those who make public use of the word, as representatives of the people of God, cannot be silent in the face of a transcendental tyranny by the princes and lords who subvert the people and provoke the people's anger.

We are not talking about the politicization of the church; nor do we intend that it align itself with a political party. On the contrary, there are signs that the church exists precisely where it succeeds in overcoming the limits of class and ethnicity and in refusing to serve racist and bourgeois interests. Therefore, these two *concomitant* openings (race and class) are the indispensable condition for the transplanted churches to be the Church. This is valid at least for the places where German Brazilians are not an absolute majority, as in a few places in Espírito Santo and Santa Catarina. What we have is an opening and not a closing, as has been supposed. It's an opening to the people of God, since it seems inevitable that those who plan to be simply people rather than people of God will exclude themselves. For example, at no time was the schism in Chile proposed by the Chilean communities (or their pastors) engaged with refugees, the unemployed, prisoners, and so on. These communities and pastors always sought to avoid the schism. After it happened, they asked Frenz if there was any chance of reunification. Frenz, already expelled from Chile, responded that the question was whether the unification would happen at the expense of the gospel. It is in this spirit that we understand M. Buthelezi's proposal for new confessional barriers, for a confession that unmasks the pseudounity of the church and gets rid of it through the questions that confession elicits. This confession is emerging. And in our view, it implies, in the case of Latin American ethno-Lutheranism, a break with the fundamental barriers we have presented. In the case of the Igreja Evangélica de Confissão Luterana no Brasil, because of various factors, this is also taking place in contradiction to an ecclesiastical configuration. Three factors appear important, since, in a disguised manner, they represent those barriers that we have mentioned: (1) ministerial uniformity (by extension, the phase that adjusts to this conformity), (2) parochial and communitarian structure (the locale of the church, its membership files, its monthly finances, etc.), and (3) formal education, when it's a function of ministerial uniformity.

Whatever emerges does so on the margins as a strange element within that complex. But it emerges . . . like a flower reluctant to [accept] good treatment, vulnerable to greenhouses, and uncontrollable in its germination.

THE DIVERGENCE BETWEEN LUTHERAN THEOLOGY AND LIBERATION THEOLOGY

Fiat justitia et percat mundus.

—Martin Luther

I. Suspicion: The Cliché of Divergence

One can say that, with only rare exceptions, the interaction between liberation theology and Lutheran confessional theology[1] (as well as other confessional theologies) has fallen into two extremes. On the one hand, there has been mutual disdain, which frequently conceals an odious reaction of one against the other. On the other hand, one can also observe an emotional fascination with liberation theology. In the second case, liberation theology is seen as a source of sacrificial expiation for a theological conscience overburdened with guilt and lost in the political and cultural ambivalences of the late phase of capitalism. In this way, it is becoming attractive to seek clarity in the social *manifestations* of sin on the other side of class struggle, in sexist discrimination, or in a darker epidermic coloration. While the

Originally published in *Estudos Teológicos* 26, no. 1 (1986): 37–58.

[1] Both terms are used here in a broad sense. Just as there are various theological factions within Lutheranism, there are also many "theologies" of liberation. I take as my starting point only the common distinction between a theology that gravitates around the doctrine of justification and one that is an intentional reflection on praxis.

attitude of mutual disdain breaks the communicative flow, the emotional fascination is followed by anti-intellectualism.

Although those two tendencies apparently offer mutually exclusive options, they are not at all incompatible. At times, a profound disdain for proposals coming from liberation theology is disguised by a sympathetic posture in regard to some themes that, because of the emphasis they receive, have reoccupied a place in theological discourse. That sympathy, therefore, is not directed toward the properly theological content of liberationist reflection but toward matters like poverty, justice, violence, dependency, marginality, and so on. When, however, one seeks a confrontation on matters traditionally central to theology and particularly when methodological questions are at issue, a real fear arises that confessional chastity is going to be prostituted. The dominant tendency—and it's even a cliché—is to say that liberation theology does not take seriously the reality of sin and that liberation theology reduces the universal condition of sin to its socioeconomic manifestations. And who would argue against the Christian concept that we are sinners and find ourselves before God under equal conditions and with equal need for the divine grace by which we are justified independent of our merit or the quality of our sins?

According to this argument, liberation theology has an ingenuous vision of the human condition and wants us to believe that sin can be conquered through political activism, solidarity with the poor and oppressed, construction of a socialist society, and so on. And, finally, one hears the coup de grace from the sympathetic executioner: "I am in favor of liberation, but it must be a radical liberation that delivers us from the most profound form of slavery, which is our sinful nature. And in that way, all the particulars of oppression will be overcome as good works flow from a genuine faith, the way a good tree produces good fruit."[2]

With that argument, liberation theology is relegated, at best, to the condition of the appendix to Lutheran theology. Liberation theology

---

[2] This position arose in evangelical circles, but now it is also appropriated by the Vatican. See the document from the Congregation for the Doctrine of the Faith, "Instructions on Some Aspects of the Theology of Liberation," 4:12–14.

might be a sort of updated edition of Luther's sermons on good works and considered legitimate as long as it assumes methodologically the doctrine of justification.

One could move from that critique to a presentation of the theoretical condition of liberation theology, reveal various problems in their various manifestations, and show how that critique often presupposes a distorted understanding of that theology. However, instead of an apology, I propose an examination of the argument underlying the critique mentioned. More important than the triviality with which liberation theology is presented is the manner in which that critique is articulated. Therefore, I make clear the suspicion[3] with which I'm operating: to the extent to which the critique of liberation theology caricatured above is representative of the Lutheran theological posture, this posture is all too eager to speak *formally* about *simul justus et peccator* and all too lacking in a recognition of the particular *content* of sin and justification. Lutherans with any grasp of theology know by heart that the discernment between law and gospel is the cornerstone of the theological art. But such discernment runs the risk of falling back into an abstract formalism.

Such formalism causes the transition from law to gospel at the expense of a differentiated and complex conception of law. In the formal schema of the law-gospel relation, the law becomes an abstract support for affirming the necessity of divine grace against the background of the universality of the sinful condition of humanity. Schematically, the formalization of the argument can be described by the following preposterous syllogism:

[3] I am not suggesting that the heuristic merits of the hermeneutic of suspicion that I am applying in this preliminary discussion justify the development of a theological argument. I want only to insist that the hermeneutic of suspicion offers a corrective to theologies that for a long time have been indifferent to the great contribution by the sociology of knowledge (from Marx to Mannheim to Scheler to Habermas)—that is, that the perception of daily reality and the representative function of common language are not a vulgarization of theoretical and conceptualist language but the expression nearest the social origins that condition knowledge.

1. The particular experience of sin makes us aware that the law always accuses (*lex semper accusat*).
2. But sin is the universal human condition in such a way that the law reveals the fall of the human being *in general*, from which only divine grace can save.

II. The Gospel Brings Us the Justifying Word of God

The transition from point 1 above to point 2, the leap from the particular and concrete content of sin to its abstract and universal affirmation, is, in my understanding, the crucial issue. In truth, that is not an original observation. Since Albrecht Ritschl and Karl Holl, Lutheran theology has insisted, with varied emphasis, that the leap to the universal also requires a return to the particular, but that return (which can be called *Lebensführung*, or personal love) has been expressed only in categories of transcendental idealism, which also denies the socioeconomic and cultural determinations of the particular experience of sin and of its rectification, in favor of an abstract Christian freedom acquired before God (*coram deo*).[4]

The Lutheran renaissance in the twentieth century, especially since Werner Elert, attempted to articulate the question of the particularity of sin in social existence by using the positive conception that Luther had of the civil use of the law (*usus civilis legis*). Luther's conception encouraged the development of a Lutheran social ethic that was, on the one hand, realistic and, on the other, conservative in the precise understanding of that term.[5] As a result, the orthodox Lutheran separation between dogmatic and ethical was restored. While the dialectic of law and gospel developed in the strict relationship of the theological use of the law (*usus theologicus*) with the gospel, the social ethic was founded on the nondialectical but positive principle of the civil use of the law while doing without any correlation with the gospel

[4] And that same criticism of the liberal solution applies as well to the conservative solution, which, though having the merit of recognizing the particular character of the sin, inflates its ethic with an individualist moralism that is abstract and foreign to the concrete conditions of human existence.

[5] See Simon S. Maimela, "God's Creative Activity through the Law" (PhD diss., Harvard, 1978).

on the sociopolitical level. The conservative principle of that ethic—which, not coincidentally, developed under the political hegemony of Nazism—was the logical consequence of the attempt to define human society on the basis of a legal concept established as the "order of creation" (*Schöpfungsordnung*), which, consequently, eliminates from the civil order the presence of a principle of newness, transformation, or redemption. The ethical maxim was the preservation of a supposed civil "order" and not its renovation.[6] The civil use of the law as a basic and unique category for analysis and definition of society creates a stable and ideal image (what should be) that floats over social instabilities and denies them. Such a negation and exclusion of the *novum* from historical and social processes in theological reflection was normative for medieval societies, with their relatively stable hierarchical structures, in which the ideal of the preservation of order was the only alternative to chaos. That, for example, explains Luther's attitude in the Peasants War.

However, when that principle is applied to modern societies, in which the fluidity of the social and political order is constitutive of the very definition of the modern state, the principle of preservation becomes a reactionary principle resulting from a crass anachronism, something like analyzing the French Revolution by using, as your analytical instrument, the ideological presuppositions of the caste system of India. Later on in this essay, we will attempt to show what the difference between a premodern society (in which Luther formulated his concept of the civil use of the law) and a modern society implies theologically.

For now, it is sufficient to recognize that the problem implicit in the transition from point 1 to point 2 is that the civil use of the law, which determines the social and primary location of the concrete experience of sin, plays only a propaedeutic role, introducing us to the "real" dialectic of law and gospel. Epistemologically, it's as if the civil use of the law served as a staircase that takes us to the sunny terrace of theology; once this terrace is reached, this staircase becomes

---

6 See Werner Elert, *Morphologie des Luthertums II*, 2nd ed. (Munich: C. H. Becksche Verlagsbuch handlung, 1953), 37–49.

superfluous or, at most, like an instrument to be preserved for use by others. But that preservation aims only at creating the conditions for the climb to the dogmatic level. In other words, the civil order must offer sufficient tranquility and peace (*pax mundi*) so that the human being can rise above earthly worries and participate in the eschatological drama of salvation and condemnation.

We should then ask, Why the leap from the level of historical existence to the level of universal and transcendent dialectic of law and gospel? Why understand history as a neutral infrastructure on which the dialectic of law and gospel is imposed? Why that cynical vision of history in which the ideal of "peace" aims only to create sufficient silence so that the gospel may resound in the convicted conscience of adamic sin? Now, the answer is surprisingly simple: because the gospel is considered exclusively universal, related only to the theological use of the law—that is, as the good news for Jews and gentiles, slaves and masters, oppressed and oppressors, women and men, all in the same manner and in total indifference to the concrete content of their sin.

Therefore, if the gospel is universal and only universal, the good news contained in it must be completely irrelevant to the differentiated and particular content of the historical experiences of human beings. The Pauline discovery of the universality of the law, which makes all people equal before grace, opened the door to the expansion of Christianity, but at times, it also undercut the particular content of the preaching and ministry of Jesus.[7] For that reason, it is not strange that metaphors like "God is red," "She is Black," or "God is in solidarity with the poor" cause scandals similar to those caused by the Jesus of the synoptics in tying salvation and condemnation to the historical praxis of his contemporaries and not to the religious law then in force.

What is frequently called the "radicality of sin" means transforming it into an abstract category so that the task of the preacher or

7 For the argument that Paul also had to rethink the relation between law and gospel from the point of view of historical concreteness, see my article "Paul's Reconstruction of Theology: Romans 9:14 in Context," *Word and World* 4, no. 3: 307–19.

theologian is to recognize the sinner by his human condition without necessarily recognizing the sin.[8] It is unnecessary to point to the ideological character of such an understanding, since the universalization of sin occasions the privatization of the faith and the loss of the public character of a religion more or less limited to the cleansing of the bourgeois religious conscience.

In reducing the dialectic of law and gospel to a formal and universal level, the theological content of social and historical existence is lost, and consequently, the concept of salvation is emptied of any particular content. This is the cause of the divergence [or failed encounter] that we have referred to. The emphasis on the particular character of the evangelical experience constitutes the fundamental theological framework of the various theologies of liberation. The fear that such emphasis on the particular might offer religious sanction to movements of a social and political kind is completely justifiable, a fact that does not mean, however, that the particularization of the evangelical content implies or even propitiates such sanctions. To think in that way would be like a Christian accusing Jesus of having been born Jewish. If that's where the divergence is, it's important to turn to the possible roots of that divergence and then elucidate the supposed incompatibility between liberation theology and Lutheran theology.

III. Applying the Suspicion: A Text from Luther

This formal leap to the universal is not at all foreign to Luther, since he defines theology as the study of the relation between the human sinner and the God who saves and justifies.[9] The theological formalization of the historical immanence of human existence could be emphasized even further with the following quote: "Ideo nostra teologia est certa, quia ponit nos extra nos" (I think that our theology is correct because it puts us outside of ourselves).[10] But despite

[8] It is ironic to note that to speak about the universal condition of sin, one must presuppose an epistemological leap to a situation prior to the very fall of the human being, since only in this way can there be knowledge of the sinful condition without having sin itself distort that knowledge. This is gnosticism.

[9] WA 40/2, 238: "homo reus et perditus et deus iustificans vel salvator."

[10] WA 40/1, 589.

those affirmations, it is known that we do not find in Luther either an organized systematic theology or a coherent methodology. In truth, he had diverse methodological motives, and the formal law-gospel relationship (i.e., justification as passive justice) was not always the ruling principle of his theological thought, even if its central role in the body of his writings is undeniable.

An article by Luther will serve to illustrate that thesis. Its selection is arbitrary and aims only to show that Luther also knew how to reflect *theologically* without abandoning the particular content of sin, a fact that implies interesting observations of a methodological character. In that text, Luther reflects on a situation that he judges to be sinful, and he attempts in his treatise to instruct pastors so that they can preach on it. It is therefore a work of theological reflection (second order of discourse); it is not a homily (first order of discourse). Hence it could be a text suitable for elaborating the formalization of the law-gospel dialectic. But that is not what we're going to find.

This treatise, written in 1540, is entitled *Exortation to pastors so that they can preach against usury.*[11] The choice of that text is not due to its being the only one in which Luther can be accused of not being very "Lutheran" but is instead due to the theme discussed in it, an economic problem that shares characteristics with the current situation and creates a certain cognitive dissonance, which is part of the hermeneutic of suspicion. That dissonance is important, as it avoids a historicist reduction, given that the situation that Luther describes shocks us by being, in many respects, current and close at hand, thus breaking the comfortable distance of three and a half centuries. The question cannot be ignored or investigated only as part of an already outmoded historical past.

It's necessary to make clear, however, that the choice of that treatise is not made on the basis of the ethical argument developed in it, as if it were possible to seek in it an anachronistic criterion that would make it possible to justify a moral crusade against modern capitalism. It is correct that during Luther's life, the economic fundamentals of capitalism were taking seed in southern Germany and northern

[11] Luther, "An die Pfarrhern, wider den Wucherz zu predigen," WA 51, 331–424.

Italy. The usurer is, in fact, the primate of our *homo pecuniosus*, the modern capitalist. But that similarity serves only as an instrument of approximation between different historical periods. In truth, there is a certain historical irony in the way Luther condemns usury. The usurer begins to dismantle the mode of medieval production and sets in motion the transition to capitalism with its "periferal benefits," like the social function of taxes, social mobility, and political autonomy. Luther's argument can even be recognized as conservative, though today it might sound revolutionary.[12]

Luther, whom Marx called "the first German economist" (a comment that, by the way, would not offend the Reformer, for whom there was no saint not versed in economics and politics), expertly defines usury. He begins by destroying the popular notion that the usurer, by loaning money, in fact serves the people. Predating modern ideological criticism, Luther affirms, "The person who takes more or gains an advantage (from what he loans) commits usury. That is not called service but rather damage committed against one's neighbor; the same as robbing. Not everything that is called service and benefit to one's neighbor actually is, since two people who commit adultery with each other render to each other a great service and satisfaction. . . . The devil himself renders to his servants great and inestimable service."[13]

Making an appeal to reason to define, with the help of philosophy (Aristotle and Seneca, in particular), the concept of equity,[14] Luther seeks to demonstrate that the unjust character of usury resides in the "antinatural" (*wider die Natur*)[15] way of producing value. It's not that this is a supernatural form of producing value. Rather, it's the expropriation of value produced by someone else's work.[16] In this sense,

---

[12] In his moral evaluation, Luther does not recognize the fact that without the usurer, there would not be the transition to capitalism, since capitalism presupposes the accumulation of capital. And compared with the previous mode of production, capitalism represents an economic, social, and political advance. This is also a weakness in the excellent study by Guenther Fabiunke, *Martin Luther als Nationaloekonom* (Berlin: Akademie-Verlag, 1963).

[13] WA 51, 338–39.

[14] WA 51, 344. For Aristotle's argument, see *Treatises on Government*, book 1, chapter 10.

[15] WA 51, 360.

[16] WA 51, 351.

it's against nature, since it alienates from the worker the fruit of his interaction with nature. Luther already introduces here the fundamentals of the concept of surplus value. It's worth mentioning that the instrumental use of monetary value still did not imply ownership of the means of production, but Luther had the merit of recognizing elements of the basic structure of capitalism operative in finance capital.

Since this process of usury tends to raise the rate of expropriation of work, Luther was not shy about passing his verdict: "Even if we were not Christians, reason would tell us—just as it tells the gentiles—that a usurer is an assassin."[17] And after demonstrating by means of secular reason ("Let's save the theology for later"[18]) that usury is unjust, Luther directs himself to Christians and, particularly, to preachers who remain indifferent to the problem. By conniving with usury, such Christians share the inheritance of usurers: hell.

The gentiles were able to conclude, by means of reason, that a usurer is a thief and assassin. But we Christians honor the usurer so highly that we practically adore him for his money:[19]

> And the attack continues on the usurer, who finds himself comfortably seated on a chair when, rather, he should be hanged from the gallows and devoured by as many vultures as the florins he stole, if at least he had so much meat that so many vultures could divide it. Meanwhile, we hang petty thieves. . . . They are thrown into the dungeons while big thieves make a show of their gold and silk.[20] . . . Therefore, apart from the devil, there is no human enemy on earth greater than a miser and usurer because he wants to be God over all men. . . . A usurer and miser wants the entire world to die of hunger, thirst, misery, and want so that he can be lord of all and that all may receive from him as from a god and eternally be his servants.[21]

---

17 WA 51, 361–62.
18 WA 51, 344.
19 WA 51, 361.
20 WA 51, 362.
21 WA 51, 399–400.

The usurer is a master of deceit; "he passes himself off as a man of great piety, more merciful than God himself and more lovable than the mother of God." And Luther concluded, "Therefore, a usurer and miser is not a correct man; he's a wolfman more terrible than tyrants, assassins, and thieves, almost as malignant as the devil. Yet he doesn't look like an enemy; he seems more like a friend and citizen who belongs to the community and who, therefore, robs and kills with greater atrocity than an enemy. So since we decapitate and punish robbers and assassins, how much more should we punish, torture, curse, and decapitate all usurers."[22]

However, if we now expect Luther to pass from the particular situation of sin to its universal condition and declare usury to be a manifestation of original sin, which levels everything out, we're in for a surprise. He even considers that possible methodological trajectory and comments, "They say that the world would not exist without usury. This certainly is true, since there never was and never will be a government so strong and rigid that it could avoid all sin. And even if a government could do that, there would be original sin, the source of all sin. . . . But if, with this argument, usurers think they're exculpated, they'll see. . . . There is usury, but woe to the usurer."[23]

The preachers who don't dare speak against usury "turn their preaching office into a farce. . . . Such individuals cannot promote the gospel."[24] And the Reformer compares such preachers, who universalize their preaching to the point of being incapable of denouncing the usurer in particular—but only sin in general—to those who want to hold back a flood with a fence.[25] "Flood" is Luther's favorite metaphor for describing socioeconomic injustice and political anarchy.

The attentive reader might note, however, that Luther is focusing his criticism on only one *manifestation* of sin, so the justifying word of God could still be directed to the usurer as a person. From Holl[26]

---

22 WA 51, 421.
23 WA 51, 353–54.
24 WA 51, 409.
25 WA 51, 353.
26 Karl Holl, *Gesammelte Aufsätze zur Kirchengeschichte*, 3 vols. (Tübingen: J. C. B. Mohr, 1928–48), 1:246–50.

and Elert[27] to Althaus[28] and Heckel,[29] this has been the "official" interpretation of Lutheran ethics in the twentieth century. But things are different in this treatise by Luther. God is not only the enemy of usury (as the particular manifestation of original sin); God is the enemy of the usurer himself.[30] The usurer is called *de jure et de facto* a nonbeliever and idolater, a fact that brings Luther to exhort preachers not to accept the usurer as Christian.[31] The Reformer argues that usurers must be denied participation in the sacraments, as well as in the absolution of sins and in the Christian community.[32] Luther even suggests something that resembles a hierarchy of sins when he says, "On earth there is no greater enemy of man (except the devil) than a miser and usurer because he wants to be God over all men."[33] The sin denounced here is not that which could be called a "spiritual" or even personal sin but a sin with a social and economic character. The usurer is not the person who *thinks* that eternal salvation is gained through works; he *acts* so that it might be so. And the criterion that Luther offers for his *theological* judgment cannot be considered as having a purely dogmatic nature: "The usurer wants the whole world to die of hunger, misery, and lack."[34]

We have only one final question. If Luther's reflection envelops on the basis of historical particularities and if the criterion for what's legal and just is found through reason, can we call that a theological reflection? According to Luther, in order for it to be theological, it has to present the correlation and the discernment between law and gospel. But can one speak of a particular manifestation of the gospel? What Luther says is concise but still surprising for a premodern thinker who could not imagine that historical transformations and the appearance of the new in social processes were immanent

---

27 Elert, *Morphologie II*, 24, 36.

28 Paul Althaus, *The Ethics of Martin Luther* (Philadelphia: Fortress, 1972), 79.

29 Johannes Heckel, *Lex Charitatis* (Darmstadt: Wissenschaftliche Buchgesellscaft, 1973), 33 passim.

30 WA 51, 422.

31 WA 51, 368.

32 WA 51, 337–68.

33 WA 51, 396.

34 WA 51, 397.

in historical processes: "If our gospel is true light, it truly needs to shine in the darkness. And the darkness will not overcome it. If we don't want suffering, if we want a transformed world (*die Welt anders haben*), then we have to go out of this world (*zur Welt hin aus gehen*) or create a world that does what we or God wants."[35] And Luther adds, "The marvelous and omnipotent power and wisdom of God is such that it needs to be perceived and grasped in our midst (*hierin*)."[36]

IV. Reconstruction and Critique

That brief review of Luther's exhortation to pastors to preach against usury offers us a sufficient basis for arguing that, at least in this case, Luther does not make the methodological leap from the particular situation of sin to its universal condition so that the evangelical word can then be expressed. The good news is not presented as a forensic "yes" to all believers and sinners (*simul*) independent of the particular content of their sins. Faith and social existence are interlaced to such a point that the peremptory affirmation cannot be made: the usurer cannot have faith, and thus it is irrelevant how pious, confessing, and faithful a Lutheran Christian he may appear to be. In that practical situation, Luther does not presume that all sin can be reduced to the sinful condition before the gospel leaves, on this old world, the marks (*Spuren*)[37] of a new world. His theological reflection is based on a particular historical experience in which justice and sin are in an antithetical relation. This antithesis, discovered in the socioeconomic parameter of history (*sub specie mundi*), certainly finds in the doctrine of justification its dogmatic development on the level of universalities, in a totalizing and eschatological dimension that Luther called *geistliches Regiment*. But the history of the struggle between oppression and justice cannot be suppressed by the universal understanding of the relation between sin and justification. This relation explains the struggle, but without that struggle, no doctrine of justification is anything more than a formal and theoretical abstraction.

---

[35] WA 51, 409.
[36] WA 51, 412.
[37] WA 51, 412.

The usurer, to take this example, cannot be *simul justus et peccator* in the way Luther defined that simultaneity (as *totus justus et totus peccator*). That definition can be affirmed only eschatologically as a profession of faith that in the end, in the totality of the creative and redemptive activity of God, grace includes all condemnation, and the totality of sin does not subtract from the totality of grace. This is the faith that nourishes paradoxical hope. It is the mystery that must remain as such. But it is not appropriate to use that mystery to offer an analytical solution to particular problems.

All the paradoxical affirmations that abound in Luther's writings and in all doxologies are nothing more than ingenious linguistic creations used to break with finitude and to give voice to the depths of the experience of faith that are situated beyond what analytical concepts are capable of revealing. Those paradoxes are, therefore, appropriate for describing an eschatological reality that embraces everything. Paradoxical language, like poetry, escapes conceptualization and analytical reasoning, which, for this reason, have no operational value for describing the finite *cooperation* between God and human beings in the context of history, what Luther called *weitliches Regiment*.

By breaking the barriers of historical and categorical finitude, paradoxical language is intuitive, and its function in theology is fundamentally doxological; it's an act of praise to God, and in that act, all the barriers of daily life are believed to be overcome. Therefore, only doxologically can one affirm a totality of the *simul* Lutheran. This act of praise can never serve as an ideological disguise for historical barriers and struggles. Only in this way can one speak about justification by faith without turning it into a word of self-justification. Only in the doxological context, in which one is offering praise to God, does justification remain an act of divine grace in whose presence human words can be only words of praise. It is by this doxological means that the believer receives the grace to observe history and nature through the masks (*larvae*) of God.[38]

[38] Ulrich Assendorf, *Eschatologie bei Luther* (Göttingen: Vandenhoeck and Ruprecht, 1967), 246.

In the world, that total simultaneity of sin and grace does not exist except in real antitheses. From the historical point of view (*coram mundo*), one can affirm only a *simul partim justus simul partim peccator*. This doesn't mean abandoning the doxological function of paradoxical language in the relation between gospel and law (*usus thelogicus*, or what Heckel called *lex iustitiae universalis contra peccatum originalis*).[39] On the contrary, it means trying to maintain the distinction in Luther between the two "governances" (*qua Regimento*) precisely for the purpose of restoring the value of doxology and the clarity of ethical discourse while avoiding the same confusion that Luther detected in Roman Christendom and in the enthusiast wing of the Reformation. Rome made theologico-political discourse into doxological discourse, whereas the enthusiasts made doxological discourse into ethico-political discourse.

We are directing our criticism particularly against the theological leap that abandons the concrete and particular reality of sin even before the gospel has been proclaimed. Such criticism already implies that a careful distinction between the two uses of the law will make it necessary for the gospel not to be restricted to its eschatological correlation with the theological use of the law. The gospel needs to have a concrete and practical function that correlates with the civil or political use of the law so that its "marks" can be "perceived and understood in our (historical) midst." Therefore, we can conclude that the gospel, according to the structure of the "two governances doctrine"—characterized here as two complementary discourses, one doxological and the other ethico-political—requires a double function corresponding to the two uses of the law. One function is doxological, and the other is ethico-political. One could borrow Luther's categories for classification of the law and speak of a *munus theologicus evangelii* (theological function of the gospel) and a *munus civilis evangelii* (civil or political function of the gospel), though that doesn't mean that only the first properly belongs to theological discourse.

It's important to point out here that in theology, there has been interest in a category that correlates with the civil use of the law ever

[39] Heckel, *Lex Charitatis*, 21.

since Melanchthon defended the third use of the law—that is, the civil law restored by Christian values for the building of a just society. Werner Elert correctly emphasizes the disagreement between Luther and Melanchthon on that point.[40] But Elert is right for the wrong reasons. The problem implicit in the defense of the third use of the law in the context of Luther's theology is that it results in a theological incoherence—and not because it leads to synergism and to utopia, as Elert claims.[41] Elert exaggerates Luther's alleged opposition to Melanchthon's affirmation that the will of God is for humans to associate (*vult Deus esse consociationem*).[42] In this way, Elert disdains the emphatic notion that Luther had about divine-human cooperation in governing history.[43] The real problem with the third use of the law is that it makes historical and social transformations possible through the ethical action of those born again by divine grace (*renati et justificati*).[44] Usually, however, Luther does not connect conversion with the responsibility for preservation and renewal of the civil law.[45] It is in that context that there arises one of the most embarrassing problems for Lutheran social ethics in a period of rapid sociohistorical transformations—namely, either one follows Elert by affirming that the civil order provides only the means for compulsion and social preservation or one follows the Reformed model that H. Richard Niebuhr appropriately called "Christ, the transformer of culture."[46] That, then, is the impasse. Either one abandons Lutheranism on questions of social ethics or one accepts an essentially conservative social ethic whose maxim is the preservation of the social order as dictated by divine creation. But such an ethic is incapable of thinking of historical and social processes as dynamic and in permanent transformation.

---

40 Elert, *Morphologie II*, 26–36.

41 Ibid., 30–31.

42 Ibid., 31–51.

43 WA 18, 754.

44 Elert, *Morphologie II*, 26.

45 See Ulrich Duchrow, *Christenheit und Weltverantwortung* (Stuttgart: Ernst Klett, 1970), 496–98.

46 H. Richard Niebuhr, *Cristo e Cultura* (Rio de Janeiro: Paz e Terra, 1967), 223–65.

Althaus tried to avoid that impasse with the introduction of his third theological category situated between law and gospel. He called it "mandate" (*mandatum* or *Gebot*).[47] With this category, he intends to explain the transformation and renewal of the law (as *lex civilis*). The divine mandate renews the law and keeps it up to date with historical development. The concept of mandate allows for explaining how, through divine intervention (*quasi ex machina*), equilibrium and peace are reestablished in the sphere of history. Such a theological artifice is, however, no more than a *petitio principii*—that is, a hypothesis that functions in the argument as a demonstration aimed at explaining, *after* the historical emergence of popular revolutions and tyrannical conquests, how God, by means of a *sui generis* intervention, reestablishes the justice that is necessary and compatible with a new historical moment, given that the former pattern of justice has become obsolete.

This proposal suffers from two ills. First, by remaining faithful to Luther's silence regarding social and historical transformations, it contradicts Luther's conviction that the historical governance of God takes place through human cooperation with God (*cooperatio hominis cum deo*).[48] In this way, incapable of remaining indifferent to the historical development of modern societies, Althaus tries to explain them by an appeal to a supernatural cause. For Luther, that was not a problem, since he shared with his era the inability to recognize that history is a process in permanent transformation.

Second, there is no metaphysical need for requiring God to act in two different manners: salvation and preservation. Once again, Luther was spared from handling that issue; being incapable of conceiving of any legal development, neither did he need a special action by God to preserve or reconstitute the civil order.[49] For Luther, the

---

47 Paul Althaus, *The Divine Command* (Philadelphia: Fortress, 1966).

48 WA 18, 754.

49 Although Luther did not have a sociopolitical explanation for historical changes, he understood that God compels some individuals—*Wunderteute, viri heroici*—to carry out extraordinary acts in moments of historical crises. These heroes need not be Christian. See Assendorf, *Eschatologie*, 260; and Gustav Wingren, *Luther on Vocation* (Philadelphia: Muhlenberg, 1957), 92. The appeal to extraordinary individuals to explain historical changes only emphasizes the lack of historical consciousness in Luther.

preservation of human institutions was the highest objective of the civil order, and for that purpose, God will institute authorities.[50] Althaus, a post-Enlightenment theologian, renews Luther's conservatism by becoming a political reactionary who turns against changes and renewals in civil society when those changes and renewals are made necessary by the historical process itself.

V. Public Reason and Equity

The argument that I have been making—namely, that contemporary interpretation of Luther requires, for reasons of internal coherence, that a law-gospel relation be developed in two dimensions (one sociopolitical with historical content and the other doxological with eschatological content)—produces a critical problem. What is the criterion that permits the distinction and the relation between law and gospel in the sphere of history? If the gospel possesses a particular function and if the good news also has a particular historical content, one cannot say that the search for peace in the world is devoid of salvific content (*pax mundi non speranda*). The attack launched by Luther against the sanctioned practice of usury was not only an expression of a profound frustration, as Benjamin Nelson claimed in his now classic study on the subject.[51] It was also an expression of a nascent hope in the possibility of creating new standards of justice that a rational being should take into consideration. When connecting the struggle against usury with the manifestation of the gospel, Luther understood the gospel as having a particular function, as being a sign or even a miracle (*semeion*). For Luther, the fundamental characteristic of the historical dimension (*weltliches Regiment*) is the appropriate use of reason (*ratio* or *Vernunft*). Ulrich Duchrow, in his still unsurpassed study of the "doctrine of the two governances,"[52] makes it clear that, with the exception of only a few passages in which coercion (the

---

[50] It's worth noting, however, that Luther's position with respect to the authorities began to change when he wrote this treatise. This change was linked to the political situation, in which it was found to be difficult to harmonize the interests of the princes with those of the emperor.

[51] Benjamin Nelson, *The Idea of Usury* (Princeton: Princeton University Press, 1948), 46.

[52] Duchrow, *Christenheit*, 495–98.

metaphor used is the sword) appears as the ultimate criterion for control of civil society, Luther's idea is that "not force but wisdom or reason should govern over both good and bad people."[53] Reason is even considered the "mestra" [teacher] of the civil law.[54] The world itself is seen positively as the "realm of reason" (*regnum rationis*).[55]

The appeal to reason as a governing and structuring agent of political history must not, however, be interpreted as an appeal to Cartesian, technical, instrumental rationality.[56] The use of reason in Luther is a function of the public persona.[57] Reason is sanctioned only when it is exercised in the public domain with the purpose of administering justice and creating more equitable socioeconomic relations, even if the creation of those relations requires legislative transformations.[58]

Since Descartes, the West has understood reason as an instrumental faculty of the intellect intended for control and dominion over nature and society: knowledge is power. Thus the understanding Luther still had of the concept of reason was lost. Martin Honecker, in his study on the "doctrine of the two governances,"[59] advanced in that same direction by suggesting that the rediscovery of the public function of reason through the theories of the Frankfurt School (especially Horkheimer, Adorno, and Habermas) truly recovered and developed Luther's understanding of reason: "To the essence of reason belongs its public character."[60] In this way, reason is once again understood on the basis of its dialogical nature and is expressed or interpreted by the contemporary concept of praxis, understood as the practical exercise of dialogue in search of universal communication between interest groups for the purpose of discerning and articulating those interests in the public forum. Even the coercive function of the state must submit to the sanction of public reason for the purpose of the "publicly

---

53 WA 30/2, 556.
54 WA 11, 272.
55 Duchrow, *Christenheit*, 498.
56 See the pertinent distinction between critical reason and technical reason in Max Horkheimer, *Critical Theory* (New York: Seabury, 1972), 188–252.
57 Duchrow, *Christenheit*, 498.
58 Ibid., 495–512.
59 Martin Honecker, *Soziallehre zwischen Tradition und Vernunft* (Tübingen: J. C. B. Mohr, 1977), 175–278.
60 Ibid., 205.

controlled and legitimated use of force for the protection of the common good."[61] The use of reason is legitimate only when maintained in the public domain for the purpose of administering justice and achieving equity even if that equity is beyond the dominion of the law.[62] The very content of the *regnum rationis* is defined by the concept of equity (*aequitas* or *Billigkeit*).[63] This concept performs its function by offering a principle for the discernment and evaluation of the causes that, when brought into the public form, are inadequately or insufficiently treated in existing legislation.[64] This means that even the civil law and mores of a society are subject to examination by the criterion of equity.[65] According to Brian Gerrish, the tight connection that Luther establishes between reason and equity results in their being almost identical.[66] Despite all Luther's scorn for Scholasticism, it's important to note the high esteem he had for the way Aristotle, in his Nicomachean Ethics, defined the concept of *epieikia* (equity). The use of the concept of equity in Luther is practically a paraphrase of the Aristotelian concept of equity as the criterion for the "rectification of legal justice."[67]

With the rise of modern historical consciousness in regard to the relativity of standards of justice and legality, the question of the "rectification of legal justice" assumes incomparable importance. One can no longer raise the question of equity apart from the constitutive forms of social and economic existence in history. The legal and moral inventory of a society is incomprehensible apart from the form of socioeconomic existence of that society and of the historical transformations it goes through.

Thus the question of equity is always relative to the possible standard of justice that that social and economic formation permits.[68] The question of equity is, then, directly linked to the question of the wealth

---

[61] Ulrich Duchrow, ed., *Lutheran Churches: Salt or Mirror of Society* (Geneva: LWF, 1977), 4.

[62] Duchrow, *Christenheit*, 498–99.

[63] Ibid.

[64] WA 19, 632.

[65] Br 3:485.

[66] Brian Gerrish, *Grace and Reason* (Oxford: Clarendon, 1963), 35.

[67] TR 6: 345; WA 44, 707; cf. Aristotle, *Ethics*.

[68] On the evolution and transformation of ethical standards, see Alasdair MacIntyre, *A Short History of Ethics* (New York: Macmillan, 1960).

produced and to the level of equality in its distribution. It's in the equation between production and distribution that the problem of equity is resolved. That is also Luther's position in his attack against usury because usury uses someone else's work for the accumulation of wealth. And that is why the public use of reason is of decisive importance. Only the public use of reason is capable of opening a public space for defending the cause of those who were victims of inequality and oppression.

Luther's understanding of reason got little attention in specialized literature, which took Luther's calling reason a prostitute to be his final judgment on the subject. Two studies broke a long silence on the subject. Bernard Lohse, in his book *Ratio und Fides*, explains the conception that Luther had of reason as paralleling his concept of works, an arrangement that permitted Luther to affirm that under the primacy of faith, both reason and works are praised.[69] Reason must be condemned when used for self-interest and for the exercise of private judgment.[70] In this way, Lohse also emphasizes the public character of reason so that its use may be sanctioned. Brian Gerrish, in his book *Grace and Reason*, advances even further on this path by suggesting that today the correct understanding of the public use of reason in Luther is that it means practical reason.[71] In this way, Gerrish not only establishes the public character of reason, its dialogical function, but also defines its application as being oriented toward the solution of problems of an ethical nature.

With these observations, it becomes easier to understand why the concept of reason in Luther must today be interpreted in terms of a communicative praxis that seeks to maximize the participation of all people in the public discourse. Such a reinterpretation permits us to reconstruct the sociopolitical dimension of Luther's theology in such a way that its concern for making the *regnum rationis* an entity of mutual service can be maintained. Beyond that, it permits us to understand that praxis in the contemporary context, in which public conversation seeks to be inclusive and emancipatory, in solidarity

---

69 Bernard Lohse, *Ratio und Fides* (Göttingen: Vandenhoeck and Ruprecht, 1958), 126–30.

70 Ibid., 54.

71 Gerrish, *Grace and Reason*, 170.

with one another and particularly with the marginalized, with the oppressed and the victims of discrimination, and with the alienated person who has lost his voice and the right to defend his cause in public.[72] Integrating into communicative praxis a person who has been silenced becomes not only the norm by which the law is renewed and legality created but also "the possible origin of God's speaking," as Helmuth Peukert has insisted.[73] It is the possible origin of God's speaking (*teo-logia*) because it permits including in the conversation the voice of those who have no voice, the clamor of those who, on the margins of life, are capable of formulating the most decisive questions about the significance of human existence in a universe that the Christian confesses is all God's creation.

Reason conceived as communicative and emancipatory praxis seeks to extend communication beyond the barriers of the dominant ideology, beyond civil law itself, which also reflects the dominant ideology. Communicative and emancipatory praxis, by including the marginalized in the conversation, creates the forum in which it becomes possible to hear the word of newness that arises like the strange voice of the victim of the moral and legal conventions themselves. Said theologically, reason becomes the public space in which the law-gospel relation develops in historical particularity. By incorporating the victim into the conversation, the law is fulfilled and also overcome as the ideological reflection of a sociopolitically hegemonic group. To give voice to the voiceless, to permit the voice of the marginalized to enter into the conversation, is the condition for the possibility of the emergence of the new that breaks the ideological hegemony of the discourse and that permits the announcement of the new. It's the use of public reason that Luther employed in the ideological critique of

---

[72] In Latin America, Enrique Dussel has defended this argument. See his "Dominação-Libertação: Um discurso teológico differente," *Concilium* 96:714–34; and *Método para una filosofia de la liberación* (Salamanca: Sigueme, 1974), 259–88. In a somewhat different form, we find this same argument in Gustavo Gutiérrez, *La fuerza histórica de los pobres* (Lima: Cep., 1979), 303–94. In general, however, this has been the argument of political theology from the North Atlantic world.

[73] Helmuth Peukert, *Wissenschaftstheorie-Handlungstheorie-Fundamentale Theologie* (Düsseldorf: Patmos-Verlag, 1976), 311.

usury. By promoting the unmasking of the ideological justification for usury, Luther opens a space in the dominant discourse for the insertion of the voice of the victim of usury.

It's important to remember that this brief sketch of practical reason implies certain consequences that have to be taken into account, given that the use of reason must always be oriented by the quest for equity. For this reason, it is important that communicative praxis find its legitimacy only when it is exercised for the purpose of greater equity in economic, social, and political relations. The conversation we have spoken about here cannot be an end in itself; it must always be exercised to achieve a more egalitarian distribution of the social and economic resources historically produced and accumulated by a society.

In conclusion, it's my responsibility to point out that the scope of the argument developed above was not meant to extract Luther's occult intentions. It did not seek to define the "true" Luther. The purpose was to show that the divergence between liberation theology and Lutheran theology on the question of the recognition of the particularity of sin and grace is not unequivocally corroborated in Luther. The treatise discussed above does not permit us to reject the historical dialectic of law and gospel in the process of liberation; neither does it make of Luther a liberation theologian. What it does do is open the possibility of a dialogue that might enable the theological reconstruction that every period requires, the same reconstruction that Luther, challenged by problems characteristic of his period, sought.

This argument's implications for what was properly theological in Luther, a theology done *in loco justificationis*, were touched upon only lightly. But one can assert that the theological act performed *in loco justifiationis* arises in the cultic context as a doxological moment, as parentheses opened in historical processes by those and for those who daily lived the historical experience of liberating grace. Thus theirs is the praise and the radical eschatological hope that dares confess in the "not yet" of history the "already" of divine justification.

THE SIZE OF PARADISE
PRESUPPOSITIONS FOR THE CONCEPT OF SIN IN LATIN AMERICAN THEOLOGY

> For three or four centuries, the inhabitants of Europe have inundated the other parts of the world and ceaselessly published collections of travel and human interest stories. I am convinced that the only people we actually know are Europeans.
>
> —Jean Jacques Rousseau

Introduction

Remembering is essential: to tell stories, locate the signs, and narrate the events associated with the scars. It's essential to remember the itinerary, the landscapes, the stones on the pathway. But it's important to note that the travelers on the pathway are diverse. There are businesspeople, whom we used to call traveling salespeople, and there are tourists and also pilgrims. Businesspeople consider the trip to be the means to an end, a necessary departure from their home for the purpose of maintaining it. Businesspeople are like missionaries or warriors; they are sent to make a delivery and bring something back in return. The place they visit has a usefulness. Tourists are different. For them, the trip is an unavoidable inconvenience in getting to their destination, the place of pleasure that allows them to bring

Originally published in *Estudos Teológicos* 38, no. 3 (1998): 239–51.

home memories and photographs. The place they visit is made up of these mementos, through which their trip is constantly reinvented. Pilgrims are the people for whom the destination is the celebration of a journey in which what matters are the adversities to be overcome. Pilgrims are people on the march for whom there is no preexisting pathway because they make their own way by walking, as Antonio Machado put it.[1] Pilgrims bring back neither an invoice nor a photograph but rather a narrative that tells where they started, the pain that led them to go on a pilgrimage, and the process by which they became liberated. So it is with theology. There are tourists, there are traveling salespeople, and there are pilgrims.

I suggest that Latin America was historically dominated by the images and invoices that the conquistadors and missionaries made of it and brought back with them. They were what I have called tourists and traveling salespeople, and they defined Latin America. In this definition, something interesting happened that I propose to examine here by trying to explain what I judge to have been the primary task of Latin American theology—that is, the definition of its condition. Thus I suggest as a proposal to be examined here that the primary task of that theology was hamartiology, the doctrine of sin and of the human condition. But this doctrine was defined within the framework of Augustine's legacy (dominant in the West), except that it had a different nuance creatively inserted into the vast biblical and ecclesial tradition. Let's see how that worked.

Why Wouldn't There Be Sin South of the Equator?

Even before the conquest (of the Americas), Europeans had imagined lands beyond the Atlantic and had cataloged them according to their own desires and fears. Even before being discovered, the Americas were the eager and desirous expression of a European idea; rather than being a place, the Americas were a nonplace, a utopia prepared to catalyze the imaginary worlds that populated the fantasy of medieval Europe, especially on the Iberian Peninsula. In the now famous formulation of Edmundo O'Gorman, Latin America was invented

[1] Antonio Machado, *Campos de Castilla* (*1907–1917*), 80.

before it was discovered.[2] Or in the words of Carlos Fuentes, it was "discovered because invented, because imagined, because desired, because, once named, America was transformed into Europe's utopia."[3] Utopias, whether positive or negative, are localities that negate the ambiguities of all other places; utopias stratify feelings and magnetize between their poles whatever is most desired or whatever most torments the imagination.[4] Things that are desired are distinctly different from things that are feared, but they are united by the implacable force of the imagination, which permits us to be detached from our own location. In reference to this phenomenon, Fernando Cervantes observes, "The power of myth over the imagination was sufficiently compelling to permit the Europeans to see exactly what they were looking for," or, we might add, what they were afraid of encountering.[5] The power that the imagination has to forge the perception of the Americas is the necessary basis for reflection on the concept of sin in the context of Latin American theologies.

What was seen and recorded, beginning with the first scribes in the New World, is immersed in an ambivalent and contradictory (though not ambiguous) attitude in relation to reality. If Columbus could believe, as he did for a time, that he had discovered the earthly location of paradise, with his description of the indigenous peoples as extremely pure and innocent prefall creatures, within a matter of days he changed his tune entirely and called them cowards, cannibals, and devil-possessed beasts unworthy of mercy.[6] Here there is no intermediate point between desires and fears, between edenic innocence and diabolical corruption. In the void between these two

---

2 Edmundo O'Gorman, *La invención de América* (México: Fondo de Cultura Económica, 1984).

3 Carlos Fuentes, *Myself with Others: Selected Essays* (New York: Farrar, Straus and Giroux, 1998), 184.

4 It's no coincidence that the most famous utopian narrative is *Utopia* by Sir Thomas More, written in the sixteenth century on the basis of a fictitious conversation with a mariner (Ralph Hythloday), who supposedly sailed with Amerigo Vespucci.

5 Fernando Cervantes, *The Devil in the New World: The Impact of Diabolism in New Spain* (New Haven: Yale University Press, 1994), 6.

6 Columbus, *Diario de Colón* (Madrid: Cultura Hispanica, 1968). See Tzvetan Todorov, *La conquista de America: El problema del otro* (Mexico: Siglo XXI, 1989), 41–58; also Cervantes, *Devil in the New World*, 6–8.

alternatives, what is properly human disappears. Even though later there are other, more nuanced representations, the basic pattern remains intact. Although the argument about the human condition of the indigenous peoples had already been resolved by about 1550, missionary strategies were shaped in accordance with the challenges identified on the Iberian Peninsula. The indigenous were thus recorded and stereotyped as Jews, Muslims, or apostate Christians ("Lutherans").[7] And the peninsular Europeans recognized that the attitudes being projected onto the "others" of the Iberian Peninsula were also being applied to the populations of the New World. The Iberians continued to invent the "other" even before discovering him. Octavio Paz describes this phenomenon with embarrassing precision: "Before we had our own historical existence, we began by being a European idea."[8]

What Europeans were then seeing (in the New World) not only had been already imagined and idealized, but also, to the extent that the real adjusts itself to the imagined, the New World was the place of the strange, the mysterious, the supernatural, in which the unexpected defied common stereotypes. Already imagined, classified, and named even before being seen, whatever was eventually seen resisted all classification. But instead of allowing the unusual to evoke new images of the new reality, the tendency in almost all the travel reports that ended up defining America for the Western world was to declare this reality, which did not harmonize with existing stereotypes, as being chaotic and belonging to an indomitable natural environment. Thus in the same way that someone who does not adjust to the law is delinquent and incorrigible, so was America.

---

[7] On this typology as descriptive of the way conquistadors and missionaries conceived of the New World based on their experience of the Old, see my essay "Conquest and Evangelization in Latin America," in *Word Remembered—Word Proclaimed*, ed. Steven Bevans and Roger Schroeder (Netteral: Steyler, 1997), 89–107. It is also not surprising that in the New World, people accused by the Inquisition received in their death sentences the notice that they "left this kingdom to become Lutherans." Jean Pierre Bastian, *Protesta y sociedad en México* (México: Casa Unidad de Publicaciones, 1983), 23; Bastian, *Protestantismo y modernidad en Latinoamerica* (México: Fondo de Cultura Económica, 1994), 41–67.

[8] Octavio Paz, *Signos en rotação* (São Paulo: Perspectiva, 1990), 127.

It did not adjust to the anthropological, biological, or cosmopolitan European norm, and thus it became the place of the strange and the mysterious. Starting with Columbus, who considered the natives to be beasts because they did not follow the rules of mercantile exchange and "donated everything they had";[9] passing through Alexander von Humboldt, with his parallelism between Europe/America and civilization/barbarism-nature;[10] and including the famous documentary by Werner Herzog about the film *Fitzcaraldo*, in which the tropical forest is the metaphor for all of Latin America,[11] the story is the same. Whatever is strange has to be bent to fit the imagination or then declared to be chaotic.

Hermann Borchard, one of the first missionaries sent by the Church of Prussia in the second half of the nineteenth century for the purpose of serving the evangelical immigrants in the south of Brazil, responds to that uneasiness as he writes aboard the steamship taking him to Rio de Janeiro. On the day that he crossed the equator, he recorded the following: "Not only will we exchange day for night and summer for winter, we'll also enter a totally new relationship that will change the concept that we've had of the world."[12] Before even arriving, he knew what he would encounter: an inverted world, strange and untamed. It's not by chance, then, that this missionary would one day confess that he was unable to find any religiosity among German immigrants: "There's no religiosity in Brazil," he prophesied.[13] By this

---

9 Todorov, *Conquista de America*, 38.

10 See Mary Luise Pratt, *Imperial Eyes* (London: Routledge, 1992), 111.

11 It's worth quoting part of the text: "There's a kind of harmony. It's the harmony of oppressive, collective assassination. And, by comparison with the articulated vileness, lowness, and obscenity of all that wilderness . . . , we have to humble ourselves before that oppressive fornication, that oppressive growth, and that oppressive lack of order. Here even the . . . stars in the sky look like a mess." Werner Herzog, "The Screenplay," in *Burden of Dreams*, ed. Les Blank and James Bogan (Berkeley: North Atlantic, 1984), 57.

12 Hermann Borchard, *Die Mission unter den evangelischen Deutschen in Suedbrasilien*, in Friedrich Fabri, *Evangelisches Zentralarchiv in Berlin*, document 123989.

13 On the basis of this diagnosis, which is commonly found among travelers from Columbus to the most recent missionaries, Borchard decided that instituting a synod would simultaneously restore the Christian faith and German identity. It's quite interesting to note that at the time he was visiting the [German] colony (1868–72) and in the same area where he was living, there arose among German

he meant either that immigrants were totally lost, incapable even of recognizing the necessity of religion, or that, based on his theory that everything south of the equator was inverted, immigrants didn't need religion, in the same way that a healthy person doesn't need a physician. In any case, immigrants were completely outside the possibility of good or evil.

Such was the way America was described and represented: on the one hand, America meant a desire, and on the other, it designated an uncomfortable sensation in regard to what is strange and feared but that is resistant to any attempt to reduce it to the familiar, to one's own world view. While the New World was known even before being found, it also represented the unexpected, that which resists any effort to control or manipulate it. With regard to the conquistadors, Contardo Calligaris writes, "Certainly there has not been, there has not existed, any place in this world that can explain so much expectation. . . . [For the conquistador] the negation of the dream is the revelation of a hell . . . the size of paradise."[14]

If European Christianity expresses itself as fallen humanity, stained by evil and guilty of sin yet capable of correcting its condition by means of grace, Latin America was perceived and described as if it were outside the bounds of the very possibility of the fall and, in a certain way, outside of guilt but also alienated from the possibility of redemption. This is what Gaspar Barleus's famous aphorism says (in a work written in 1647 at the request of Mauricio of Nassau after he retook Brazil): *ultra equinoxialem non peccavit.* That there is no sin south of the equator is a declaration that emerges like an omen. In a situation so different from what was expected—but at the same time so identical to what the imagination was creating—Latin America was radical evil, a state of absolute corruption, and simultaneously the impossibility of the existence of evil. These are

Protestant immigrants one of the most important messianic movements in Brazil, led by a charismatic woman, Jacobina Maurer. For Borchard, with a Prussian agenda in his hand and a male hierarchy in his head, this movement could certainly not be religion. See the work of João Guilherme Biehl, "Jummerthal—o Vale da Lamentação: Crítica à construção do messianismo Mucker" (MA thesis, Federal University of Santa Maria, 1991).

[14] Contardo Calligaris, *Brasil, país do futuro de quem?* (unpublished text), 9.

two extreme situations yet united in the sense that in neither one is sin conceivable. Sin is possible neither in hell nor in paradise, so in this way, hell and paradise are interchangeable. Barleus's statement is a critique both of the violent practice of the conquistadors and of the Romantic vision of the good savage.

The vision that the West had of sin—that is, its myth, its originating voice[15]—permitted Mediterranean and European civilization to demarcate for itself a space of ambiguity, flanked in the imagination by the duo of heaven/paradise on one side and hell on the other. In that space of ambiguity, the human journey would evolve. Sin makes life dangerous, but grace guarantees the promise of rescue and freedom. Where the danger grows, there also is the redeemer, in the words of Friedrich Hölderlin.[16]

It was exactly that space that America was denied by the conflation of paradise and hell. Just as in the medieval notion of limbo, the place where innocent children went who died before being baptized, the Americas were also a place deprived both of suffering and of pleasure. They were the place of the impotent god—impotent because innocence cannot be condemned, but impotent also because those whose names have not been written in the Book of Life cannot be redeemed. Differently from purgatory, limbo does not allow for negotiating a possibility of blessing or curse. In limbo there is neither politics nor economics. It's the infinite place in which the parallel margins of hell and paradise overlap and in which both of them and neither of them exist at the same time.

---

[15] I'm thinking here of a fragment from the philosopher Xenophon of Colophon from the fifth century BCE, in which he defines the importance of myth as recounting the story from which we came, of what went wrong, and of where we are going: "It's close to the fire during the winter that, stretched out on a soft bed, the stomach well fed, drinking sweet wine and chewing garbanzo beans, we should ask such questions as: Who are you? And where do you come from? How old are you, my friend? How old were you when fear arrived?" *Os filósofos pré-socráticos*, introduction, translation, and notes by Gerd A. Bomheim (São Paulo: Cultrix, 1972), 33 (fragment 22).

[16] "Nah ist / Und schwer zu fassen der Gott / Wo aber Gefahr ist, wächst / Das Rettende auch." Friedrich Hölderlin, *Gedichte/Hyperion* (Muenchen: Wilehln Goldmann, 1978), 138.

Limbo is the imaginary, inverse copy of the ambiguous sphere in which the life choices between good and evil are negotiated, thus opening a space flanked by the margins of hell and paradise. But it is certainly a space of opportunities and risks that European civilization defined as its story, a fable of European conception with a long history. Irenaeus of Lyon had already defined sin as daring plus irresponsibility, an idea confirmed by Augustine when he described history as a journey on this earth in search of salvation. This idea receives more radical expression in the medieval theory of happy guilt (*felix culpa*), in which the sinner receives greater grace precisely for having sinned. It's found also in Luther's theory of temptation (*Anfechtungstheorie*), in which being put to the test and even sinning with daring manifests the greater power of grace. Finally, Milton celebrates this notion in the epic poem of the West, *Paradise Lost*, when he ends his narrative with the expulsion of Adam and Eve from the garden of Eden and with the following words, which are far from being an unconsoled lament:

> They looked back, contemplating the eastern side of paradise, their
> happy former place, having been dismissed by that flaming blade;
> the gate was guarded by menacing faces and incandescent arms.
> They shed a few natural tears but dried them rapidly; the world was
> before them so that they might choose their place of rest, with
> Providence as their guide.[17]

Claiming the Fall

In the New World, European imaginings inflated the borders (of paradise and hell), thus reducing the ambiguity of history and swallowing

[17] John Milton, *The Poetical Works* (New York: Leavitte and Allen, 1850), 1:400. Translator's note: I have translated back into English the Portuguese-language version that Westhelle was citing.

the space needed for wandering in search of possibilities. Paradise and hell, hell and paradise, simultaneously conquer the earth. America is the *finis terrae* [land's end] in the precise sense of being the mythical-topographical limit of the world but also the place where the earth, as the theater of the history of the world, is consumed by paradise and/or by hell. Thus America is also the *finis historiae*, a "terrain without history," in the words of Euclides da Cunha.[18]

America, as a European epigraph, however, has not been forever deprived of its own historical consciousness, of its narrative, of its foundational myth. The intention of my commentaries is to point out that whatever historical consciousness Latino(a) Americans have is contingent on and secondary to the manner in which we insert ourselves into European history, or the manner in which we resist that insertion, even if that is done anthropologically, as we take nourishment by metabolizing European idealizations. Which is to say, even the notion of sin and fall has already been contaminated by Western metaphysics. The problem is how this notion can be deconstructed and rebuilt on a new site, with new parameters.

Our Latin American conception of sin—the recognition that we also inhabit the ambiguous realm of our own historical condition—is then the ironic result of our having raised ourselves up to the state of fallenness. Like those men and women who are sympathetic to European hubris—that is, eurocentrism—and who live in a locality that is at the same time suspended in paradise and relegated forever to hell, historical consciousness is converted into a way of affirming the perversity of our own condition. But this is a function of hope and not of resignation. As a response to the fact of our having been formed, imagined, and recorded as a European idea, such hope assumes two faces that represent the options with which America sought to raise itself to the state of fallenness: the assimilationist face and the liberationist face of American historical consciousness. In both cases, the basic characteristic is the commitment to recover the right to the fall, the right to work and dream and share the experience of those who

[18] Euclides da Cunha, *A margem da História* (Porto: Lello e Irmão, 1946).

were exiled from paradise but who look to the future with the fundamental gifts of the fall: hope and responsibility.

Of the two ways of claiming the fall—demanding history and ambiguity, hope and responsibility—the most common is assimilationist. Here I won't discuss it except to mention, in passing, that its intention is to recover the meaning of the fall and of historical ambiguity by engrafting the destiny of America into European history by accepting the European myth as foundational. Assimilationism seeks to insert the New World into the Western tradition, which, since Augustine, conceives of history as progress (*procursus*), a journey forward by those who are guided by providence in this earthly existence. In this view, sin and guilt are an inherited tendency to stray and wander on this journey instead of marching onward according to the designs of the Western world. But sin and guilt also promise possibilities of redemption. This point of view receives its secular version in the defenders of colonialism (Sepúlveda), in nineteenth-century positivism (Comte), in the developmentalism of the twentieth century, and finally in the neoliberal notion of modernization and globalization. The neoliberal notion has been influential throughout Latin America and triumphant in the United States and Canada so as to make North America an overseas campus of Europe. For this triumph, they adopted a concept of sin that qualifies as sin only when kept in the private sphere and that, when it emerges in the public sphere, frequently metamorphoses into benefits, as Adam Smith formulated it so well: private greed becomes public benefit.[19]

What interests me here is the liberationist version of historical consciousness. Not very different from the assimilationists, the liberationists tore down the wall between paradise and hell, thus creating the space for ambiguity. But they didn't do it to insert Latin America within the European historical project. Rather, they did it to create a geographical meaning, an autochtonous awareness of regionality and spatiality. That awareness of regionality and spatiality represents

[19] The expression "private vices made public benefits" is from Bernard de Mandeville but is based on Adam Smith's *The Wealth of Nations*, ed. Bruce Mazlish (Indianapolis: Bobbs-Merrill, 1961), 152–53, 166.

a pleading, if we may call it that, for the right to sin, the right to live in ambiguity and to assume the consequences in freedom. What was being sought in this endeavor was the voice of America.[20] It's no coincidence that many of the theological texts produced under the label of liberation theology insist on this sense of regionality by adding to their title the expression "from Latin America."[21] This sense of spatiality treats sin not as a private attitude, something that one does or fails to do, but as an experience of circumstantial participation. Thus sin is not defined primarily as hubris—that is, the desire to be the center of the world—but as the condition of being in the world not only as a subjective act (a lack of something), nor as an objective corruption, a stain about which nothing can be done, but as an intersubjective structure.[22]

This spatial sense of existence allows us to formulate the notion of sin in an unusual manner. Thus Enrique Dussel can say that original sin is "the constitutive sin of our being, from its origins and from our birth."[23] And the constitution of this being is determined "by the place that we occupy in the social fabric."[24] This, then, is original

---

[20] Ironically, that was the name of a radio program that disseminated the assimilationist project.

[21] Unlike Kierkegaard, who considered the real Christian to be a contemporary of Christ, in Latin America we have the opposite, as a Brazilian anthropophagic movement in the 1920s pointed out in its manifesto: "We insisted that Christ be born in Bahia or in Belém do Pará." Oswald de Andrade, "Manifesto antropófago," in *An Anthology of Brazilian Prose*, ed. R. L. Scott-Buccleuch and Mário Tèles de Oliveira (São Paulo: Ática, 1971), 388. Something similar is also found in the canticles of the Nicaraguan Mass or in the poetry of Carlos Mejia Godoy: "Cristo ya nació en Calapaguina, de Chepe Pavón y una tal Maria."

[22] The first formulation that Latin American theology adopted to express its condition (now already dated) was the theory of dependency, which was transfigured in theology as a mythical expression of the Latin American condition. The seminal works of that theology invariably open with a discussion of the theory of dependency. See, for example, Gustavo Gutierrez, *Teologia de la liberación* (Lima: Universitaria, 1971); Hugo Assmann, *Opresión-liberación: Desafio a los cristianos* (Montevideo: Tierra Nueva, 1971); Enrique Dussel, *América Latina: dependencia y liberación* (Buenos Aires: Fernando Garcia Cambeiro, 1973); and José Míguez Bonino, *Doing Theology in a Revolutionary Situation* (Philadelphia: Fortress, 1975) [Brazilian edition: *A fé em busca de eficácia: uma interpretação da reflexão teológica latino-americana sobre libertação* (São Leopoldo: Sinodal, 1987)].

[23] Enrique Dussel, *Ética comunitária* (Petrópolis: Vozes, 1986), 32.

[24] Ibid.

sin, inherited sin, which establishes itself in the institutions through which and within which we are born. Thus there exists an "institutional transmission of sin." Henceforth we reject any attempt to attribute sin only to an individual. Such sin would be an abstract construction: "Speaking abstractly, one can truly say that Jack the individual sinned. But, concretely, Jack is the father of Alexa, the brother of John, the teacher of his students, a citizen of his country, and so on. Never—not even before God—is Jack alone and without company. . . . In the same way, Jack's mistakes or sins are, concretely, never alone."[25]

This analysis by Dussel, so direct and harsh, is not a rhetorical instrument or an irresponsible excuse for concealing the individual vileness of the human being. Rather, his analysis records a rupture with the mode of interpreting the origin and transmission of sin based on the biological paradigm; his analysis reformulates sin in a social paradigm, in which the body of sin is primordially the social body.[26]

Not abandoning the notion of original sin but rather recovering its concrete significance, the Catholic bishops gathered in Puebla, Mexico, in 1979, were able to speak about the audacious form of "the structural dimension of sin" or about a "situation of sin": "Structures that generate injustice have been imposed upon our peoples."[27] And again, "to a personal attitude of sin . . . there always corresponds, on the level of interpersonal relations, an attitude of egotism, of pride, of ambition and envy. . . . Consequently, situations of sin are established that, on a world-wide level, enslave many people and adversely affect the freedom of all."[28]

---

[25] Ibid., 31–32.

[26] That model as we know it goes back to the time of Augustine but becomes particularly problematic when, in the eighteenth century, the modern subject emerges who can be abstracted from all relations. Such an individual either would have to reject original sin because it contradicts the basic experience of the modern human being (the belief in autonomy) or would have to spiritualize sin in order to be able to make a connection between original sin and sins of little importance.

[27] *Evangelização no presente e no futuro da América Latina: Conclusões da III Conferência Geral do Episcopado Latino-Americano: Puebla de los Ángeles*, México, 27-1 to 13-2 from 1979, 3rd ed. (São Paulo: Paulinas, n.d.), 437, 198.

[28] *Evangelização no presente*, 328, 170.

The bishops took care in their formulations not to make the structures or situations of sin equivalent to original sin itself, thus avoiding direct criticism of the Augustinian tradition. Personal sin and social sin are, however, so closely related as to be analytically inseparable. You cannot analyze one without the other.

In this way, the bishops succeed in linking the discussion of sin with the biblical conception—still maintained in the first centuries of Christianity—that Augustine reformulated masterfully while, at the same time, imposing upon that conception a new interpretative approach.[29]

Bringing the social and the individual together reintroduces into the discussion about sin and the fall a social and even cosmic dimension in which the reality of evil, mythically expressed in the notion of the devil, again has importance. Not only idolatry but also demonology recover theoretical standing. The metaphysical position of Augustine, for whom evil is nothingness, is not rejected, thus avoiding Manicheism. But evil, nevertheless, is not nothing, even if it's not an ontic reality per se. Between being and nothingness, there arise structures that, though not possessing ontic character, define themselves as a structure maintained through a nexus of intersubjective relations. Irenaeus called this the "reign of apostasy."[30] This reign, without implying an ontic dualism, can be described as a domain or "hamartiosphere," and according to Dussel, this hamartiosphere has a structural mark that sustains it simply by the intersubjective inversion that human beings engage in within it. Thus it has no ontic value, since it doesn't exist by itself. It is, however, real and not an illusion or an entity or a mere apparition.

João Batista Libânio sums up what this concept of sin represents in the history of the interpretation of sin by calling attention to three traditional understandings of the concept of sin. The first understanding is as something objective, an inherited blot such as is normally represented by the notion of hereditary sin in the tradition of

[29] That is, Augustine represents, in relation to the Christianity that preceded him, a deviation that became hegemonic, as Elaine Pagels argues. Elaine Pagels, *Adam, Eve, and the Serpent* (New York: Vintage, 1988), esp. chapters 5–6.

[30] Irenaeus, *Against Heresies*, book 5, chapter 1.

Augustine. The second is the Enlightenment version, in which sin is interpreted as a subjective lack, a failure of courage, or a laziness that prevents us from making full use of reason in an autonomous and responsible way.[31] The third concept, which Libânio finds best expressed in Latin American theology, synthesizes the two others while maintaining their objective reality, which, however, consists of intersubjective connections.[32] I find no better way of expressing Libânio's idea than through [the Zen-like prose of] João Guimarães Rosa, which turns the binary constructions of Western metaphysics on their head: "Whatever is not God is the devil's domain. God exists even when there is no domain, but the devil doesn't need to exist in order to have one."[33]

Sin versus Sins

The problem is that this intersubjective structure becomes vague, spongy, and difficult to locate when it is designated by broad, loose terms like *dependency* or *market* or *political system* or *capitalism* or *neoliberalism* or *globalization* and so on. These terms tend to absorb everything that traditionally is attributed to individual responsibility in regard to sin, thus creating a situation in which attribution of responsibility disappears. The result is an apparent return to Manicheism, dividing the world between those who organize and participate in structural sin—the oppressors—and those who suffer under its dominion—the victims. This problem has been detected in Latin American theology, especially by feminist theologians, starting with the work of Valerie Saiving and Judith Plaskow, who identify in the theology done by men the importance of denouncing systems of injustice but also a tendency to romanticize the victims without recognizing that our own lack of self-affirmation and our own failure to

---

[31] See Immanuel Kant, *Was ist Aufklärung*, in *Ausgewählte kleine Schriften* (Hamburg: Felix Meiner, 1965), 1.

[32] João Batista Libânio, *Teologia da libertação: Roteiro didático para um estudo* (São Paulo: Loyola, 1987), 142–46.

[33] João Guimarães Rosa, *Grande Sertão: Veredas* (Rio de Janeiro: José Olympio, 1967), 49.

assume responsibility make us accomplices of the same unjust system that we denounce.[34]

It is in response to this question that the work of Juan Luis Segundo is instructive. In his intricate analysis and exegesis of Paul's Letter to the Romans, he clearly recognizes this problem: "I arrived at the reading of Romans with a hermeneutically decisive hypothesis . . . : that structural sin was not only *outside* of us, and that, in spite of our protests of innocence, sin dwelled in us, who were in some way part of it and its accomplices."[35]

In Segundo's Christology, he develops some of the basic themes of Paul's theology: sin, law, and grace. Allow me to jump immediately to his conclusion and then briefly reconstruct his principal steps: "But we did not invent a new sin when we spoke about political and social structures of sin or structural sin, which is the same thing, because this approach does not involve attributing to abstract and impersonal systems or structures a term like 'a sin,' which can justly be applied only to individuals. Paul taught us precisely to avoid the (political) mistake of confusing Sin, the dehumanizing structure that enslaves and treats us like things, with the sins that man commits when he is in the Flesh."[36]

To arrive at this conclusion, Segundo observes that Paul distinguishes clearly between the sins that individuals commit and Sin, which the apostle interprets as "the kingdom of Satan." Segundo tells us that Sin, in Paul, is the "(anthropological) personification of Satan . . . and only a sketchy attempt at demythologizing."[37] The sin of Adam is not interpreted genetically but instead appears as a mythological version that gives an account of the inauguration of the reign of Sin. Thus Paul creates the perfect antithetic parallelism between the two Adams, since the second Adam inaugurates the reign of grace just as the first Adam inaugurates the reign of Sin. In an

34 See Valerie Saiving Goldstein, "The Human Situation: A Feminist View," *Journal of Religion* 40, nos. 100–112 (abr., 1960); and Judith Plaskow, *Sex, Sin and Grace* (Lanham: University Press of America, 1980).

35 Juan Luis Segundo, *O homem de hoje diante de Jesus de Nazaré: Tomo II 1: História e atualidade: Sinóticos e Paulo* (São Paulo: Paulinas, 1985), 627.

36 Ibid., 629.

37 Ibid., 343–44.

argument that is surprisingly close to Luther's, Segundo demonstrates that for Paul, the problem is not the fact that human beings want to sin or desire sin but that they are not free to avoid sin. The basic idea is that sin is not a generic term for all the sins that a person commits, but it's what comes with the force of death. And here death is not a merely biological event but rather everything that separates intention from the effective consummation of an act. The price of sin is death in the sense that death is the lack of discernment. In Segundo's words, "If man could recognize in what he does the intention he first had, then his action would necessarily be good because it would also be free. And vice-versa."[38] Death comes in when, through our successes, we hide the fact that we have done neither what God wanted nor what we ourselves had intended to do.

To make a long argument short, the sins that a person commits are not in a strict sense occasioned by original sin but are a symptom of it. This is the reason the law has a double face. On the one hand, it increases offenses (Rom 5:20) and permits the power of sin to be recognized. In this way, the law will make the human being despair about what he can accomplish with his personal good works.[39] On the other hand, the works of the law are a way for human beings to believe that sin can be conquered, since these works conceal the symptoms of sin in the same way that concealing the symptoms of a disease makes diagnosis more difficult or impossible: "The supposition is that man must awaken from his delusion and seek another way out, which cannot be anything but the way of faith, the surrender to grace, and the rejection of any attempt at a negotiated salvation."[40] All of this is possible because sins fight against Sin in the same way as the symptoms of an illness make it impossible, or at least more difficult, for us to deceive ourselves about being sick.[41]

---

38 Ibid., 519.

39 Ibid., 455–56.

40 Ibid., 456.

41 Ibid., 454. Note, however, that the medical analogy used by Segundo, that of illness and symptoms, betrays his basic intention—that is, that of affirming that, if structural sin resides in us, our actions are also responsible for perpetuating it. If we act in such a way that we achieve our intentions, sins are also constitutive

Coda

How can this conclusion by a Jesuit, one who is apparently afflicted by Lutheran anxieties, offer a response to the Latin American dispute as I have described it above? Remember that I presented this dispute as a search for space in which there could be a history, however ambiguous, that could challenge the imposed and recorded images that deny such a space. The responses given are of two different shades. One, the assimilationist, was mentioned only in passing. The other, the liberationist, sought, through the notion of structural sin, to create a sense of ambiguity (despite sometimes running the risk of falling into duality). In returning to Paul, Segundo completes the cycle by distinguishing between Sin as the universal condition of all creation and sins as a symptom of this condition. The recognition of those symptoms, by means of the law, allows us to diagnose the structures of sin and death and thus confront them—not combatting the symptoms through "works of the law" but acquiring freedom "by means of faith" and by "yielding to grace." Once again, by insisting on the structural dimension of sin, the liberationist focus opened a place for historical ambiguity, a place where one can arrive at a recognition of evil. And by developing the dialectic of sins and Sin, it became evident that through works of the law, sins can conceal Sin. This is nothing more than the work of the devil, which in an arrogant way was announced in Barleus's aphorism *ultra equinoxialem non peccavit*. The concept of sin in Latin America is a plea to abandon an imaginary paradise for a real life of risk and danger or, perhaps better stated, a plea to abandon an imposed hell for the sake of a fantastic hope. But that hope can be named only by the voice of a people who know and narrate the history of their errors, their vileness, their fall.

It is by that voice that evil is named, and when named, it can also be exorcized. In the seventeenth century, the great Jesuit preacher and missionary António Vieira, commenting on Mark 9, which tells the story of the exorcism of the mute spirit that possesses a young man, says in reference to Brazil something that could be true for

---

of Sin since there exists between the two a dialectical relationship and not simply a causal one.

Latin America generally—namely, that the spirit in Mark 9 is the same spirit that took Brazil's voice and left it unable to name its own condition. After being recorded by traveling salespeople with their invoices and by tourists with their photos, Latin America—with its theology, its literature, its arts, and its science—seeks a narrative by pilgrims who walk through these lands, learn to map them, and along the way, relate their condition. The goal is to get out of this condition, but that cannot be done without narrating it, thus making it one's own and knowing it as one's own. In the words of Riobaldo from Guimarães Rosa's *Grande Sertão*, "We have to get out of the sertão [Brazil's semiarid wilderness]! But the only way out is by keeping watch over it from the inside."[42] In that narrative bit, one discovers that paradise has the dimensions of hell and that someone has falsified the boundaries of the territory of hope.

[42] Rosa, *Grande Sertão*, 212.

SUBJECT INDEX